Reiner Schürmann
Selected Writings and Lecture Notes

Reiner Schürmann

Modern Philosophies
of the Will

Lecture Notes for Courses at
the New School for Social Research

(Fall 1980/Spring 1987/Spring 1992)

Edited by
Kieran Aarons and Francesco Guercio

DIAPHANES

Reiner Schürmann
Selected Writings and Lecture Notes

Edited by Francesco Guercio, Michael Heitz,
Malte Fabian Rauch, and Nicolas Schneider

1st edition
ISBN 978-3-0358-0307-5
© DIAPHANES, Zurich 2022
All rights reserved

Layout: 2edit, Zurich
Printed in Germany

www.diaphanes.com

Table of Contents

Syllabus 7

List of Abbreviations 9

Edition Guidelines 15

Historical Introduction 17

PART I   Rationality and Irrationality of the Will 27
1.   Kant: the good will and practical reason
2.   Schelling: the rational will and the "dark will"
3.   Nietzsche: will as the self-affirmation of the subject
4.   Heidegger: the analogy 'technological rationality : thinking = the will to will : the will not to will'

PART II   The Ontological Turn in the Philosophy of Will 75
1.   Schelling [missing]
2.   Nietzsche: being as "imposed" by the will
3.   Heidegger

PART III   Legislation and Transgression 109
1.   Kant: from the good will to the legislative will: the three formulae of the categorical imperative

APPENDIX   The Time of the Mind and the History of Freedom. Review of Hannah Arendt, *The Life of the Mind* 117

Notes 125

Editors' Afterword 155

Tentative Chronology of Reiner Schürmann's Courses at the New School for Social Research 181

Lecture Notes of Reiner Schürmann at the NSSR— Pierre Adler's Inventory (1994) 190

Editorial Statement 192

Syllabus

Through Kant, Nietzsche, and Heidegger, this seminar traces the development of the relation between the will and the law as self-given. Topic areas include: the ontological turn in the philosophy of the will; from obligation to self-overcoming, to 'decision'; the will's playful character and the problem of teleology; the will as principle of morality (Kant), of life-forms (Nietzsche), and of technology (Heidegger); the formal-identity of legislation and transgression of the law.

The seminar will trace three 'strategies' in the development of the philosophy of will from Kant to Heidegger: viz. rationality and irrationality of the will, the ontological turn, and law.

List of Abbreviations

Immanuel Kant

AA   *Akademie-Ausgabe: Kants Gesammelte Schriften*, 23 vols. (Leipzig: Preußische Akademie der Wissenschaften, 1902–).

GMS   *Grundlegung zur Metaphysik des Sittens* (Riga: 1785) in *Akademie-Ausgabe: Kants Gesammelte Schriften*, (Leipzig: Preußische Akademie der Wissenschaften, 1902–), I Werke, vol. IV, 385–473.

GMM   *Groundwork of the Metaphysics of Morals*, trans. H. J. Paton (New York: Harper Torchbook, 1964) re-ed. in *The Moral Law: Groundwork of the Metaphysics of Morals*, trans. with a preface, commentary and analysis by H. J. Paton (London and New York: Routledge Classics, 2005).

Friedrich Wilhelm Joseph Schelling

Cl   *Clara oder über den Zusammenhang der Natur mit der Geisterwelt.* Aus dem *Nachlass*, hrsg. von K.F.A. Schelling (Stuttgart und Augsburg: J.G. Cotta Verlag, 1862).

HF   *Of Human Freedom*, trans. J. Gutmann (London: Living Time Media Int'l, 2005), revision of J. Gutman's trans. (Chicago: Open Court, 1936).

SW   *Sämmtliche Werke*, Hrsg. K.F.A. Schelling, I Abtheilung Bde. 1–10, II Abtheilung Bde. 1–4 (Stuttgart und Augsburg: J.G. Cotta Verlag, 1856–61).

SW, I, 7 *Philosophische Untersuchungen über das Wesen der menschlichen Freiheit*, in *Sämmtliche Werke*, Hrsg. K.F.A. Schelling, I Abtheilung Bde. 1–10, II Abtheilung Bde. 1–4, (Stuttgart und Augsburg: J.G. Cotta Verlag, 1856–61, Part I, vol. 7, 331–416).

Friedrich Wilhelm Nietzsche

Schürmann cites Walter Kaufmann and R.J. Hollingdale's translations of Nietzsche, although he often modifies these or else translates directly from the German. In this volume, every effort has been made to maintain reference to the English editions preferred by Schürmann. When citing from the *Nachlass* (*Posthumous Fragments*), Schürmann references Nietzsche's *Die Unschuld des Werdens*, ed. by A. Baeumler (Stuttgart: Kröner, 1931/1978), 2 vols. Where possible, we

LIST OF ABBREVIATIONS

have referred these passages from the *Nachlass* to the now standard edition by G. Colli and M. Montinari, *Kritische Gesamtausgabe Werke und Briefe* (Digital edition, ed. P. d'Iorio, available at nietzschesource.org).

BW	*Basic Writings*, ed. and trans. W. Kaufmann (New York: Modern Library, 2000 [1967]). From *BW*, the following are cited:
BGE	*Beyond Good and Evil*;
GM	*On the Genealogy of Morals.*
eKGWB	*Digitale Kritische Gesamtausgabe Werke und Briefe*, ed. P. d'Iorio, of Friedrich Nietzsche, *Werke–Kritische Gesamtausgabe*, eds. G. Colli and M. Montinari (Berlin/New York: de Gruyter, 1967–) and *Nietzsche Briefwechsel, Kritische Gesamtausgabe*, eds. G. Colli and M. Montinari (Berlin/New York: de Gruyter, 1975–). The fragments from the *Nachlass* (*Posthumous Fragments/Nachgelassene Fragmente*)—are cited as *eKGWB/NF*, followed by the year, group, and number.
NF	*Nachgelassene Fragmente/Posthumous Fragments*, cited from the Colli-Montinari edition (*Kritische Gesamtausgabe Werke und Briefe*); in the German as *eKGWB/NF* followed by the year, group, and number.
GS	*The Gay Science*, trans. W. Kaufmann (New York: Vintage Books, 1974).
PN	*The Portable Nietzsche*, ed. and trans. Walter Kaufmann (New York: Viking Penguin, 1982 [1954]). From *PN*, the following are cited:
TI	*Twilight of the Idols*;
TSZ	*Thus Spoke Zarathustra. A Book for None and All.*
WP	*The Will to Power*, trans. W. Kaufmann (New York: Vintage 1967). Every fragment is specified in the original German as *WzM* (*Der Wille zur Macht*) followed by § (section) and referenced to the Colli-Montinari edition (*Kritische Gesamtausgabe Werke und Briefe*) in note as *eKGWB/NF*, followed by the year, group, and number.

Martin Heidegger

Schürmann quotes Heidegger from the latter's published works before the completion of *Le principe d'anarchie: Heidegger et la question de l'agir* (1982) and—albeit he often modifies existing translations or directly renders from the German—usually gives reference to the available French and English editions. In this volume, the list of both German and English abbreviations provided by Schürmann in the typescript—as well as in *Heidegger On Being and Acting*—

LIST OF ABBREVIATIONS

has been maintained and reference to the now standard Heidegger's *Gesamtausgabe* has been added.

German

FD	*Die Frage nach dem Ding* (Tübingen: M. Niemeyer, 1962, VII).
GA	*Gesamtausgabe* (Frankfurt a.M.: V. Klostermann, 1975–).
GA 2	*Sein und Zeit*, ed. Friedrich-Wilhelm v. Herrmann (2008²).
GA 5	*Holzwege*, ed. Friedrich-Wilhelm v. Herrmann (2003²).
GA 6.1	*Nietzsche* I, ed. Brigitte Schillbach (1996).
GA 6.2	*Nietzsche* II, ed. Brigitte Schillbach (1997).
GA 7	*Vorträge und Aufsätze*, ed. Friedrich-Wilhelm v. Herrmann (2000).
GA 8	*Was heisst Denken?*, ed. Paola-Ludivika Coriando (2002).
GA 9	*Wegmarken*, ed. Friedrich-Wilhelm v. Herrmann (2004³).
GA 10	*Der Satz vom Grund*, ed. Petra Jaeger (1997).
GA 12	*Unterwegs des Sprache*, ed. Friedrich-Wilhelm v. Herrmann (2018²).
GA 13	*Aus der Erfahrung des Denkens*, ed. Hermann Heidegger (2002²).
GA 14	*Zur Sache des Denkens*, ed. Friedrich-Wilhelm v. Herrmann (2007).
GA 15	*Seminare*, ed. Curd Ochwadt (2005²).
GA 16	*Reden und andere Zeugnisse eines Lebensweges*, ed. Hermann Heidegger (2000).
GA 41	*Die Frage nach dem Ding: Zu Kants Lehre von den transzendentalen Grundsätzen*, ed. Petra Jaeger (1994).
GA 47	*Nietzsches Lehre vom Willen zur Macht als Erkenntnis*, ed. Eberhard Hanser (1989).
GA 55	*Heraklit*, ed. Manfred S. Frings (1994³).
GA 79	*Bremer und Freiburger Vorträge*, ed. Petra Jaeger (1994).
Gel	*Gelassenheit* (Pfullingen: G. Neske, 1959).
Hw	*Holzwege* (Frankfurt a.M.: V. Klostermann, 1950).
MHG	*Martin Heidegger im Gespräch*, interview with Richard Wisser (Freiburg/Br.: K. Alber, 1970).
N I	*Nietzsche* (Pfullingen: G. Neske, 1961), vol. I.
N II	*Nietzsche* (Pfullingen: G. Neske, 1961), vol. II.
Rc	*Der Ursprung des Kunstwerkes* (Stuttgart: Reclam, 1960).
SD	*Zur Sache des Denkens* (Tübingen: M. Niemeyer, 1969).
SAF	*Schellings Abhandlung Über das Wesen der menschlichen Freiheit* (Tübingen: M. Niemeyer, 1971), IX.
Sp	*Nur noch ein Gott kann uns retten* (interview) in *Der Spiegel*, 5.31.1976, 193–219.

LIST OF ABBREVIATIONS

SvG *Der Satz vom Grund* (Pfullingen: G. Neske, 1957).
SZ   *Sein und Zeit* (Tübingen: M. Niemeyer, 1957⁸), XI.
TK   *Die Technik und die Kehre* (Pfullingen: G. Neske, 1962).
US   *Unterwegs zur Sprache* (Pfullingen: G. Neske, 1959).
VA   *Vorträge und Aufsätze* (Pfullingen: G. Neske, 1954).
VS   *Vier Seminare* (Frankfurt a.m.: V. Klostermann, 1977).
WhD *Was heisst Denken?* (Tübingen: M. Niemeyer, 1954).
Wm   *Wegmarken* (Frankfurt a.m.: V. Klostermann, 1967).

English

BT   *Being and Time*, trans. John Macquarrie and Edward Robinson (New York: Harper & Row, 1962).
BWr   *Basic Writings*, ed. D. Krell (New York: Harper and Row, 1977).
DTh   *Discourse on Thinking*, trans. J.M. Anderson and E.H. Freund (New York: Harper & Row, 1966), 93 pp.
EGT   *Early Greek Thinking*, trans. David Farrell Krell and Frank Capuzzi (New York: Harper & Row, 1975), 129 pp.
EPh   *End of Philosophy*, trans. Joan Stambaugh (New York: Harper & Row, 1973), 110 pp.
Isp   *"Only A God Can Save Us Now"* (interview with *Der Spiegel*), trans. D. Schendler in *Graduate Faculty Philosophy Journal* 6 (1977): 5–27. This interview has also been translated as *"'Only a God Can Save Us': Der Spiegel's Interview with Martin Heidegger,"* trans. M.P. Alter and J.D. Caputo in *Philosophy Today* 20 (1976): 267–284.
IW   *"Martin Heidegger: An Interview"* (with R. Wisser), trans. V. Guagliardo and R. Pambrun in *Listening* 6 (1971): 34–40.
N i   *Nietzsche I: The Will to Power as Art*, ed. and trans. David Farrell Krell (New York: Harper & Row, 1979), 263 pp.
N ii *Nietzsche II: The Eternal Recurrence of the Same*, ed. and trans. David Farrell Krell (New York: Harper & Row, 1984), 289 pp.
N iii *Nietzsche III: Will to Power as Knowledge and as Metaphysics*, ed. David Farrell Krell, trans. Joan Stambaugh (New York: Harper & Row, 1984).
N iv *Nietzsche IV: Nihilism*, ed. David Farrell Krell, trans. Frank A. Capuzzi (New York: Harper & Row, 1982), 301 pp.
OTB   *On Time and Being*, trans. Joan Stambaugh (New York: Harper & Row, 1972).

LIST OF ABBREVIATIONS

OWL   *On the Way to Language*, trans. Peter D. Hertz and Joan Stambaugh (New York: Harper & Row, 1971).

PLT   *Poetry, Language, Thought*, trans. Albert Hofstadter (New York: Harper & Row, 1971).

QB   *The Question of Being*, trans. William Kluback and Jean T. Wilde (New York: Twayne, 1958).

QCT   *The Question Concerning Technology and Other Essays*, trans. W. Lovitt (New York: Harper & Row, 1977).

WCT   *What Is Called Thinking?*, trans. Fred D. Wieck and J. GlennGray (New York: Harper & Row, 1968).

WTh   *What Is a Thing?*, trans. W. B. Barton and Vera Deutsch (Chicago: Regnery, 1967).

Edition Guidelines

In order not to overload Schürmann's text with marginals or footnotes, all notes have been rendered as endnotes. Only bibliographical references to Kant, Schelling, Nietzsche, and Heidegger have been maintained within the text. All other references—by Schürmann and by the editors—are to be found in the endnotes. The edition marks are the following:

No marks: bibliographical references by Schürmann

‹ __ ›: infra-text handwritten additions by Schürmann

‹ ill. ›: illegible text

[__]: Editorial notes

" __ [__ R.S.] __ ": addition by Schürmann to quotes

" __ [__] __ ": addition by the editors to quotes

[* __ ?*]: editors' guess/reconstruction for partially readable text

{ __ }: handwritten marginal notations by Schürmann (*Marginalia* to the typescript)

{ ‹ " __ " › }: crossed-out text by Schürmann

All emphasized text within quotation marks (*italics*) should be considered as emphasized by the author(s) of the quote unless specified otherwise.

Reiner Schürmann, *Le principe d'anarchie: Heidegger et la question de l'agir* (Paris: Éditions du Seuil, 1982; Bienne and Paris: diaphanes, 2013) / *Heidegger on Being and Acting: From Principles to Anarchy*, trans. Christine-Marie Gros in collaboration with the Author (Bloomington and Indianapolis: Indiana University Press, 1987) are referred to as *PA* (diaphanes edition) and *HBA*, respectively.

Reiner Schürmann, *Des hégémonies brisées* (Mauvezin: Trans-Europ-Repress, 1996; Zurich and Berlin: diaphanes, 2017) / *Broken Hegemonies*, trans. Reginald Lilly (Bloomington and Indianapolis: Indian University Press, 2003) are referred to as *DHB* (diaphanes edition) and *BH*, respectively.

Historical Introduction

What I would like to do in this seminar is to work out a few concrete historical turns by which certain philosophical shifts—one could say, certain shifts in our civilization—become apparent. To take the matter in such broad terms,[1] one can nevertheless characterize the development in the philosophy of the last two centuries by a movement away from rationalism. The first challenge to rationalism bears an English signature: empiricism. As you know, it is the conflict between Leibniz's rationalism and Hume's empiricism that sets off the Kantian critical system, as an effort to assign to each his legitimate share.

But what happens after Kant, and to a large extent due to Kant, is what one could call the triumph of the ‹ willing › subject. Kant attempts to balance the rationalist and the empiricist claims by showing that each of these two doctrines addresses a specific set of subjective conditions of knowledge: the first, the conditions provided by reason, and the second, the conditions provided by sensibility. But it is this turn towards the subject—transcendentalism, in a word—that interests me with respect to a certain number of consequences. Kant's question is, quite naturally from what I have said: how can reason and sensibility be brought together? How can rationalism and empiricism be synthesized? How are a priori synthetic judgments possible? The challenge to the predominance of reason in the Western history of philosophy—in Western man—is thus taken up and answered by Kant by laying bare 'functions' in the subject. One could also say: strategies in the subject. It is Kant who coins the phrase of the 'subject as legislator,' as prescribing laws to nature ‹ by having reason [and] sensibility cooperate. ›

It is easy to see how this legislating subject—like a spider in a Hollywood movie that has come across potent victims and grows into a monstrous tarantula—develops after Kant: once the balance of empiricism, i.e., of experience in sensibility, is abandoned, there is no reason to remain content with the finitude of the subject. Thus the 'absolute mind' of the Idealists, the 'overman' of Nietzsche, and finally even the 'global reach' of technology can be seen as unbridled offspring of the transcendental turn in modern philosophy.

It is the hypothesis of this seminar that from Kant, to the Idealists, to Nietzsche, to contemporary technology, it is the will that comes to determine primarily and at times exclusively the human subject. Man's self-imposition under the labels of 'spirit,' 'overman,' and 'technological man' is an act of the will. The rise of empiricism had put into question man's self-understanding as 'rational animal.' With the post-transcendentalist developments that I have just sketched, he comes to understand himself more and more exclusively as the willing animal to whom nature must conform.[2]

* * *

How has the will gained this prestige? And first of all: what is the will? I should like to place the will into a few historical contexts, and by means of an introduction to the modern developments look back a little at its history.[3] I will briefly try to trace what we today call the will through three prior philosophical settings: the 'ethical' context, with Aristotle; the 'religious' context with Augustine; and the 'epistemological' context with Descartes.

a. The ethical context: Aristotle

As is well known, the Greeks have no word for 'will.' The verb *boulomai* rather means 'having the desire to,' 'wishing,' 'preferring.' The verb *ethelō* or *thelō* means 'being ready to act,' 'being decided,' 'having made up one's mind' (although the two verbs frequently mean the same thing). Nevertheless, one can say that Book III of Aristotle's *Nicomachean Ethics* contains much of what the later tradition will call 'voluntary.' In Book III, Ch. 3, Aristotle opposes what we do 'deliberately,'[4] ‹ διάνοια, › [*diánoia*] to what we do not do deliberately. "We deliberate about things that are in our power and can be done; [...] for nature, necessity, and chance are thought to be causes, and also reason and everything that depends on man."[5] Here is clearly enunciated the distinction between the voluntary and the involuntary: reason is that type of cause that is deliberate, and therefore, we can say, voluntary; nature, necessity, and chance are those types of causes that are not deliberate and thus involuntary. What do we do involuntarily? Aristotle defines [the term as follows]: all that we do naturally (knee-jerk reflex), as necessitated by, for instance, external constraint[6] (at gunpoint), or, by chance, i.e., without knowing the circumstances (Oedipus killing his father). The post-Aristotelian tradition characterizes the voluntary mainly by these two features: *internality* of the cause for action, and *knowledge* about its circumstances. This is the first basic distinction:[7] between what we do knowingly and [what we do] unwittingly.

Within the realm of what we do knowingly or deliberately, Aristotle furthermore distinguishes between what we wish and what we prefer.[8] The realm of what we prefer is inscribed—like a smaller circle—within the realm of the deliberate.[9] The generic term is 'wish,' i.e., the optative: precisely *boulēsis*. But all our wishes are not necessarily dependent on ourselves alone (winning a contest, being spared by a plague). Some wishes are impossible to fulfill (to be immortal). You see that this generic term, then, indicates the megalomania of desire, by which Descartes will explain error, and Sartre the infinity of our projects (ultimately, to be god). What is 'desirable in general' may please the mind or the body. The preferable restricts this vast field of wishful thinking. Its sphere coincides with that of our proximate efficacy, with what we can actually achieve, where we are masters of the means. You see how this distinction anticipates the later notions of choice and decision. I choose, I decide among, alternatives that are actually within my reach. Thus the two ingredients of the will here are freedom from constraint and choice among alternatives.

Of this Aristotelian notion of choice or decision, the generic term, I said, is wish, or desire. The specific difference is not difficult to identify: it is that about which we can deliberate. More precisely: that realm where I can select means towards a determinate end. Thus one could define the voluntary as 'deliberated desire,' whereby deliberation is over the means, and desire of the ends.

This way of defining the voluntary by genus and specific difference is the classical answer to the problem of rationality and irrationality in the will. We will see—in some detail—how modern philosophers, and first of all Kant, have tried to maintain the specificity of the will with regard to reason, and yet not yield to the total irrationality of the will. Aristotle's solution to this problem is clear from the description I have given: the generic term, desire, draws on forces that are not rational. But desire is not the will.[10] Deliberate desire, i.e., the will, is thus tamed desire, tamed irrationality, irrationality rationalized. In the Middle Ages, there will be ferocious struggles between 'intellectualists' such as those who then call themselves Aristotelians (and later, Leibniz) and the 'voluntarists' who draw on the neo-Platonic, Augustinian line. In Aristotle, the two elements, intellect and desire, are not in conflict, but harmonized in his understanding of the will as 'deliberated desire.'

You also see that this way of answering the issue of the will is neither psychological, since it is not meant to be an account of experience, nor metaphysical, since it does not rest on a theory of substance. It is properly *ethical*. Indeed, it is meant to answer that question which was foremost on the Greeks' mind: how can I live well? Description is balanced by prescription. Aristotle describes how megalomania is will without deliberation, and at the same time he prescribes the middle road, the *mean* between excess and deficiency. This doctrine of the mean is the basis, as you know, of his theory of virtues. And one can say that it is in the inquiry into the virtues that Aristotle's doctrine of the will—although this term does not exist in his writings—receives its full development. The proper usage of the will, then, is *phronēsis*, practical wisdom. And the theory is anchored in ontology in as much as our actions are the *'erga'* into which our actuality, *energeia*, translates itself. In this sense one could say that the will, for Aristotle, is what reveals being as actuality.

b. The religious context: Augustine

Augustine has been called the philosopher who 'discovered' the will (H. Arendt).[11] This is a little overstated, as we have seen in looking at Aristotle's *Nicomachean Ethics,* and as one would also see—in another fashion—in Plotinus, *Enneads*, VI, 8. But to the Aristotelian notions (as translated into our vocabulary) of freedom

and choice, of desire and deliberation, Augustine adds three elements that remain decisive for the entire tradition that follows.
— The first of these three elements is provided by a reflection on evil. Whereas for the Latin masters of Augustine—e.g., Cicero—evil was a problem of deficiency, of a lack of good, of the abuse of good,[12] for Augustine it is a positive act. This act is called by him '*aversio*,' turning away from the 'light within us,' as he says—turning away from God. The opposite movement of the mind is '*conversio*,' turning towards that light, which is nothing other than truth. What is new here is the 'infinite' role given to the individual. It is not by chance that Augustine was the first to write '*Confessions*': he is the discoverer of the will as that capacity by which we can lose ourselves. Hegel puts this contribution of Christianity very clearly in his *Philosophy of Right*:

> The critical and central point that distinguishes *Modernity* from *Antiquity* lies in the right of the subject's *particularity* to find itself satisfied or, which is the same thing, the right to *subjective freedom*. This right, in its infinity, is expressed in Christianity, where it becomes the real universal principle of a new form of the world.[13]

A new form of the world indeed, in which the fate of the individual subject becomes all-important. And in Augustine the right to particularity is entirely a matter of the will as infinite.

The will has the terrible power to negate itself, to will its annihilation, called damnation, to radically say no. Positively, its power is likewise awesome: Augustine does not hesitate to say that by turning inwards towards the truth in us, and upwards towards the divinity above us, we become God. This boundless either/or is something that the Aristotelian concept of choice did not include. Evil is an act, and not a thing, as for the Manicheans against whom [Augustine] polemicizes. But it is an act that inclines us to nothingness.

— The second element in Augustine that has modeled the philosophy of the will after him, at least until Kant, is the concept of a pure will. Kant will interiorize this pure will, or purely good will, and base his entire moral doctrine upon it. In Augustine, the pure will is God's, but it serves as a paradigm for man. Man is conceived

21

of against this background of pure will, linked in God to absolute knowledge and absolute power. The absolute is the model for the finite. Thus Augustine, although from two different points of view, holds that the human will is both infinite and finite. Infinite not in the sense of what I called the megalomania of desire, but infinite in its capacity for God, it is *capax Dei*. Finite not in that it can only elect a limited amount of goals to achieve, as in Aristotle, but finite in that it is never pure. The will is finite, for Augustine, due to the other faculties of man: our intellect guides it poorly, and our body obeys it poorly. If our intellect clearly saw the good, and if our body created no obstacles by desire, the will would be as absolute as God's.

— The third element derives directly from this infinity-finitude of the will: that is, the will is divided against itself. It wills the good, and yet there is something within itself—and not only in our intellect or our body—that does not will the good, that resists it. This is the famous opposition between 'willing and nilling,' *velle-nolle*. On this point I simply refer you to H. Arendt's *The Life of the Mind*, *Vol. II: Willing*, sections 8 ("The Apostle Paul and the impotence of the Will") and 10 ("Augustine, the first philosopher of the Will").[14]

Together, these three elements show the human will midway between desire, which is the element of the will's dispersion, and reason, which is its agent of unification—of 'sublimation,' perhaps. The will directed outwards is 'dissolute,' aiming at many things and ever-new goals; but the will that obeys reason, the will that is turned inwards, is simple, aiming ultimately at one single object, which Augustine calls the *lumen veritatis* [the light of truth]. Will constantly stands at a crossroads: it can follow what is spiritual in us, but also what is bodily. Hence the dramatic insistence on evil: ‹ the will › can altogether turn away from the light of the mind. To be spiritualized, it can model itself after the pure will, which is divine and which is its paradigm, its goal. And so standing at the crossroads, it remains, as long as we live, *divided*, in constant struggle with itself. The freedom of choice, *liberum arbitrium voluntatis*, is thus reduced to an awesome either/or.

No one set the stage of the drama of the will as clearly and as dramatically as Augustine. Also, it should be clear that his basic intuition—learned, of course, from the Apostle Paul—remains predominant until Kant, and including Kant: namely, that man is half carnal, half spiritual.[15] This middle-position assigned to the will, between reason and appetites, gives it its decisive role. You see how the problem of the rationality or irrationality of the will is posed here: the will can submit to desire and appetite, and then it is irrational, but the will can also obey reason, which makes it rational. The will, for Augustine, is rational when the mind commands it; hence the need for training of the will, *exercitatio animi*. I should add, though, that Augustine has a very unitary view of man. Thus desire, will and reason are not three layers or faculties or agencies. It is always I who wills, who desires, who understands. Or, to state it otherwise, the will is of itself rational and irrational.

One has to say, additionally, that the will is the agent that unifies man. Just to mention the distinction between inner and outer man: it is the will—and that means, here, a spiritualized way of life—that joins the two into harmony. Or according to the many triads of the mind: again, it is the will, one of the three elements of the mind's ternary structure, that makes the mind one.[16]

c. The epistemological context: Descartes

In Antiquity—early, classical, and late—the problem of the will was entirely confined to man's way of life; in other words, to the question, 'how should I live?' In Early Antiquity, for instance, in Sophocles' last play, *Oedipus at Colonus*, the hero is shown meditating on the preceding drama, *Oedipus Rex*. He says: it is not deliberately that I committed the monstrous deeds that have produced my ruin.[17] At the same time, he confesses that it is deliberately that he resisted the discovery of the truth—once it became all too evident. And we have seen how, in Aristotle, the problem was altogether an ethical one. Likewise in Augustine and the Middle Ages after him, where the issue is that of a god-like life.

All this changes with the rise of modernity, i.e., with Descartes. The problem of the will primarily arises no longer within debates about 'how should I live?,' but rather about another question: 'what can I know?'[18] The context, then, is an epistemological one. More precisely, the will serves no longer to account for *evil*, but for *error*.

This new context is not without relation to the preceding one. Whereas earlier, what was at stake was the foundation of the good (or evil) life, what is now at stake is the foundation of proper knowledge. And the framework of this new inquiry is the theory of judgment. Its classical locus is Descartes' Fourth Meditation. As one may expect, the problem of the rationality and irrationality of the will now becomes more crucial than ever.

The model of knowledge is exact science. How is it possible, the question goes, for the mind to be mistaken—be it in the sciences themselves or in other types of knowledge? How are false judgments possible? The question, 'how are true judgments possible?,' had been resolved earlier by the theory of the Cogito, of clear and distinct ideas, and God. What Descartes looks for now are the causes of error. Thus the inquiry is located within the quest for 'true knowledge.' And it is the will that bears the entire responsibility for error. Whenever there is error, it is the will that has misled us. How does this happen? And first of all, why is it that the understanding cannot be held to err?

> By the understanding alone I neither affirm nor negate anything, but I only conceive the ideas of things that I may affirm or negate. Now considering understanding in this way, one may say that no error is ever found in it, as long at least as the word error is taken in its proper sense.[19]

The proper sense of error would be 'wrong idea.' But that precisely cannot happen, since the understanding "only conceives the ideas of things" which are then affirmed or negated. The ideas as such cannot be false. There are no materially false ideas in our mind. Descartes is not saying either that will, which is the cause of error, is in itself rotten, or something of the kind. "Will consists merely in that we can do something or not do something (that is, affirm or negate, pursue or not pursue). Will consists in the possibility to act in such a fashion that, to affirm or negate, to pursue or not to pursue, those things that the understanding proposes to us, we feel no exterior force constraining us."[20]

As a simple faculty, will is thus innocent, too. But it is not innocent in its usage. When I am mistaken or deceived, my will is not contained within the boundaries of the understanding. Here, then, is Descartes' account of the possibility of error in the 4th Meditation: "I extend my will to things that I do not understand, to which—being of itself indifferent—it very easily goes astray."[21] Here the will is seen as an indifferent energy, so to speak, which drives the mind beyond what it understands. When the understanding does not discover something with perfect clarity, the will easily pushes our judgments beyond the limits so set by reason.[22]

Here the will is the active moment in judgment, whereas the understanding is the passive moment in it. The will is discovered by analysis, i.e., by taking apart those elements that are required to reach a judgment. We do not have an experience of the will, we have an experience only of judgments. In order to account for error, Descartes decomposes judgment into two causes: one that is limited by clear and distinct ideas, i.e., the understanding, and one that is without limit or restraint, i.e., the will. One can define the will as the power of contraries, since it can proceed one way or the other—in agreement with the ideas of the understanding or in disagreement.[23]

What has to be retained is the disproportion between reason and will. We find the old megalomania of the will—that I can will to be anything and everything—and the restraining agency of reason. However, as compared to Aristotle and Augustine, the stage is now narrower: it is limited to epistemological problems—or, in the general itinerary of the *Meditations*, to the problem of whether God can be a deceiver. In order to clear that possibility, Descartes has to give an account of the genesis of error, and that is the locus of the will. The philosophy of the will in Descartes responds to the question: 'why is there anything else but truth?' And the response provided is neither ethical, as in Aristotle, nor religious, as in Augustine. It is neither metaphysical—since we do not know, says Descartes, the end of creation—nor psychological, since the will cannot be experienced as such. The response is epistemological, proceeding by way of an analysis of judgment. This concludes my historical introduction ‹ : [the] will set loose. ›

With these three turning points—Aristotle, Augustine, Descartes—the stage is set for Kant's solution to the problem of the rationality and the irrationality of the will from which the *Groundwork* begins.

PART I

Rationality and Irrationality of the Will

In this part of our course—the first of three—we will look at a strategy in philosophy that leads from Kant to Heidegger. This strategy—if I may borrow from Leni Riefenstahl—is that of the 'triumph of the will.'[24] In the context of the 18th and 19th centuries, this strategy follows altogether the line of one key problematic, i.e., that of the relation between reason and its opposite (desire, sensibility, wish, body, emotions, or in whatever terms the principle of irrationality may be couched). The one who has most explicitly wrestled with this problem of the rational and the irrational nature of the will is Kant.

1. Kant: the good will and practical reason

Very early,[25] apparently already in 1753,[26] Kant affirms that there is nothing good in man but a good will. This is in contradiction to the tradition of Leibniz, Wolff, and even Aristotle—that the will is good when enlightened by ‹ the torch of › reason. In this more traditional view, it is precisely reason that is good alone, since it illuminates the will. In terms of the history of ideas, this is to say: at the age of 29, Kant had already left the rationalist influence in moral matters; in speculative matters, this took him about 20 years longer (the theory of synthesis between sensibility and understanding in *Critique of Pure Reason*).

Indeed, rationalism[27] holds the view that morality is impossible without science. Rational ethics means, for Leibniz, that ethics must derive from knowledge. Rationality thus implies that the will be guided not only by deliberation, as for instance in Aristotle, but that the will be informed by theoretical reason, modeled after the pattern of mathematics. What is good in man, for Leibniz—to put it briefly—is reason in its scientific activity. And action is moral when it is guided—when the will is guided—by a clarity of intuition that is the same as in mathematics.

Against this rationalist doctrine, Kant—particularly in the very first chapter of the *Groundwork*—holds that the good will suffices by itself for morality. But let us take this important issue step by step. First we should look briefly at some earlier texts of Kant.

a. The pre-critical writings and the question of moral evidence

The question, to state it again, is the following: in order to be moral, is it necessary to first gain rational evidence, i.e., knowledge? In a way, this question answers itself: whatever I wish to undertake, it is clear that I have to know what I am doing, I have to know (this was one of Aristotle's discoveries) the context, the antecedents and consequences of what I may do. Leibniz's conclusion thus sounds plausible: in order to be fully moral, I would have to know the general course of things scientifically, and if possible, with a divine intuition. I would have to encompass the entirety of human history with my eye. And indeed, according to Leibniz, God alone, who knows all things, is fully moral. As for man, his action will be more moral as his knowledge is clear and encompassing.

Kant will hold throughout his life that, yes, an evidence is required for moral action. However, this evidence is of a totally different kind than cognitive evidence. In his later vocabulary: practical reason is irreducible to theoretical reason. And also, yes, something supra-sensible is necessary for morality, but supra-sensible does not mean supra-natural. The good will is of itself supra-sensible.

This conviction is enforced by Rousseau,[28] who writes in *Émile* that "we can be humans without being scholars."[29] This means: there are those that are knowledgeable, and those that are less or not at all. 'Being human,' i.e., being moral, cannot depend on one's degree of knowledge. In Kantian terms: the realm of morals is independent of theory. The will is independent of cognitive evidence. The good will has its own evidence, which is a moral evidence. This type of evidence has nothing to do with the model of evidence in mathematics.[30] Long before the so-called critical turn, Kant thus separated himself from the school out of which he had come. Wolff, indeed, had taught that it is through demonstration that we can prove morality. The way to decide whether our conscience is good or not is logical argument, a deduction from premises according to syllogisms. This view of reason, for the early as well as for the later Kant, is too narrow.

To establish his insight into the rationality proper to the will, Kant first turns to a theory of affects. In a treatise of 1763, *Untersuchung über die Deutlichkeit der Grundsätze der natürlichen Theologie und der Moral* (On the Evidence of Principles in Natural Theology and in Morals), Kant attempts to oppose the two different kinds of evidence—theoretical and practical—in terms of sentiment.[31] In this text, reason appears as assigning form to morality, while sentiment assigns matter to it.[32] That is to say: when I reflect upon my affects or feelings a peculiar evidence arises, one which is not comparable to that in mathematics. The junction of reason and feeling is the operation by which moral evidence is obtained. You see that moral evidence is thus distinguished from theoretical evidence, with the help of an element that is foreign to reason, irrational. Moral evidence arises in the juncture of irrational feelings with a rational act. And it is the will that functions as unifier. Thus the will partakes both of irrationality and rationality—the influence of English authors such as Hume and Shaftesbury and Hutcheson is quite obvious.

Indeed, in these authors Kant had read ideas that were rather in conflict with his pietist upbringing. He read there that the moral ideal does not consist in vanquishing one's inclinations at all, but rather in tempering, balancing them so as to achieve peace in one's feelings. Kant discovered a view according to which the will espouses rather than combats our natural tendencies. The will is rational, then, when and in so far as it establishes harmony among our affects. What, then, is the moral evidence in these terms? Kant states it clearly and espouses this solution in some pre-critical writings: when our egotistical and altruistic propensities are balanced, moral evidence arises from inner sense, a kind of inner certainty. In these writings, Kant holds that any feeling can produce virtue; the moral good arises from rational equilibrium among sensible inclinations. As you know, this will no longer be his opinion in 1785, in the *Groundwork*.

At the same time, in these early writings, Kant separates himself already from the English doctrines of sentiment or "moral sense": he recognizes that in the will as tempering agent, there lies a drive for absolute obligation. A feeling will always only produce action in a relative fashion—when the object is there. But it may not always be given to sensibility.

In fact, with this idea of absolute obligation Kant embarks already on a road, concerning the will, that differs decisively from the utilitarian and empiricist premises of the English authors. The chief point is this: Kant departs from them at the precise moment that the agent of will is at stake. For Hume, virtue—i.e., the act of the will—is the means to reach happiness by establishing peace among our feelings. But with the idea of absolute obligation his intermediary agency of the will—between reason and sensibility, or between happiness and an affect—cannot hold. ‹ In fact, the will is separated from the problematic of happiness, or *telos*, end, matter, object altogether. › The peace felt in the inner sense cannot be the criterion of morality if morality is universally obligatory. In fact, the will is separated from the problematic of happiness altogether. In fact, without saying so in the early texts, Kant already gives to moral evidence the characteristic of reason—but he decidedly follows the British by holding that morality is never to be made dependent on knowledge, on science. You see how he agrees and at the same time disagrees with Hume in moral matters. On theoretical, 'pure,' matters, too, he will agree and disagree with Hume, although in another sense.

What[33] you have to remember from these early texts is that virtue, and with it the will, is clearly seen from the start as something unique when compared to theoretical reason. And yet, the will has a rationality of its own, which Kant expresses sometimes in terms of sentiment, at other times in terms of obligation. The crucial turn in 1785 will consist in the discovery that obligation and sentiment cannot both be considered rational, or as providing what I called moral evidence. It is impossible to reconcile sentiment and universal moral principles.

The last step that I want to briefly mention before beginning our reading of the *Groundwork* is contained in *The Dreams of a Spirit-Seer* (polemic against Swedenborg). In his critique of illuminism,

Kant mentions that there is one kind of evidence for which we have indeed neither empirical corroboration nor mathematical certitude, i.e., moral evidence. And he expresses this evidence in terms of the will: the moral good is evident to us when our individual will is in agreement with the universal will. Now moral sense—he still speaks in those terms—is the organ by which we discover a much more radical harmony than that among feelings: we sense, Kant says, that our individual will is subordinated under the universal will.

In this text, the universal will has nothing to do with the traditional notions of general will: it is not the will of all, but the systematic nature of the will. The universal will is closely connected with a notion that we encounter in the *Groundwork,* namely, the "kingdom of ends." By the universal will, as opposed to the individual will, I belong to a community of rational beings. The will, here, is the connection among rational agents. When Kant speaks of the submission of the individual will to the universal will in *The Dreams of a Spirit Seer* we are not far from the definition of the kingdom of ends: "every rational being [... R.S.] must regard himself as making universal law by all the maxims of his will, and must seek to judge himself and his actions from this point of view" (*GMM*, 100).[34] Here you see at work one of the key ideas in Kant's practical philosophy, namely, that of universalizability. If I will an object *A*, and if I can will that any rational agent in my situation should be able to will that same object *A*, then I can say that my individual will has submitted itself to the universal will.

Let us retain these elements from Kant's pre-critical philosophy of the will (leaving aside the brief adoption of "sentiment" and "moral sense"):

1. The specificity of the will as compared to both sensibility and—more importantly—theoretical reason;

2. The self-sufficiency ‹ [or] autonomy › of the will in terms of moral goodness;

3. Moral evidence as distinguished from cognitive evidence;

4. The rationality of the will has to be ‹ (formally) › defined by universal obligation, rather than ‹ (materially) › by the desire for happiness.

Part I

b. The "good will" in the
Groundwork of the Metaphysics of Morals

The purpose of this first writing of Kant's after the 'critical turn' (1785; *Critique of Pure Reason*: 1788) on 'practical philosophy' results from what I have said about the pre-critical texts: it is to establish what he calls the "moral fact" as a "fact of reason." This means that—now within the original framework—Kant has to separate off morality from any other 'fact,' i.e from experience; he also has to separate it off from any other form of 'reason,' i.e. speculative or theoretical reason. For the two tasks he calls upon the notion of "good will." We will read the *Groundwork* today in order to learn about the will. Thus this is not a course on Kant's moral philosophy in general. We will only read those sections that directly deal with the problem of the will.

In the Preface, Kant states the 'critical' intention of the work:

> Do we not think it a matter of the utmost necessity to work out for once a pure moral philosophy entirely cleansed of everything that can only be empirical and appropriate to anthropology? That there must be such a philosophy is already obvious from the common Idea of duty and from the laws of morality (*GMM*, 57).[35]

The critical point of view consists in looking at the conditions of morality within ourselves rather than at facts of moral decision making (which would be the task of empirical anthropology). And the first condition we discover is that everyone knows of morality, i.e., we are all familiar with what Kant here calls duty and the laws of morality. Let us not discuss these terms here but simply retain that Kant's intention is to examine morality 'purely,' without an eye to what people actually experience and do, and to examine it as something known to all.

With these two premises, he can introduce immediately, as he does in that Preface, the issue of the will: the pure laws of morality "must gain entrance into the will" (ibid.),[36] and "the metaphysics of morals has to investigate the Idea and the principles of a possible *pure* will, and not the activities and conditions of human willing as such, which are drawn from the most part from psychology"

32

(*GMM*, 58).[37] Against anthropology and psychology, which rest on experience, a metaphysics of morals must investigate how a pure will is possible. Thus the philosopher is not the only one to raise questions about the will. But he does so, without giving consideration to the concrete conditions of the will,[38] e.g. maturity, social context, ideological milieu, etc. The philosopher, Kant adds, "pays attention to the different sources" (ibid.)[39] of faculties within us: that is precisely the transcendental-critical method.

In what sense can he claim that morality is a fact known to everyone? We have seen that it is not a fact in the sense of experience. This is to say, Kant cannot claim that we all know about morality because we all act morally.[40]

The moral fact[41] is the fact of moral judgment.[42] What we are all acquainted with, is not moral behaviour—in the strictest possible sense, that may even never have existed on earth—but moral judgement. However, judgment is not a matter that one can experience as one observes people cheating ‹ on › one another. Thus moral judgment is a fact, known to all, but not an empirical fact.

Please note the parallel with the *Critique of Pure Reason*: Kant never puts into question the moral fact here, nor experience there. In either case, what he never puts into question is a judgment: the scientific judgment in the context of pure theoretical reason, the moral judgment in the context of pure practical reason.

It is this context—the critical enquiry into subjective sources and the conviction that everyone is acquainted with moral judgment—that you have to keep in mind when you read the very first sentence of the book after the Preface: "It is impossible to conceive anything in the world, or even out of it, which can be taken as good without qualification, except a *good will*" (*GMM*, 61).[43] How are we to understand this linking of the good will to the critical method on the one hand and to the universality of the moral fact on the other?[44]

The answer[45] is simple, and the first chapter of the book supports it in detail: Kant looks, not for the causes of moral action as a psychologist or anthropologist does, but for its conditions of possibility. And there is only one such condition, i.e., the good will. The critical method does not lay bare causes, but the foundation or condition in us (link between good will and transcendental criticism); and since this condition does not depend on experience—talent, knowledge, culture—it is also universal (link between good will and the moral fact in common consciousness). Now, universality and necessity, when they are not predicated of forms of sensibility (time and space), pertain to reason. Thus because it is ‹ (a) › not a fact of experience and (b) universally shared, the good will has to be a 'fact of reason.'[46]

Good will cannot be explained by egoism, which is the mark of sensibility: hence it must be explained by reason. But how can the good will be assimilated to the rational will? That is the question that Kant raises at the beginning of Chapter I.

c. Chapter I of the Groundwork:
good will and rational will.

What is the most startling about the beginning of the text is its apo-deictical tone. I already quoted the first sentence: "It is impossible to conceive anything in the world, or even out of it, which can be taken as good without qualification, except a *good will*." This state-ment is never proved in the text. And we know why: Kant follows the evidence of common consciousness.[47] The fundamental truth about the will in its relation to morality need not be established through long reasonings. Actually it *cannot* be established. It is the moral evidence that every rational being—"in the world or out of it," i.e. rational beings other than ourselves—possesses. Kant's starting point is an absolute, reached immediately. It is not the topic of any discussion.

This is how you have to understand the title of the first chap-ter: "Passage from ordinary rational knowledge of morality to philosophical."[48] Ordinary rational knowledge states: there is noth-ing good in the world except a good will. What, then, can 'philo-sophical' knowledge of morality be? In other words, what is the transition *towards* that the title enunciates? We have heard about philosophy in the opening sections of the Preface to the *Ground-work*. The first sentence there reads:

Ancient Greek philosophy was divided into three sciences: *physics, ethics* and *logic*. This fits the nature of the subject perfectly, and there is no need to improve on it—except perhaps by adding the principle on which it is based" (*GMM*, 55).[49]

What can this principle be? We read about it further down in the Preface: we are "to pay heed to the difference of the sources" (*GMM*, 58). This[50] is in line with the general movement of the transcendental turn: examine those sources or faculties in the subject out of which the theoretical fact—i.e. experience—as well as the practical fact—i.e. the moral evidence—are possible.

The transition from ordinary knowledge of morality to philosophical knowledge of morality is thus clear: the task is to disentangle the sources within ourselves that eventually produce the moral evidence that everyone possesses.

Concretely, this task will be carried out by the discussion of the most traditional of topics in moral philosophy, namely, that of happiness. Philosophers have traditionally held that moral evidence arises from everyone's desire for happiness; the question now is: is it the will to be happy that provides the ordinary knowledge of morality? Happiness is what we desire. Thus right away, the question of morality is couched in terms of the rationality and the irrationality of the will: is the absolutely good will a matter of desire, and hence of irrationality, or of rationality?

This assignment of the ordinary evidence about the good will to either sensibility (i.e. desire, appetite, affect) or to reason thus properly constitutes the philosophical task.

The passage from ordinary knowledge to philosophical knowledge will be completed when we know whether the will—of which everyone knows that it alone is morally good—is, as such, irrational or rational. Whether it is the will as desiring happiness that makes us morally good or the will in some other, rational, competence. This is the starting point and the sense of the title of the first chapter. Once again, the evidence that the good will alone constitutes what we call morality is never put into question. What is put into question, and what constitutes the nature of philosophical knowledge, is: what is it that makes the will good? Reason or ‹ instinct? › Reason or ‹ un ›reason?[51]

In the second sentence of this first chapter, Kant rejects the two traditional ways of answering that question. The first is the Leibniz-ian and Wolffian way. You remember that the rationalists taught that morality depends on science. I have to gain a kind of knowledge that is as clear as mathematics in order to then act morally. To this, Kant replies: "Intelligence, wit, judgment and any other *talents* of the mind we may care to name" will never make for moral perfection (*GMM*, 61).[52] The second solution that Kant rejects is the Aristotelian one: morality does not coincide with virtue. Indeed, he says,

> Courage, resolution, and constancy of purpose, as qualities of temperament, are without doubt good and desirable in many respects; but they can also be extremely bad and hurtful when the will is not good which has to make use of these gifts of nature" (ibid.).[53]

The essence of moral life cannot consist in the virtues: indeed, moderation in emotions or in passions, courage, etc., can quite well be put into the service of evil. Thus neither talents nor virtues will ever make the will good.

On the contrary, it is the will that has to make talents and virtues morally good. It "has to make use of these gifts of nature." In other words, the good will cannot be referred to anything outside itself for evaluation—neither to gifts of intelligence nor to gifts of moderation. I can have courage in robbing a bank; I can have temperance in eating and drinking to remain clear-headed in setting up an illicit business, etc.[54]

Intelligence (or science) and virtues can be called good only insofar as they serve something good: insofar as I do something with my gifts. That is precisely the ordinary knowledge of morality: that intelligence and virtue are not good in themselves, that they need to be oriented towards an end that is good, and that only that can be called good which is so by itself. Thus the will cannot be called rational because reason would assign the will its end. That was the traditional rationalist solution: reason has to hold the torch, and the will has to follow, ‹ to select, › what reason shows it.

"A good will is not good because of what it effects or accomplishes—because of its fitness for attaining some proposed end; it is good through its willing alone—that is, good in itself" (*GMM*, 62).[55] This idea is, of [course], most Greek: only that which can be called simply good, *haplôs agathon*,[56] is good by itself. But what you have to see is that Kant understands the will not as *aiming* at this *bonum simpliciter* as everyone [did] before him, but that the will—a certain quality of it—is now what is called purely and simply good. You see the move of subjectivation already mentioned.

This doctrine—that a good will is good not because of what it accomplishes, but "through its willing alone"—has often been misunderstood. One must not believe that Kant wants to say: whatever you do has no importance. Only the intention or the inner disposition is what counts. Kant says clearly here that the good will is "not, admittedly, a mere wish, but the straining of every means so far as they are in our control" (ibid.).[57] The good will is not 'wishful thinking,' day-dreaming; it tends with all its power towards the fulfillment of an end. But it is the moral *value* derived exclusively from our inner disposition which Kant calls the good will ('disposition,' *Gesinnung*, is one of the related terms in the *Critique of Pure Reason*).

Indeed, intention and inner disposition alone count towards the moral quality of our acts—but these are concepts of analysis; that is to say, in an act that always tends towards a concrete end, what is the element that makes it good? The disposition, the intention, the good will, 'meaning well' alone.[58]

Nietzsche[59] will say of this subjectivation of the Platonic *haplôs agathon*, in Kant: "At bottom, the old sun, but seen through mist and skepticism. The idea has become elusive, pale, Nordic, Königsbergian" (*PN*, 486).[60] Moral perfection no longer lies in the objective excellence of our behaviour, visible to the eyes of all inhabitants of the city, as for the Greeks; moral perfection lies in the purity of the heart (in Rousseau's terms).[61]

Now comes the move that, for our purpose, is decisive. Kant formulates it in a strange way, as a rhetorical suspicion:

> Yet, in this idea of the absolute value of a mere will, [...] in spite of all the agreement that it receives from ordinary reason, there must arise the suspicion that [...] we may have misunderstood the purpose of nature in attaching[62] reason to our will as its governor (*GMM*, 62).[63]

Thus ordinary reason agrees that a good disposition, i.e., the will alone, has absolute value. But what if ordinary reason is mistaken? And, he explicates further: what if ordinary reason is mistaken about the fact that nature has attached reason to our will as its pilot?

Never mind the rhetorical question—it is immediately negated and forgotten. But the content is important, namely, to say that only the good will has absolute moral value is to say that "nature has attached reason to our will as its governor." This is what we must examine. The affirmation constitutes the core of the problem of rationality and irrationality of the will. Indeed, by this formulation we learn, as if by a detour, that the good will of which Kant has been speaking for a while is nothing other than the rational will—will subjected to reason alone.

This is the exact point where the title of the first chapter comes to apply. Kant has followed what he considers ordinary reason to know. Now he proceeds to the "passage from ordinary rational knowledge of morality to philosophical."

Up to now[64] we have heard—and common reason is supposed to know—that the good will is the good in itself. Now we hear—and that is the result of 'philosophy'—that the good will is reason.

This crucial step is only understandable within the general framework of Kant's critical thinking. For Kant, there is nothing other in man than either sensibility or reason. To be sure, each of these two "stems of knowledge"[65] is in itself complex: sensibility encompasses in its theoretical activity the five outer senses and the inner sense; and reason, in its theoretical activity, *Verstand* and *Vernunft*.[66] In the mind's practical activity these two stems are now put in parallel, with instinct on the side of sensibility and the good will on the side of reason. Now, instinct has been characterized (at least in the context of the critical writings) by everything that the good will is not: instinct has an object, a *telos*, the good will is self-sufficient; instinct always requires something given, material, whereas the good will is merely formal. Thus since the good will is not instinctual, it can only be rational.[67]

Teleology, or teleocracy, is the decisive factor in this disjunction. For Kant, to speak of a goal to be attained is to speak of inclination, sensibility, desire—of faculties that are irrational. Most philosophers would agree that voluntary action is that action which is subject to reason. But most philosophers would not agree with Kant in saying that moral reason finds its goal in itself, i.e. in making the will good.[68]

This much has to be clear in order to understand Kant's solution to the problem of the rationality and irrationality of the will: to desire is always to desire something, an inclination towards something; but to will is not—formally, at least—to will something. It is rather a matter of general disposition.[69] This ‹ negative › criterion, teleocracy (the rule of ends), is what makes for Kant's so-called rigorism. He says indeed:

> Suppose now that [for] a being endowed with reason and will the real purpose of his nature were happiness. In that case, nature would have hit on a very bad arrangement by choosing reason in the creature to carry out this purpose. For all the actions he has to perform with this end in view would have been mapped out for him far more accurately by instinct (*GMM*, 62–63).[70]

This is of course a hypothetical argument: suppose nature had in view only our happiness and nothing else. In that case we would not have needed reason and will. Now, since we also have reason and will, our destiny, so to speak, goes farther than the mere quest for happiness. And this more noble destiny, everyone knows it: it is to be moral rather than happy.

Or, in the terms which are now Kant's: our real destiny is to do our duty rather than be happy. What Kant has to say about duty in this first chapter, ‹ pertains › directly to the topic of the will. What counts is a double duty, one primary and the other secondary. Our primary duty is "the culture of reason" (*GMM*, 64).[71] That is, making our will good. Our secondary duty is towards happiness. The first is unconditional, the second conditioned.

The concept of duty,[72] Kant says, "includes that of a good will, exposed, however, to certain subjective limitations and obstacles" (*GMM*, 65).[73] Duty thus can be defined as the necessitation of our subjective, individual will by reason. It is opposed to inclinations and fears. Thus the battlefield of morality is marked out by an either-or: either the will follows duty, and then it is rational and good, or it follows inclinations and fears ‹ alone ›, and then it is irrational and evil.[74] My individual will becomes rational when it overcomes "certain subjective limitations and obstacles," i.e., inclinations. Thus it is duty that makes the will rational.

Kant frequently opposes our specifically human case to the case of rational beings in general. Here he speaks of the "holy will" (*GMM*, 81)[75]—both the will that is *heil*, integral, and *heilig*, holy. Well, even such a perfect will would be subject to the moral law, but it would not resist the moral law "through certain subjective limitations and obstacles." Human duty has this particular feature that it requires submission[76] of our tendencies to reason.

You see the purpose in Kant's introducing here this new concept, duty. It serves to further determine in what sense our will has to be rational; in what sense it is as if threatened by irrationality; and what we have to do to make it genuinely rational. One distinction that he uses in this respect is between acts that are morally "in conformity with duty" and acts done "from the motive of duty" (*GMM*, 65).[77] And he gives the example of the grocer who may act in conformity with duty by not overcharging his customers—but his motive may be mere interest, so that they will come back. Only that will is good which determines acts done "from the motive of duty."

Some critics of Kant have claimed that according to his doctrine of duty only that action is moral which is opposed to my inclinations and normal tendencies—only those actions, in other words, that hurt. Such a view of Kant is totally wrong. Once again, the purpose of Kant's enterprise is analytical. He lays bare that element in our actions that makes them moral, and this element is now called duty—which is the proper term for the will's conformity with reason. But Kant also says quite explicitly in these pages that it is part of our duty to preserve one's life, to be good to one's friends and to preserve one's happiness: all things that one would consider precisely not to hurt.

Kant never ever says that the good will is corrupted when it follows our tendencies. He only says that when the good will follows our tendencies there is no way of analyzing the moral or immoral quality of an act. Thus the will is good indeed insofar as it is rational; but the rationality of the will may on many occasions be in perfect harmony with our inclinations and desires. In other words, it in fact frequently happens that our inclinations conform with duty. Only, in such cases it is not this conformity with duty that makes for the rationality of the will and moral quality. You see the continuity on this part with some pre-critical writings: our tendencies and inclinations may be altruistic, well-meaning. Except that now he says: that is not what makes our actions good. Thus Kant's rigorism is due to the necessities of analysis rather [than] to obligation. We do not have the ‹ systematic › obligation to combat our inclinations. His rigorism is not normative.

We can now summarize[78] some chief aspects of Kant's teaching about the rationality and the irrationality of the will. He does so himself, as a matter of fact, at the end of this first chapter. I briefly focus on the four notions of formalism, respect, representation, and maxim.

Formalism. This means that the rules of the good will can only be a priori. Or, stated otherwise, that it is not any given content of an act that makes it morally good. Stated still otherwise, it is not something particular, something actually given to us as a matter of desire, that makes an act good but something universal: and that is found only a priori in reason. It is the moral law as spelled out by the law: you must always be able to universalize your maxim.

Respect. Duty is that necessity in acting which results from pure respect for the moral law. Thus the conformity of sensibility and reason, in the practical domain, is properly described by this notion of respect. Respect is a feeling. It is that feeling by which we acquiesce to the moral law. Thus it has to be opposed to inclinations and fears. These are determined by things empirical whereas respect is determined by reason alone. The will, as rational, is accompanied by the feeling of respect. One cannot have respect for a content of action, or even a goal, for the effect of the will. Respect ‹ is › only for that element which makes the will rational—for reason as the principle of action.

Representation.[79] What is it now that reason does with regard to the will so that Kant can state here again that it is "in the will of a rational being alone that the highest and unconditioned good can be found" (*GMM*, 69)?[80] Reason represents the law to itself. Paton renders this as "idea" instead of "representation"—which is truly misleading (if you keep in mind Kant's technical usage of the term "idea"). What Kant wants to say is: reason is not necessary to act according to a goal; we heard that instinct is much better equipped for such teleology. Rather, reason is required to represent to itself the law, a law which instinct can only follow immediately, without representation. Here then comes Kant's proper solution to the problem of the rationality of the will: reason is the condition for the good will because the good will is possible only in such a being that can represent the law to itself, render it present to itself so as to have it constantly before its eyes. This representational characteristic of reason will appear closely related to the triumph of the will in modern philosophy, and particularly in technology as Heidegger sees it: to represent is then the basic trait of technical rationality.

<u>Maxim</u>. This is an individual rule that I implicitly formulate for myself in any action. Example of the grocer: if I want to keep my customers, I had better not cheat. The rational maxim is that which can be universalized without contradiction (i.e., the categorical imperative).[81]

2. Schelling: the rational will and the "dark will"

Schelling's essay *Of Human Freedom* (1809) announces a decisive turn in the philosophy of the will. We will see later that this turn can fully be understood only in ontological terms: what occurs with Schelling is the ontologization of the will. At this point I merely want to show how this essay presents the relation between will and reason. The overall thesis is easily summarized: reason turns into one kind of will.[82] The way, however, that this thesis is reached and substantiated, is not so easily shown. I will first place the essay within Schelling's general development.

RATIONALITY AND IRRATIONALITY OF THE WILL

a. Philosophy of nature,
transcendental philosophy, philosophy of identity

Schelling is usually depicted as the first idealist who has really "overcome" the Kantian transcendental subjectivism.[83] Fichte is, then, presented as the subjective idealist and Schelling as the "objective" idealist. By this is meant that spirit, with Schelling, comes to be independent of the subject—as it was, in other ways, for classical metaphysicians. The situation is, however, a little more complex: as we shall see, the entire problem of the will hinges, for Schelling, on subjective affirmation, and subjective in the very individual sense of personality or individuality.

What is meant by 'objective idealism' applies best to Schelling's first period: *Ideas for a Philosophy of Nature* (1797), *A First Project of a Philosophy of Nature* (1799). In these works, Schelling attempts to consider nature in its totality. After neo-Platonic authors (we will frequently encounter reminiscences of this tradition—it goes back via Spinoza and Giordano Bruno to Nicholas of Cusa and, from there, via many intermediary figures, to Plotinus), he represents nature as a hierarchical whole. From general matter up to the human mind, he views nature as a process of perpetual becoming. The human mind is "the eye by which the spirit of nature contemplates itself."[84] Thus knowledge is inseparably subjective *and* objective—knowledge of the self, as in Kant and Fichte, and knowledge of the things themselves in nature, as in earlier metaphysics.

To show the unity of subjective and objective knowledge, Schelling undertakes a double itinerary: from object to subject, and this is his "philosophy of nature"; from subject to object, and this is his "transcendental philosophy." The point is that one without the other is mutilated and impoverished.[85] Hence the harsh criticism of Kant—even until the later essay, *Of Human Freedom*, which begins:

> [T]he contrast of Nature and Spirit was at first readily taken up as such. This way of looking at the matter was adequately justified by the firm belief that reason is found only in man, the conviction that all thought and knowledge are completely subjective and that Nature altogether lacks reason and thought, and also by the universally prevalent mechanistic attitude—even the dynamic factor which Kant revived having again

PART I

passed over into a higher mechanism [..., R.S.] The time has come for the higher distinction or, rather, for the real contrast, to be made manifest, the contrast between Necessity and Freedom, in which alone the innermost center of philosophy comes to view (*HF*, 1).[86]

Transcendental philosophy by itself, in other words, leads us astray since it can only conceive of nature as a mechanism obeying subjectively imposed laws. In the essay *Of Human Freedom,* Schelling takes this up again and again: [*SW*, I, 7,] 346, 348, 351f, etc. For Schelling, then, nature is something that is really encountered—not posited. Nature is furthermore so rich that its very variety of forms is a proof of its otherness with regard to the subject. This turn to an objective idealism is Kant turned against himself: with Kant, the Schelling of this early period holds the "ideality" of nature; but against Kant, this now means that nature is itself spiritual, that it is objective spirit. Nature is something autonomous and spiritual: autonomous because we encounter it, come upon it, and spiritual because of its intrinsic order and life.[87] Schelling:

> So-called dead[88] nature is nothing else but an intelligence that is not yet ripe. This is why in all its phenomena the intelligible character transpires, although as yet unconscious. Thus nature reaches its highest goal, viz. becoming entirely an object for itself, only by the highest and ultimate reflection in itself: this is nothing else but man or more generally what we call reason. By reason, indeed, nature returns completely upon itself [cf. the neo-Platonic *reditio completa,*[89] R.S.], and it becomes manifest that originally nature is identical with what in ourselves is known as intelligence[90] and consciousness.[91]

Thus Schelling considers the mechanistic view of nature—prominent from Descartes to Kant—as reductive. Against this view, he means to rehabilitate the autonomous life of the organic (for which Kant has no categories[92]) as well as everything individual and singular. It is on this last point, as we will see, that his solution to the problem of the rationality and irrationality of the will depends.

In his transcendental philosophy (*System of Transcendental Idealism,* 1800), which is the counterpart of his philosophy of nature,

44

Schelling follows the opposite itinerary: not from nature to subject (or spirit), but from the life of the spirit to objective nature.

> The pure life of spirit does not satisfy our hearts. There is something within us that desires essential reality [...] The artist does not take rest in the mere thought of his work, but only in its physical representation.[93] [...] Likewise the goal of all ‹ longing ›[94] [*Sehnsucht* - important term later in the essay *Of Human Freedom*, R.S.] is perfectly physical in as much as it reflects[95] what is perfectly spiritual (*Cl*, 178).[96]

Thus behind the life of the mind we discover the life of nature as essentially different. In the *System*, he then develops how the physical "reflects" the spiritual: to each level of reality corresponds a level of self-consciousness. I do not insist.

The philosophy of identity focuses on this same relation between freedom and nature—this time, however, to assert their essential identity. Nature is spirit made visible, and spirit is nature as invisible.[97] But seen from either side, it is the same essence that is at stake. This thesis of identity rests on a theory of truth as conformity. How would conformity be possible if, in the judgment that conforms to a given reality, the "ground" were not the same as in that reality? We would be forever unable to know whether our judgments correspond to something real if we did not presuppose an original identity between mind and nature—what Kant, because of his mechanistic assumption, had to deny. "In all that becomes, be it of whatever species, the subjective and the objective, the ideal and the real are always together, only to diverse degrees."[98]

It is the philosophy of identity that paves the way for the problem of the will and its rationality. Indeed, identity between subject and object requires a common ground, which Schelling calls divine; and the problem of the will is right away raised in connection with the absolute (as was the case, here again, with the first philosopher of the will, Plotinus; cf. *Enneads* VI, 8).

The main problem in the philosophy of identity can be stated in a very traditional way: how does the manifold arise from the one? It is for a solution to this problem that Schelling has to postulate a certain identity and a certain difference within the divine absolute. Absolute indifference differentiates itself, he says. Even

PART I

more: absolute unity is possible only among multiplicity; the absolute First needs the manifold to appear as one, as undifferentiated, indeterminate. The process of self-differentiation is spelled out in very classical terms again: the *noesis noeseōs*, mind contemplating or intuiting itself, from Aristotle. The degrees of the universe arise from divine self-intuition. This construct is highly reminiscent of Plotinus, Proclus, Scotus Erigena.

At the beginning of the essay *Of Human Freedom*, of which we have to speak now, Schelling enters into a detailed refutation of the charge of pantheism. This strange way of entering into the topic of the will and of freedom cannot be understood except against the background of the philosophy of identity—with the seemingly inevitable consequence that the absolute is entirely present in the subjective and in the objective domains, that it *is* their conjunction.[99] This is not what Schelling holds, although it is not easy to refute the charge. Later, in the so-called *Spätphilosophie*, or Gnosis, he will not tire of arguing against the emanation of all things from the one, and for God's free will. The essay *Of Human Freedom* stands on the threshold between the philosophy of identity and the—very obscure—late philosophy.

b. The absolute will

You[100] have seen how the problem of the absolute arises for Schelling: out of a dissatisfaction with the transcendental method and the need to account for the autonomy of nature—with its variety of forms, its own vitality, and hence the particular. The absolute appears as the "ground" that unites subject and object, or freedom and nature.

But how does the absolute account for the individual, the ‹ singular ›[101]? To push this question to the extreme, which is the key-issue in the essay *Of Human Freedom*: how does the absolute account for the possibility of evil? Indeed, it is evil that is seen by Schelling as the ultimate obstacle for reason. The charge is now that metaphysics up to German Idealism was unable to account for evil: "It is impossible for dogmatic philosophy to recognize the [positive, R.S.] character of evil since it has no concept of personality, that is of selfhood elevated to spirituality, but only an abstract concept of the infinite and the finite" (*HF*, 39).[102] You see how the problem of evil is tied to individuality, personality. Quite as nature, life, history, evil is something positive: "Something positive is required which must of necessity be assumed in evil, but which will remain inexplicable as long as a root of freedom is not recognized in the independent basis of nature" (*HF*, 40).[103] This freedom in the independent basis of nature is the will of the absolute—or the absolute *as* will.

The traditional solutions given to the problem of evil are unsatisfactory because they rest either on a merely formal opposition between finite and infinite, as mentioned in the first quote above, or on the equally formal opposition between reason and sensibility. In the first case, evil is what is finite (and thus merely a restriction of the infinite, nothing positive, a 'privation'); in the second case, evil is what is unfree: reason is the realm of freedom, and sensibility, the realm of evil:

> According to current views, the sole basis of evil lies in the world of senses or in animality [...] This notion is the natural outcome of the doctrine in accordance with which freedom consists in the mere mastery of the intelligent principle over the desires and inclinations of the senses, and the good is derived from pure reason. Accordingly, it is obvious that evil can have no freedom (ibid.).[104]

The aporia that Schelling faces in this essay is the following: either we explain evil as philosophers have done since Plato, i.e., through recourse to the oppositions between infinite and finite as well as reason and sensibility; but then evil is located in what is finite, what can be intuited by the senses, and it is nothing positive, not a consequence of our freedom. Or we trace evil back into the very ground of nature, i.e., into God, and then the goodness of the divine being is done away with.

This, then, is the point where Schelling sees no other solution than to introduce an element of irrationality into the divine ground itself. The absolute will cannot be altogether rational, light, '*logos*.' If that were the case, what would be the root of evil in the world? And—to say it again—Schelling understands evil to be something concrete, positive, and hence freedom more than '*libertas indifferentiae*,' the freedom of choice (Buridan's ass): "The real and vital conception of freedom is that it is a potential for good and evil" (*HF*, 21).[105]

To understand the potential for evil in human freedom, then, Schelling thinks that we have to assume a double will in the absolute itself. One will is rational, the other is 'dark.' This latter will is the source for all evil and guilt in history. He is always quick to add, however, that this is by no means to say that there is anything evil in the absolute itself: "Notwithstanding this general necessity, evil remains man's own choice; this ‹ ground › cannot cause evil as such, rather every creature falls through its own guilt" (*HF*, 50).[106]

Here we have a peculiar solution to the rationality and irrationality of the will: both terms designate one aspect of the absolute. Not only is the will promoted with Schelling (as already before him with Fichte) to the rank of ultimate ground, but it is—as ultimate ground—the locus where reason and non-reason enter into a conflict. One consequence of this position is that where there is the rational, there also is the irrational; where there is truth, there also is untruth. We will see this simultaneity taken up first by Nietzsche ("truth is a lie") and then by Heidegger ("the history of truth is a history of errancy and error").

One quote to illustrate the identification between absolute and will:

> In the final and highest instance there is no other being than Will. Will is primordial being, and all predicates apply to it alone—groundlessness, eternity, independence of time, self-affirmation! All philosophy strives only to find this highest expression (*HF*, 19).[107]

The most arduous task in reading Schelling is what has to be explained now, namely the identity and difference in the absolute, or, as Schelling says, "the only correct dualism, namely a dualism which at the same time admits a unity" (*HF*, 88n.11).[108] What is this dualism in the absolute? After Jakob Böhme (and thus indirectly, Meister Eckhart), Schelling distinguishes between God as existing and God in his 'ground.' In Neoplatonic terms, which are quite appropriate here, he distinguishes between the One beyond reason and being, and the *Noûs*, which is reason and being.[109] "This ground of his existence, which God contains within himself, is not viewed as absolute, that is insofar as he exists" (*HF*, 27).[110]

Schelling operates a disjunction between the 'ground' of God, or rather 'in' God, and the absolute, which is here said to be God's 'existence.' The ground is also called God's nature. This is actually not new in the history of philosophy: the neo-Platonists and Meister Eckhart had opposed God's nature[111] and his being as the ineffable and the knowable; or as 'Godhead' and 'God.' But they had not tied this disjunction to the account of human freedom and the possibility of evil in history. But many of the phrases that Schelling uses to express the dynamic unity between God's ground and God's existence stem from that direction: e.g., the 'longing' of the ground to break forth into existence; or the longing of the dark will to break forth into the light.

> Things have their ground [J. Gutman translates it as 'basis,' R.S.] in that within God which is not God himself, i.e., in that which is the ground of his existence. If we wish to bring this being nearer to us from a human standpoint, we may say: it is the longing [*Sehnsucht*, R.S.] which the eternal One feels to give birth to itself (*HF*, 28).[112] [113]

The ground is then called "the unfathomable unity," and "this longing seeks to give birth to God" (ibid).[114]

And now comes the decisive move: the ground and God, or God's nature and God's existence are opposed as one will to another will. The ground is dark, and it is deprived of reason: "Regarded in itself, it is also will: but a will within which there is no understanding, and thus not an independent and complete will" (ibid.).[115] What would be the complete will? That which is thoroughly rational. "Understanding is actually the will of willing," "Der Verstand ist eigentlich der Wille im Willen" [ibid.].[116] It is clear that the two are here fused. The will of the existent is entirely one with reason; but the will of the 'ground,' the 'dark' will, is merely adumbrating reason: "not a conscious but a prescient will, whose prescience is understanding" (ibid.).[117]

This distinction within the absolute serves as the framework for the understanding of both nature and history. In nature, that is, in the visible world, the elements of disorder, disease and death are traced back to the dark will in the absolute:

> Following the eternal act of self-revelation, the world as we now behold it is all rule, order, and form;[118] but the unruly lies ever in the depths as though it might again break through and order and form nowhere appear to have been original, but it seems as though what had initially been unruly had been brought to order. This is the incomprehensible ground of reality in things, the irreducible remainder which cannot be solved by reason (*HF*, 28).[119]

Schelling thus traces the 'fall' back into the absolute will, the fall from reason. It is less the explanatory role of disorder and evil that interests us here than the simultaneity, in the absolute, of rational and irrational willing. The ground in the absolute, as constituted by what the Gnostics called a "primordial fall" is not only *'Urgrund,'* primordial ground, but also *'Ungrund,'* abyss.

The bright, rational will in the absolute encompasses everything, it is the universal will; but the blind, irrational will is disorderly, chaotic, seeing only parts rather than the whole, it is the individual will. Hence the (very Eckhartian) imperative: "Man must die to everything proper to him." "Der mensch muß aller Eigenheit[120] absterben" (*HF*, 50).[121]

3. Nietzsche: will as the self-affirmation of the subject

It is out of the question, here again, to present Nietzsche's entire reflection on the will: quite as for Kant, it is the will from the point of view of rationality that is our topic. We will see, however, that this is not exactly a marginal approach to Nietzsche. First, it will be important to place this approach within the general framework of the course, i.e., the rise of the transcendental ‹ legislative › subject as the basis for the "triumph of the will" in modern philosophy. Then, we will examine the question of the will as a faculty, and lastly, if it appears that man is the 'willing animal,' we will ask what becomes of reason.

a. Nietzsche's critique of the will as subject to an ideal

I take the following aphorism as my starting point—you will soon see why:[122] "Christianity and Judaism: the Ideal is posited outside ourselves, with the highest might and commanding: [...] May each of us feel as the creator of his own image? Hardly so!" (*NF*, 1880,7[64]).[123]

Nietzsche speaks in these lines of the ideal. What is an ideal? In *The Will to Power*, there is an interesting answer: "The 'idealist' (that is, the ideal-castrate) emerges from a quite definite reality [...] The castrator formulates a number of new self-preservative measures for men of a quite definite species" (*WP*, 120f.).[124] As usual, Nietzsche declines to answer the question of essence, *viz.* 'What is the ideal?,' and rather points to the concrete historical conditions and to the type of man for whom the ideal counts at all: 'What type of man?' He is naturally called the "idealist," and later, the "ideal-castrate," as opposed to the "castrator." The castrator is clearly the Christian or Jewish teacher who "posits the Ideal outside ourselves." And why is he a "castrator"? Because due to such fixation "each of us" cannot feel "as the creator of his own image."

Thus the establishment of an ideal at first sight looks destructive. But the lines from *The Will to Power* do not speak of destruction at all. On the contrary: "the castrator [= the moralist, to be brief, R.S.] formulates a number of self-preservative measures (*Erhaltungsbedingungen*)." The function of the ideal seems essentially ambiguous: it is set up "outside ourselves," i.e., by others; it commands with "the highest might"; it "castrates," i.e., it forbids us to "feel as the creators of our own image," of ourselves. And yet it is life-preserving, thus somehow also beneficial...at least "for men of a quite definite species."

One can systematize these thoughts in the following way—and Nietzsche, does so himself: there is a history of the ideal. In the *first* stage of this history it is "posited outside ourselves, with the highest might and commanding." This is the Christian and Jewish origin of morality. And if you recall that Nietzsche calls Christianity "Platonism for the people" (*BW*, 193),[125] we can say that the first stage, in which the ideal is exterior, is both biblical and Platonist. The *second* stage is that of Kant: "a fanciful visionary

PART I

of the concept of duty" (*WP*, 60),[126] which is to say, the ideal has become interiorized. In the key text on this topic, "How the 'True World' Finally Became a Fable," Nietzsche says of Kant: "At bottom, the old [Platonic, R.S.] sun, but seen through mist and skepticism. The idea has become elusive, pale, Nordic, Königsbergian" (*PN*, 485).[127] That is to say, the ideal has become a function within the mind—practical reason, precisely, in so far as it legislates for itself, binds itself with the moral law. The *third* stage is that of the 19th century, of science. Nietzsche sees his own age as having 'rid itself of the domination of ideals.' How? By the triumph of science. This is to say, he adds, of reason: "The true world [...] *unknown*. Consequently, not consoling, redeeming, or obligating: how could something unknown oblige us? (Gray morning. The first yawn of reason. The cockcrow of positivism)."[128]

Now Nietzsche sees the will as precisely this setting-up of ideals:

> To will is to command (*Wollen*, i.e., *Befehlen*): but to command is a certain affect (this affect is a sudden explosion of power)—tight, clear, focused on one single thing, with the inner conviction of superiority, assurance that obeying will ensue; 'freedom of the will' is the 'feeling of superiority in the one who commands' with regard to the one who obeys: '*I* am free, and *he* must obey' (*NF*-1884,25[436]).[129]

To will is to command.[130] Now you understand the lines that I began with: "Christianity and Judaism: the Ideal is posited outside ourselves," i.e., by the moralists of the biblical and Platonist brands. But the Kantian brand is a matter of commanding too. Put simply, in Kant the ideal is not posited outside but rather inside ourselves. There it is still more inescapable and demanding. It is no longer the rabbi or the priest who commands, or Moses or Jesus: now I legislate for myself, I command myself. Such is the result of the rationality of the will in Kant as seen by Nietzsche. In his earlier metaphor: the castration is self-inflicted, I am both castrator and castrated.

You see the movement of interiorization: the ideal becomes transcendental. In Nietzsche's view, this is to say, the commanding becomes an act within the subject. As such, the Kantian thesis of the rationality of the will[131] deserves the same criticism, if not worse, as the biblical and Platonist moralists. They all perpetuate one and the same human type: the type that wants to obey, the slave morality, the herd.

And yet[132] there is a great discovery in the Kantian turn towards the subject. You remember the rhetorical question that I began with: "May each of us feel as the creator of his own image?" With Kant, Nietzsche has to say: yes, to some extent. Precisely because of the self-imposition of the moral law or the ideal, I am the creator of my own image. Which is to say, again in Nietzsche's terminology: Kant has discovered the 'artistic' nature of reason. "To be thoroughly truthful [..., RS.] that is the *tragic problem of Kant*. Now art achieves a totally *new* dignity [..., RS.]. The *truthfulness of art*: it alone now is sincere" (*NF-1872*,19[104]/[105]).[133] The active spontaneous nature of the subject—its artistic nature—is Kant's great discovery.[134]

One has to see together this exaltation of the creative subject and the old tyranny of the ideal in order to understand Nietzsche's view of Kant. Kant has seen—in the categorical imperative, particularly—that the will commands itself, and therefore his notion of the will is artistic. But he wants this command to be universal and necessary—transcendental, that is—and therefore Kant is "in the end, an underhanded Christian (*ein hinterlistiger Christ*)" (*PN*, 484).[135]

What Nietzsche spells out concerning the rationality of the will is that the will has a history. This history arises from the various ways it is tied to reason: in Plato—and in the "Platonism for the people"—the will is rational in so far as it obeys an Ideal outside ourselves, which is intelligible in itself. Thus, at this first stage, there is a distinction, an otherness, between reason and will: the "old sun" of the Republic commands, and the Platonist obeys. On the second stage, with Kant, the will itself becomes artistic, it commands itself over itself. Such is the meaning of Kant's identification between reason and will,[136] under the concept of 'practical reason.' However, Kant is not a man of the 19th century, Nietzsche adds, and therefore Kant "invents the transcendental world *in order that* a place remains for 'moral freedom'" (*WP*, 310).[137] Only in the third stage does reason discover its true locus: the positive sciences. With that discovery, the very instinct of seeking domination by ideals becomes historically impossible: the 19th century has 'rid itself of the domination of ideals,' that is, "the first yawn of reason, the cockcrow of positivism."

This itinerary by which ‹ reason has become scientific and › the will has progressively untied itself from reason, comes to fulfillment only in the next stage—himself. In the text, "How the 'True World' Finally Became a Fable," this is how that stage is described: "The 'true world'—an idea that is no longer good for anything, not even obligating [...] (Bright day, breakfast; return of *bon sens* and cheerfulness; Plato's embarrassed blush; pandemonium of all free spirits)" (*PN*, 485).[138] Nietzsche then adds another stage, which we will have to look at later. What counts at this point can be summarized in the following four points:

1. Nietzsche discovers that the will is 'rational,' not naturally, but historically. And from the biblical and Platonist beginnings, the will's connection with reason has been one of submission, obedience;

2. Kant's turn towards the subject—his 'Copernican revolution'— becomes radicalized in Nietzsche from the point of view of the rationality of the will: Kant has discovered the creative, 'artistic'role of the will, but has perverted it in pseudo-Christian, pseudo-Platonist ("the old sun") ways;

3. With Nietzsche's radicalization of the Copernican turn, the will comes into its own, i.e., it becomes legislative without the representation of an ideal;

4. If the will is to be "creative," "artistic," "affirmative," it comes to stand for the subject itself. The subject affirming itself: that is the will for Nietzsche. Man = the willing animal.

b. Nietzsche's negation of the will as a faculty

All this may sound plausible—until we read texts like this one: "Freedom or no freedom of the will?—There is no such thing as 'will'; it is only a simplifying conception of the understanding, as is 'matter'" (*WP*, 354).[139] In other words, once one begins speaking of 'the understanding,' *Verstand*, one will also speak of 'the will,' 'matter' and other faculties or constituents that are opposable to 'understanding' and 'reason.' But for Nietzsche, this entire complex has to fall: reason with its opposites, i.e., will, sensibility, body, matter, etc. And once these handy oppositions are dismissed, the venerable question of freedom or unfreedom of the will cannot even be raised any more. How is one to understand this? And why should this entire apparatus be dismissed?

Here are two more texts from *The Will to Power* about the non-existence of the will. They may clarify things a little:

> *Weakness of the will*: that is a metaphor that can prove misleading. For there is no will, and consequently neither a strong nor a weak will. The multitude and disgregation of impulses and the lack of any systematic order among them result in a 'weak will'; their coordination under a single predominant impulse results in a 'strong will' (*WP*, 28).[140]

And here is the second text:

> 'The subject': interpreted from within ourselves, so that the ego counts as a substance, as the cause of all deeds, as a doer [...] The belief in substance, accident, attribute, etc., derives its convincing force from our habit of regarding all our deeds as consequences of our will—so that the ego, as substance, does not vanish in the multiplicity of change.—But there is no such thing as will.— (*WP*, 270f.).[141]

Whereas earlier we had reached as a first conclusion the equation, in Nietzsche, between subject and will—man is the willing subject—we now hear that there is neither subject nor will. The subject is a mere "interpretation," he says, a "belief," a "habit." Elsewhere he even says that the subject is a fiction (*WP*, 269).[142] And the will: "there is no such thing as the will." Now it is not only the subjective apparatus of reason and the understand[ing] versus the will, the senses, and the body that collapses; the 'objective' apparatus of substance and accidents, too, is only a "belief."

And yet Nietzsche speaks of a weak or a strong will, a will that is negative and one that is affirmative. As a reminder, we can probably say that the weak will is the one that needs an ideal as posited outside of ourselves, as in Platonism, Judaism, and Christianity; and a strong will would be that which has become "artistic," "creative," "affirmative."

But how does he speak of a weak and a strong will? "The multitude and disgregation[143] of impulses and the lack of any systematic order among them result in a 'weak will': their coordination under a single predominant impulse results in a 'strong will'." Instead of a subject and its faculties, we hear about impulses and their coordination. And in the second text I quoted, we hear furthermore: subject and substance are inventions "so that the ego does not vanish in the multiplicity of change." Thus Nietzsche views the subject as intrinsically manifold and in motion, in transformation.

This is not new: all philosophers have seen a multiplicity in the human subject—multiplicity of 'parts' of the soul, or of 'soul and body,' or faculties of the mind, etc. What is new is that in Nietzsche, the concept of a multiple subject makes it impossible to retain the idea of a substantive subject as for the metaphysicians; it also makes it impossible to retain a transcendental subject, as for Kant: indeed, ‹ because › of the multiplicity that constitutes the subject, it cannot be transcendental, a system of enduring forms. Rather, we hear that the systematic order that constitutes the subject can be coherent or incoherent—thus certainly not universal and necessary, as are the conditions for knowledge in Kant. "'Subject,' 'object,' 'predicate': these distinctions are *fabricated*" (*WP*, 294).[144]

There clearly is something of an atomism in Nietzsche: he views the subject as the result of impulses entering into aggregations that are either strong or weak, [coordinated or] disintegrating. Here, then, is what I consider to be the key text about the dissolution of the will as a consequence of the dissolution of the subject (I have abbreviated this important fragment): "[What counts is] the preservation and enhancement of complex forms of relative life-duration within the flux of becoming" (*WP*, 380).[145] The 'subject' thus is one configuration of the flux of becoming, but a flux that is irreducible to either subjective or objective change. Nietzsche also calls these forms of relative life-duration within the flux *Herrschaftsgebilde*, forms of domination. "'Forms of domination': the sphere of that which is dominated, continuously growing or periodically increasing or decreasing according to the favorability or unfavorability of circumstances (nourishment—)" (ibid.).[146] And it is from this view of the subject that there follows the conclusion: "There is no will: there are only punctuations of will that are constantly increasing or losing their power."[147]

We are to understand, it seems, that there is no will as an X outfit of the subject because there is no such thing as a stable subject. And yet Nietzsche speaks of the weak and the strong will. But the strong will, we heard, is the "coordination of impulses under one predominant impulse." It is clear what the will must be understood to be, then: it is the factor that ‹ results from › integrated[148] impulses into a certain 'type' of personality—depending on inner forces such as beliefs, habits, etc., as well as on outer forces such as nourishment, etc.

With the impossibility of speaking of the subject as one, it is clear that 'reason' as a faculty disintegrates together with the will. If all faculties are fictions, if the subject is a fiction, then the very question of the rationality and irrationality of the will seems out of place. And yet Nietzsche speaks of order and system among the forces that the will indicates. The coordination of impulses "results" in a strong will. The will can certainly not be held to be 'rational' or 'irrational' if the entire problematic of an enduring subject as substrate of the faculties is a metaphysical fiction—a fiction for the sake of that type of man that needs stability within the flux of becoming, a stability derived from some form of the ideal. And nevertheless, we have to raise the question: what becomes of reason in its correlation to the will once the latter is understood [starting from] "forms of domination"?

c. Affirmation as the clue to the 'rationality' of the will

The problem of the region between reason and will is one of the topics Nietzsche addresses in the section, "The Will to Power as Knowledge" (*WP*, Bk. III, Ch. I, 261–324). We will see that this problem can no longer be raised in terms of the irrationality or rationality of the will, once the will itself is negated as faculty and understood rather as the self-affirmation ‹ of forces ›. Whatever may remain of rationality or reason, it will have to be transvaluated quite as the will has been transvaluated: from a faculty to a basic trait of "forms of domination." With Nietzsche, we have to put "will" in quotes.

Quite as he did for the will, then, Nietzsche sets about putting reason as a faculty into question. I will follow, here, a fragment in that section of *The Will To Power* entitled "The Tremendous Blunders" (*WP*, 285f). In it, Nietzsche enumerates a few tenets of what he considers common doctrine in the Western tradition. The first of these "blunders" (*Fehlgriffe*) is "the absurd *overestimation of consciousness*, the transformation of it into unity, an entity: 'spirit,' 'soul,' something that feels, thinks, wills" (ibid.).[149] "Reason," too, in quotation marks.

Consciousness is overestimated when it is held to be something that feels, thinks, wills. Thus 'consciousness' stands for the spiritual substance which he had already rejected in texts quoted earlier, and thinking, willing, feeling are seen as the acts or attributes of that substance. You remember that for Kant—for the early Kant in a different way than for the late Kant—the problem of willing hinged entirely on the will's relation to feeling, on the one hand, and to thinking on the other. His early solution was to locate it on the side of feelings and emotions (under the influence of the British Empiricists), and his later solution, to identify it with thinking in the broad sense, i.e., with practical reason. Thus even though consciousness may not be held to be a substance called 'spirit' or 'soul,' it remains "absurdly over-estimated" when considered as a totality of functions, as in Kant.

The second "blunder": "Spirit as cause, especially wherever purposiveness, system, coordination appear" (ibid.).[150] Here it is the identification between order ‹ —teleology— › and reason that is challenged.

You have to see to what extent this tenet too is one that has gone unquestioned in the Western tradition: it is the nerve of the proofs of the existence of God, whether they start from the order in the cosmos, or the order in the human soul (from motion or from degrees of being). Where there is order, there must be an ordering mind: such is the metaphysical conviction that Nietzsche puts into question here, calling it a slip of the hand (*Fehlgriff*). Again, Kant had begun challenging this tacit assumption in the *Critique of Pure Reason*, by showing that from the world-order (the physico-theological argument) one cannot prove a demiurgical or creator-mind, and in the *Critique of Judgment*, with his notion of purposiveness without purpose. But he only began this overturning, since he replaces talk of 'causal ground' with that of 'conditioning ground.' The mind in its structured acts provides, not the cause, but the condition for "purposiveness, system, coordination."

The following "blunder"—the third—indicates how reason has been "overestimated": by the estimation of high and low, of degrees of being: "Consciousness as the highest achievable form, as the supreme kind of being, as 'God'" (ibid.).[151] By contrast, we may get a hint, then, of Nietzsche's new valuation or estimation: there will be no supreme kind of being; no higher and lower kind of being even. And with these three premises—substantiality, causality, hierarchy—Nietzsche can approach the topic of will. Indeed, substantiality entails a certain concept of will: as an act of a spiritual substance. Likewise, causality entails a concept of will: will as producing effects, as a cause. And hierarchy, too, entails a concept of will: namely as the principle of motion upward, as Platonic eros; or as the principle of outward appearance, as the 'willing ground' in the late Schelling.

Here, then, is the fourth "blunder": "The will introduced wherever there are effects" (ibid.).[152] This sounds of little consequence. But this identification between will and causality leads us to the heart of Nietzsche's solution to the problem—which we now have to place in quotation marks—of the "rationality and irrationality of the will." How is it that the metaphysician introduces the will wherever there are effects? And what does Nietzsche oppose to this causal concept of will? These are the two lines of inquiry to be pursued now (I do not comment on the two remaining "blunders").

In pointing out the link between will and causality, Nietzsche speaks again with Kant against Kant. Here is a revelatory fragment from the *Nachlass*: "Any (causal) sequence still requires interpretation: the 'natural law' is but an *interpretation*. 'Cause and effect' go back to the concept of '*doer* and *deed*.' And whence *this* distinction?" (*NF*-1886,7[34]).[153] The first part of this fragment is Kant [being] more Kantian than ever: causality, or "cause and effect," is but an interpretation; Kant would say: a form that reason prescribes to Nature. The "natural law," or the law of nature, thus cannot be something read in the world, but it is introduced into the world by the subject. And here is how Nietzsche turns Kant against himself: he seems to ask: 'from where do we get the idea of introducing such forms as cause and effect to begin with?' Nietzsche's answer, in this text and in many others, is: from our experience of acting. We discover that we do something and that what is so done is "a deed"—something autonomous, there for all to admire. Causality is but the projection of a certain experience upon the entirety of phenomena. Hence "natural law" is an interpretation derived from the distinction between doer and deed. "And whence this distinction?"

The next piece gives the answer: "Belief in causality goes back to the belief that it is *I* who effects something, to the separation of the 'soul' from its activities. Thus, an age-old superstition!" (*NF-*1885,1[38]).[154] The age-old construct that the will is something 'upon' that substance called 'soul' accounts for our belief in causality. The "fourth blunder" stated: "the will introduced wherever there are effects." This blunder has its ground in a certain classical solution to the problem of the rationality and irrationality of the will, namely, that the will is something 'upon' the rational soul. Once the separation of the 'soul' from its activity appears as a fiction, causality itself is but a belief, a fiction, too. This is certainly taking Kant beyond Kant.

It seems, at this point, that the entire metaphysical language about the will has to be abandoned: that it is a cause, that it is the soul's activity, that it produces deeds, that it depends on reason ... But Nietzsche never abandons or merely dismisses what he calls "age-old superstitions." He transvaluates them. How, then, does he transvaluate the relation between will and reason, once the 'subject' has appeared to be a fiction?

One way of seeing the transvaluation of the rationality of the will is to focus on the distinction between 'active' and 'passive.' The texts about this opposition are numerous. Here is one: "What is 'passive'? To be *hindered* from moving forward: thus an act of resistance and reaction. What is 'active'? Reaching out for power" (*WP*, 346f.).[155] We already heard that Nietzsche retains the distinction between strong and weak will; now we see that this distinction corresponds to 'active and reactive' or 'active and passive.' The weaker will is "hindered from moving forward." The stronger will "reaches out for power." For this movement forward, this reaching out for power, Nietzsche has another term: affirmation, ‹ yes-saying ›. The will as the movement forward, as reaching out for power,

60

is not a faculty upon the mind or the soul. It is a certain system, an 'order,' which unifies the aggregate of forces that make up the "forms of domination." That is what the will comes to stand for once Nietzsche has dismantled the metaphysical constructs relating will and reason as two faculties.

With this notion of affirmation, we have again reached the heart of the topic of this course. It is the 'subject' (now in quotes) as *Herrschaftsgebilde* that affirms itself, and this affirmation is what Nietzsche calls the "will." And we are also at the heart of the topic of the problem of rationality and irrationality: affirmation gives an order, a direction to forces. You remember Fragment 46 from *The Will to Power* (*WP*, 28): "There is no will [...] The multitude and disgregation of impulses and the lack of any systematic order among them result in a 'weak will'; their coordination under one predominant impulse results in a 'strong' will."[156] The will, one could paraphrase, is the differentiating factor that arranges forces into coherent or incoherent constellations.[157] And not just forces in the sense of human impulses: "In place of 'sociology,' *a theory of the forms of domination*" (*WP*, 255).[158] "I beware of speaking of chemical 'laws': that smacks of morality. It is far rather a question of the absolute establishment of power-relationships: the stronger becomes master of the weaker" (*WP*, 336).[159]

Will is the differentiating factor among all and any configurations of power-relationships. As such, Nietzsche calls it "will to power"— which has nothing to do with the human will to overpower.

This self-affirmation of the subject was prepared by Kant—but again, only prepared. I have shown how Kant's notion of legislative reason makes the subject "creative," "affirmative," "active," in Nietzsche's terms. This was the very content of the so-called Copernican revolution in Kant: phenomena must conform to the laws that the subject prescribes to them, rather than the subject conforming to 'nature.' But Nietzsche, in line with his general ambivalence about Kant, has something nasty to say about this Copernican revolution: "Since Copernicus, man has been rolling from the center towards X" (*WP*, 8).[160] Kaufmann indicates a parallel in *Genealogy of Morals*, III, 25:

Has the self-belittlement of man, his *will* to self-belittlement, not progressed irresistibly since Copernicus? [...] Since Copernicus, man seems to have got himself on an inclined plane—now he is slipping faster and faster away from the center into—what? into nothingness?" (*BW*, 591).[161]

Thus, the phrase about Copernicus only confirms that the ideal in Kant, or subjective legislation, is ultimately not at all man's self-expansion or self-enlargement—man's self-affirmation—but, on the contrary: Copernicus' heliocentrism goes very well with "the old sun" in Kant, "seen through mist and skepticism—elusive, pale, Nordic, Königsbergian" (*PN*, 485). Kant's awkward use of the Copernican metaphor (for anthropocentrism) tells the truth: a disguised heliocentrism.

About the will-to-power we shall have to say more in the second part of this course, on the ontological turn of the will. At this point what counts is to have understood the identification, in Nietzsche, between will and self-affirmation (the 'self' understood as a formation of domination); and that the 'rationality' of the will so transvaluated consists in "more!": "the *feeling of increase* (*das Mehrgefuhl*), the feeling of *becoming stronger*" (*WP*, 344).[162]

Let me take as the guiding text about 'affirmation' his fragment from *The Will to Power*, which at the same time will allow for the transition to my last point about Nietzsche, in this section:

> If becoming is a great ring, then everything is equally valuable, eternal, necessary.—In all correlations of Yes and No, of preference and rejection, love and hate, all that is expressed is a perspective, an interest of certain types of life: in itself, everything that is says Yes (*WP*, 165).[163]

d. The Eternal Recurrence as the will's rationality

The lines just quoted indicate how Nietzsche views self-affirmation: as Yes-saying. This Yes-saying is not just any kind of agreement. It is opposed to what in this he calls "perspectives." "In all correlations of Yes and No, of preference and rejection, of love and hate, all that is expressed is a perspective, an interest of a certain type of life." We heard something about 'types of life' already earlier.

"The castrator formulates a number of self-preservative measures for men of a quite definite species" (*WP*, 120f).[164] A species and a type designate the same thing: that figure of man which was earlier characterized by its need for an ideal, for its need for a 'valuation' of high and low. The mind is high, the body is low. This valuation or esteeming is at the origin of what Nietzsche now calls a perspective. Thus we can paraphrase the first part of the quote from § 293: wherever men say Yes to some forces or beings and No to others, where they love this and hate that, where they prefer, for instance, what is moral over what is immoral, a "perspective" is created. By such perspectivism, Nietzsche describes the entire Western metaphysical tradition. That was what philosophers and sages were all about: telling us what was to be accepted and what was to be rejected.

To such perspectival Yes-saying, Nietzsche opposes another Yes-saying. "In itself, everything that is says Yes." Thus in "everything that is" there is no perspective. Which is another way of saying that values, that representations of hierarchies are created by man for man—and for the sake of dominating, 'castrating' men. But what does it mean that, "In itself everything that is says Yes"? The first sentence gives the answer: "If becoming is a great ring, then everything is equally valuable, eternal, necessary."

You have to see the opposition between Nietzsche's thinking as expressed in these lines and the Western tradition. The tradition has taught us that there are some things that are valuable, some that are eternal—as opposed to things corruptible—and some that are necessary—as opposed to things contingent. What would philosophy be without these basic distinctions? And yet, Nietzsche claims that everything is equally valuable, eternal, necessary. What can he mean?

There is a condition to this thought that everything is equally valuable, that everything that is says Yes. "If becoming is a great ring..." Thus Nietzsche emits something like an hypothesis. He imposes a trial on us, on our will: "Whoever wants to have a single experience once again must wish all of them again."[165] This is one of many versions of the Eternal Return: here it is expressed from the point of view of the will. I must will to relive all things. In the terms of Zarathustra: "Was *that* life? Well then, once again..."

(*PN*, 269).[166] You see that such an affirmation of all things is essentially different from perspectival affirmation. Nietzsche speaks of the "great Yes" and opposes it to the 'Yes' of the ass (see the "The Ass festival," *Thus Spoke Zarathustra*, Part IV, [425–429] vs. the "Yes-and-Amen song" in Part III, "The Seven Seals," [340–343]). Likewise, the "great will" is the will that can will things to come back eternally.

For our purposes, only this line of thought about the eternal recurrence is of importance: as a test, for the will, or as the expression of the "great will," or again, as the order, the geometry, of the will. Geometry, because the will is viewed here by Nietzsche as at the center of a circle. The quote that I read earlier stated: "If becoming is a great ring...," that is, if all things come back eternally—or, as a test for the will, if I can will that all things return eternally, then they are all equally valuable, eternal, necessary.

This same metaphor, the ring or the circle, is also implied in another section from *Thus Spoke Zarathustra*. In the "Prologue," Nietzsche spells out the three metamorphoses of man (rather two!): from the camel to the lion to the child. This should be read in parallel with the following fragment from *The Will to Power*:

> 'Thou shalt'—unconditional obedience in the Stoics, in the Christian and Arab orders, in the philosophy of Kant (it is immaterial whether to a superior or to a concept). Higher than 'thou shalt' is 'I will' (the heroes); higher than 'I will' stands: 'I am' (the gods of the Greeks) (*WP*, 495).[167]

With the transition from "thou shalt" to "I will," you have the step from an obedience to moralists, castrators, and idealists to the creation of perspectives, of values, to the willing of values; but with the transition from "I will" to "I am" the will itself is transformed. This is the step from perspectival willing to the "great will." And only this latter is the self-affirmation that Nietzsche is interested in.

The transition towards the great will, the great Yes, the great affirmation, is the discovery of the equality in beauty, or in value, of all that there is. Now, where does one have to stand in order to so affirm all forces, all possible occurrences? At the center of the ring. It is from the hub of the wheel that the circle looks all the same. The correct understanding of the circle-metaphors in Nietzsche thus derives from the history of transcendental philosophy: the subject placing itself in the center and 'esteeming' all things equally, that is the will. And the will's rationality consists in this geometrical order around man, or around the great Yes.

In one fragment, Nietzsche writes: "My doctrine declares: the task is to live *in such a way* that you must *want* to live again— you will *anyway*" (*NF*-1881,11[163]).[168] I do not insist here on the last words. But the test-character of the eternal recurrence comes through quite clearly: can you bear that all things return? This is the test of the great will. To say: 'Yes, I can will it' is to bring to completion the movement inaugurated by Kant's Copernican Revolution: the centrality of the subject in the phenomenal world.

One can see this centrality as the supreme anthropomorphism, and actually as the very doctrine of technology: man declaring himself the master over all things. Technology would then be the concrete realization of the eternal recurrence, the victory of man's will over all things. But one can also read this circularity of all things around man as, on the contrary, something like their letting-be. Then Nietzsche's teaching would amount to not doing violence to them at all, but to will that they be what they are. "In itself, everything that is says Yes": there may be an indication here that Nietzsche wants us not to overpower all things—this would be the second stage in the metamorphoses, that of the lion or of the "I will"—but to let them manifest themselves in the order that is theirs for a time.

At any rate, what is at stake is the end-form of transcendentalism and of the relation between will and reason. Neither the will nor reason are understood by Nietzsche as faculties of man. Rather, the "great will" is self-affirmation to which no negation can correspond, and the "great reason" is the eternal recurrence to which no corruption can correspond. With technology, according to Heidegger, this rationality of the will has gained worldwide extension.

PART I

4.[169] Heidegger: the analogy "technological rationality : thinking = the will to will : the will not to will"[170]

a. The common opinion: decisionism

> We are still far from thinking the essence
> of action *decisively* enough.
> Heidegger, "Letter on 'Humanism'"[171]

There is a common thesis concerning the problem of the will in Heidegger that can be summarized in three steps. (1) In *Being and Time*, the will is rooted phenomenally in care, and therefore in Dasein's existential openness. The voluntary and the involuntary, then, are opposable as the authentic is to the inauthentic.[172] In this view the phenomenon of the will is linked to the existential determination called resoluteness or resolve. When being-there is authentically resolved it wills something: its own (*eigen*) possibilities. Its *Eigentlichkeit*, authenticity, consists in making these resolutely its own. In that way, the will is not a faculty but a phenomenon concomitant with the modifications through which I attain my ownmost, most originary truth. (2) But on the other hand, still according to that *opinio communis*, Heidegger deconstructs the very notions of truth[173] that might function as regulative measures for resoluteness, namely, its normative notions. Truth deconstructed—unconcealment—yields no standards, no guide for the possible impulses of the will. These impulses shoot forth blindly, as it were, into the dark. Hence a certain underlying decisionism[174] in the young Heidegger. (3) After the 'turn,' this decisionism would lapse into its contrary, 'letting-be.' Heidegger would no longer recommend that we will resolutely so as to exist authentically, but that we will not to will so as to unlearn objectivation, representation, prehension—the entire mechanism of essentially technological thinking. The topical shift from resoluteness to releasement would, it may be added, not have occurred without difficulty. Thus in the essay "The Origin of the Work of Art" (1935) the two themes, voluntarist and anti-voluntarist, would curiously coexist, so much so that more than twenty years later, Heidegger would feel obliged to append an explanatory supplement to that essay. He would then strive, if somewhat tortuously, to reconcile the opposition between 'willing' and 'letting' by tracing both back to "existing man's ecstatic commitment to the unconcealment of being."[175] That he should have taken the trouble to state several times that "the resoluteness thought of in *Being and Time* is not decided action"[176] would indicate precisely how artificial the retrospective harmonization of these two positions remains, how disturbing a problem it raised for him. In short, 'the turn' would be accompanied by an "abdication of this will, of this self-assertion in the face of Being."[177]

b. The epochal sense of "decision" [178]

All this may be plausible. But what that common opinion does not say is more telling with regard to action as the condition for thinking than what it does say.

To begin with the most elementary, it says nothing about the word *Entscheidung*,[179] decision, itself. The German, like the English, derives from a verb that means 'to separate,' 'to cut.' To separate and cut what? "Thinking has not yet risen out of the separation (*Scheidung*)[180] between the metaphysical being question, which inquires into the being of entities, and that question which inquires more originally into the truth of being."[181] The separation here sets apart two types of questions. The first is 'metaphysical,' the second no longer is. It is therefore also a separation between two eras. These lines say clearly enough that questions invented by man do not decide anything essential at all; that two historical questions set themselves up as separate even before he can intervene; in other words, that the decision, understood as a separation, a cut, a break, is economic.[182] It cuts out an age, a historical order of presence, a world. "The world is that opening which unlocks the broad tracks of the simple and essential decisions in the destiny of a historical people."[183] A decision is, then, first of all, a matter of collective destiny. It is the disjunction between two ‹ epochal ›[184] eras ‹ two historical worlds ›.

Every essential decision is not only ‹ epochal ›,[185] it is also aletheiological.

The world is the lighting of the tracks of the essential injunctions with which all decision complies. Every decision, however, bases itself on something unmastered, hidden, confusing; otherwise it would never be a decision.[186]

An economic decision[187] contains something hidden and confusing, inasmuch as every pre-understanding is confused and dark. But such a decision is also essential because it 'lights' concealedness, wrests 'world' from 'earth,' *alētheia* from *lēthē*, and thereby opens the space where human decisions can occur at all and where understanding can articulate pre-understanding. A constellation of truth determines the tracks—the variables that structure an age—through which the economic injunctions reach us. Concretely, for example, the decision or disjunction from which the post-modern age was born (experienced by Marx in 1845, by Nietzsche in 1881, and by Heidegger in 1930) established technological breakthroughs, the very idea of progress—not in morality (Kant), but in the techniques of mastery—as the conveyer for our age of what is true and false, to be done and not to be done.[188] One could say that these injunctions produce the concrete and structured order of presencing-absencing, the aletheiological order that marks an age. Here, Heidegger designates that order as the set of 'tracks' (*Bahnen*) according to which a historical cut-off structures a given economy. The concept of 'track' underscores the systemic nature of *alētheia*.

As aletheiological and therefore systemic,[189] any essential decision is necessarily non-human. Here are a few examples of what Heidegger calls historically "decisive": "fundamental words" such as "truth, beauty, Being, art, knowledge, history, freedom"[190]; "a transformed fundamental position"[191]; "constructive thinking"[192]; "the thought of the eternal return."[193] In each of these cases an economically disjunctive decision[194] precedes all possible volitional decisions. The relation between the two types of decision, conditioning and conditioned, appears best in the following example:

For Marx it has been *decided in advance* that man and only man (and nothing besides) is the issue. Whence has this been decided? How? By what right?[195] By what authority?—These questions can be answered only by going back to the history of metaphysics.[196]

Hence philosophical humanism itself is also the product of a prior decision which is economic, not human.

What I am calling economic decisions here, those which situate each and every human decision, Hannah Arendt described in the following terms:

> We may very well stand at one of these *decisive* turning points of history that *separate* whole eras from each other. For contemporaries entangled, as we are, in the inexorable demands of daily life, the dividing lines between eras may be hardly visible when they are crossed; only after people stumble over them do the lines grow into walls which irretrievably shut off the past.[197]

Conditioning decisions set apart networks of interaction. Thereby they both open up and restrict all possible voluntary, conditioned, decisions. They enjoin or tell us ('condition' stems from *dicere*, to say) what is essential in our age. As indicated in the first line of the "Letter on 'Humanism'" cited in the epigraph above, decisive thinking is therefore essential thinking: "We are still far from thinking the essence of action *decisively* enough." If the essence of action consists in its compliance with the plies in the history of being, with the economic decisions, then voluntary action *can* or *cannot* be essential. At the turn which sets apart the modern and the post-modern regularities, this means that action can choose to follow or not to follow the disjunction that seems to be growing into walls today. It can renounce the principles[198] and adhere solely to the economic transmutations. This kind of action[199] alone, possible only in the age of closure, would be essential, originary.[200] "Are we in our being-there historically at the origin?"[201] This is, Heidegger adds, a question of "comportment," of "an either-or and its decision."[202] The step back from the conditioned to the condition is clear. Just as thrownness precedes every project, so an essential, disjunctive, historical-destinal, economic, aletheiological, non-human, systemic decision precedes all human or voluntary decisions, all comport-ment. These decisive conditions are always "confusedly" pre-understood by us, and thus make every understanding and every deciding possible. Heidegger also calls the context-setting decision a crisis. "The thought [of the eternal return, R.S.] must not only be thought each time out of an individual's creative moment of decision, it belongs to life itself: it constitutes a *historical decision*—a *crisis.*[203] The 'critical' decisions, in that sense, account for the changing conditions of life itself. They differ from the 'creative' decisions as life differs from any momentary act. In Nietzsche all these terms are obviously heavily overdetermined. In Heidegger, the concept of decision is primarily topological. A crisis assigns us our site. The economic disjunctions that we may espouse or not espouse[204] in praxis *situate* that praxis. It is this economic, topological significance in Heidegger's usage of *Entscheidung* and related terms that makes the charge of decisionism[205] difficult to sustain.

The will can follow the economic flow or not follow it, observe its own context or decontextualize itself. If, as has been shown, the last epochal principle, whose efficacy culminates in technology, is the subject reduplicating itself as will to will—if for our age being is willing—then the will, too, is primarily contextual and only secondarily behavioral. What does it mean, in our age of closure, to follow the economic modifications? It can only mean to follow the context-setting will in its epochal decline, to dismiss it as the last metaphysical stamp, as the being of entities, as the mark of our age. It means to "renounce willing voluntarily."[206] Such is the practical condition for us to be, "in our being-there, historically, at the origin." It consists in saying: "I will non-willing."[207] This twofold notion of the will, economic and behavioral, shows once again the practical a priori for thinking: revoking the epochal principles.[208]

But what would uncompliant comportment be, the one that abstracts itself from its economic context and aspires to consolidate the rule of principles? Is it even possible *not* to espouse the historical decisions as defining our condition? Hannah Arendt is probably not mistaken when she evokes Anaximander's *adikia*, injustice, in this regard. Heidegger understands *dikē*, justice, as a harmony in presencing, as the jointure (*Fuge*) between arrival and withdrawal. *Adikia*, then, is disjointure. "Disjointure means that whatever lingers awhile becomes set on fixing itself in its stay, in the sense of pure persistence in duration." The 'unjust' entity disjoins itself from the finite flow of absencing-presencing-absencing and "holds fast to the assertion of its stay."[209] The present insists on its presence, consolidates it, persists against absence. It con-sists with other entities against the movement of originary arrival, which is ever new and conjoined with departure. This essence of the will by which it is set on constant presence stands in agreement with conceptual, i.e., 'grasping' thought, but it is opposed to 'thinking' in the sense of the last transitional category. When, in the closing age of philosophy, the human will becomes absolute, willing nothing but itself, it shows forth its insurrectional nature.[210] "The will acts like 'a kind of coup d'état,'" Hannah Arendt wrote.[211] It is that force which seeks to establish the self as permanent and time as lasting.[212] If 'justice' means for each thing to arrive and depart in accordance with the economies, 'will' is the name for rebellion against that justice. Put in a simple correlation: constant presence is the very issue of willing, just as the event of presencing is the very issue of thinking. Willing and thinking are thus understood not as faculties of the mind, but as modalities of disclosing the world. If one recalls, now, that it is the epochal principles that claim constant presence most of all, it becomes obvious, too, that principial acting is hubris. The Greek word *hubris* stems from *huper*, 'beyond,' 'across.' Principial acting is hubristic since it oversteps our finite condition expressed in the temporal difference between presence and presencing.

Heidegger seeks a counter-will to that absolute, rebellious, will. The mere possibility of "willing not to will" places action before the alternative either to let itself be carried by the economies or to rebel against them, thereby immobilizing the event of presencing on a fictitious mainstay. Of the two options, ecstatic transport or enstatic support, only the former is thoughtful. Voluntary decisions either abandon[213] themselves to the epoch-making disjunctive decisions or they harden themselves against those decisions. Such hardening is the source of all thoughtlessness.[214] Both Hölderlin and Nietzsche dared to 'let—to abandon—themselves to the movement of transition in which the modern age, and perhaps the metaphysical age, comes to an end.[215] [Nietzsche's] *Mitdenken*, the thinking accompanying that shift, is telling. It reveals that practical decisions can approach, as it were, asymptotically, the historical decision. In that lies the advantage of transitional ages, when practical releasement becomes a concrete possibility; when action can retain as its sole measure the varying constellations of *alētheia*; when it is possible to will non-willing because for an entire civilization the hubris of principles has lost its credibility.

The concept of decision in Heidegger entails several answers[216] to the problem of the will. (1) In the primary, essential sense, a decision is the historical separation, cut-off, or crisis between two economies of presence, their severance. The reversals within metaphysical history as well as the turn beyond metaphysics are such aletheiological, non-human decisions. (2) The contemporary crisis sets apart the economy of the final metaphysical principle, the will to will, and a possible economy, one deprived of any standard-setting principle.[217] Economically speaking, the turn is that decision in which the will is given up[218] as the increasingly exclusive stamp of Western civilization. (3) Individual and collective decisions, our voluntary acts, are always inscribed within the horizon of economic decisions. Humanity is 'used,' 'utilized' (*chreōn*, Anaximander), for and by these trenchant incursions. (4) Within the transient horizon thus carved out, action is faced with an either-or: voluntary acts comply with economical transitions or they "hold fast to the assertion of their stay." The truly ultimate products of such holding-fast are the epochal principles. In temporal terms, that either-or means that being is experienced as constant presence or as event-like presencing. (5) The response to this either-or gives rise to 'philosophy'[219] or to 'thinking' respectively. The willful quest for constant presence, then, is to be relinquished if, at the end of philosophy, the issue for thinking is event-like presencing. To will non-willing is the practical condition for "thinking of being."

Thinking springs from two forebears, two types of conditions. Its economic condition might be opposed to its practical condition as a conditioning is opposed to an a priori. Heidegger defines the condition qua conditioning as the setting up of a world. "Wherever the essential decisions of our history occur—taken up or foregone by us, misknown or retrieved by new inquiry—there the world worlds."[220] The setting up of a world, its 'worlding,' is the *economic* condition within which we can take up or forgo, misknow or retrieve, the decisions that have made history. If a thinking is at all possible that transgresses its predominant conditioning, the stepping stone for such a transgression must again be provided by the economy. Such is the case with technology, whose 'worlding' is actually the most principled and potentially anarchic. The *practical* condition for such an other thinking to arise is best described by the transformation of the a priori, 'willing,' into the a priori, 'letting.' This is a transmutation of one willing into another, of willing as absolute because it wills itself, into "that willing which, renouncing willing, lets itself be committed (*eingelassen*) to what is not a will."[221] The acting that eventually shatters metaphysical conditioning introduces us fully into what Heidegger here calls *die Gegnet* [*sic*, R.S.], the "open expanse"—none other than the economy emancipated from principles.[222] "When we let ourselves be committed to the releasement [turned, R.S.] toward the open expanse, we will non-willing."[223]

Heidegger is not content with examining what happens to the question, What is to be done? at the end of metaphysics. He also asks: What is to be done at the end of metaphysics? In his answer, he does not urge decision for decision's sake. Neither does he advocate love in order to combat hatred, nor expropriation of the expropriators in order to combat injustice. He urges the express downthrow of the epochal principles[224] that are already foundering economically. This downthrow of what is already falling must be understood otherwise than as a willful, 'decisive,' 'resolute,' "efficacious" (*tatkräftig*) enterprise. For Heidegger, non-willing and releasement are more subversive than any project of the will that "wills to actualize and wills effectiveness as its element."[225] [226]

PART II

The Ontological Turn
in the Philosophy of the Will

2.[227] Nietzsche: being as "imposed" by the will

What[228] we will try to do in this section is to understand Nietzsche's concept of "will to power" as an ontological concept—as the off-spring of the ontological turn in the philosophy of the will first seen in Schelling. To read Nietzsche this way is not something that goes without saying. But to speak of the 'ontology of the will to power' makes sense, at least if one inserts Nietzsche into the lineage in which we read him now: between the 'German Idealists' and Heidegger's critique of technology as full-fledged identification of being ‹ = Rationality = › with Willing.

To speak of the 'ontology' of the will to power is to pick up a problem as old as Greek philosophy—"What is being?" Nietzsche, we will see, can be read as answering that question by equating being with willing.

And yet, if we look at only the best known texts, we hear Nietzsche say on the contrary: "being is an empty fiction" (*PN*, 481; Cf. *WP*, 330: "a world of being invented").[229] This is a rather strange answer to 'the' metaphysical question. And yet, it is an answer. Nietzsche confronts the metaphysical question par excellence. He inscribes his own thinking in the line of Western metaphysics. But he does so by calling it an 'empty question'—thus bringing metaphysics to its end. In this line one can claim, with Heidegger, that Nietzsche is 'the last metaphysician.' How so? § 617 from *The Will to Power* begins this way: "To *impose* upon becoming the character of being—that is the supreme *will to power*" (*WP*, 330).[230]

Thus being is something that is imposed, ‹ fictionalized, invented › something accomplished by us. How do we accomplish such imposition? Keeping in mind Nietzsche's rejection of 'the' ontological question, we can describe how classical ontologists have imposed being upon becoming: by setting up a world of being, of true being, an ideal world. As we heard in the first reading of Nietzsche:

"With the 'true world' we have also abolished the apparent world" (*PN*, 486).[231] We thus have two modalities of imposing being upon becoming: metaphysically, the construction of an ideal world; critically, the abolition of the ideal world, the abolition of its opposition to the apparent world—the abolition of that way of dealing with the question of being.

The point, now, is that there is in either case a doing, a willing. Declaring the ideal world to be true being—then revoking such a declaration.

Let us step back a moment. For Kant,[232] the question, 'What is being?', is answered, one might say, by pointing to the subject. That is at least what I suggested at the beginning of the course: with the Copernican revolution, the subject comes to the fore as legislating upon all that there is. The objectivity of the object has its ground in the subjectivity of the subject.[233] The subject 'constitutes' what can appear, and that is to say: what there is. With Schelling,[234] this triumph of the subject receives its name: the will as the absolute. The ground of all things, of the being of all things, lies in the process of willing. Will now accounts for all that there is and for the way everything is—namely, finite, capable of failure and death, evil, and guilt.

In either case—Kant's or Schelling's—to ask about being is to ask about the subject. To be sure, the subject in Kant is merely human, and in Schelling it is only secondarily human. But the question of being is always a question about the subject, it is a question about the subject's relation to itself: in a Kantian context, the subject is related to itself in such a way that it legislates for itself; in Schelling, in such a way that its will is divided: both dark and light, evil and good.

Against this very general background, Nietzsche's position can be described easily. I should like to look for that at the section in *Thus Spoke Zarathustra*, "On the Afterworldly":

> 'That world' is well concealed from humans—that dehumanized inhuman world which is a heavenly nothing; and the belly of being does not speak to humans at all, except as a human (*PN*, 144).[235]

The 'true world' of Platonism or of Christianity, 'being in itself,' is concealed from man. As an 'ideal' it is even dehumanized and inhuman.

But being speaks to man "as a human." In more technical terms, being presents itself to man only in terms of a relation to subjectivity. Being 'in itself,' however, is "a nothing." Nietzsche then adds these lines: "This ego and the ego's contradiction and confusion[236] [still] speak most honestly of its being—this creating, willing, valuing ego, which is the measure and value of things" (ibid).[237]

> A new pride my ego taught me, and this I teach men: no longer to bury one's head in the sand of heavenly things, but to bear it freely, an earthly head, which creates a meaning for the earth. A new will I teach men: to will this path which man has walked blindly [..., R.S.].[238]

Here the reduction of the question of being to "willing, creating," and to "the ego"[239] is quite clearly stated. All being is being in relation to subjectivity, more precisely: to the willing human subject. The 'Copernican turn' is even described beautifully by Nietzsche when he writes: "Things that have a constitution in themselves—a dogmatic idea with which one must break absolutely" (*WP*, 302).[240] This is a nice way of summarizing the shift from an ontology of substance to an ontology of subject; and the shift from an ontology of the rational subject to an ontology of the willing subject is stated clearly in the section, "On the Afterworldly" from *Thus Spoke Zarathustra*.[241]

Let's go back then, to the section with which we began, the section "On the Afterworldly." Immediately after the passage which I read earlier, Zarathustra continues with these words (one of the most important themes for our present problem): "Verily, all being is hard to prove and hard to induce to speak. Tell me my brothers, is not the strangest of all things proved most nearly?" (*PN*, 144).[242] Then he continues, "Indeed this ego and the ego's contradiction and confusion still speak most honestly of its being—this creating, willing, valuing ego, which is the measure and value of things" (ibid.).

(1) Since I think this passage is of much importance, I want to try to stay with it for a moment to suggest a number of points which seem to come out through it. First of all, we are told in this passage

that the ego, the I, is the measure and value of things. This means that *the ego, the self, the I, is that through which things are measured in their being.* The ego is that in reference to which things are measured in their being. Or to put it differently, it says that *the self is that by which the being of things is determined.* In other words, you see, the passage suggests that the being of things, not only has reference to subjectivity, not only is for a subject, as we were saying before, but furthermore that the being of things is projected, is constituted, by subjectivity. And Nietzsche already says that in the statement with which we began: "Being is a fiction."[243]

In the *Twilight of the Idols*, this is quite explicit (*PN*, 495). Nietzsche says, "[Man, R.S.] posited 'things' as 'being' in his image in accordance with his concept of the ego as a cause." He constituted the things as being. And then he adds, "small wonder, that later he always found in things *only that which he had put into them.*"[244] These are almost the same words that he used in the essay *On Truth and Lie.* Man then, posits being. Subjectivity posits being and the subject does so specifically in terms of the concept of being. It says here in this passage:[245] man posited things as being in his image in accordance with his concept of the self. He posits the being of things in terms of his relation to himself.

So we can say that precisely as in German Idealism, the subject's relation to itself is the ground of its relation to an object.

(2) Finally, in this passage, Zarathustra says that all being is "hard to prove; is hard to induce to speak" (*PN*, 144). Why is this so? Why is being hard to prove? Well, of course, in the light of what we've just said, we can say that all being is hard to prove, hard to induce to speak, because what it says is only the echo of our own voice, to put it in terms of the imagery of the passage. Because, in other words, we find in things not being in itself, but rather, as Nietzsche says in *Twilight of the Idols*, "what we put there." I might suggest that, here in this statement, the issue is precisely the same as [when] we dealt with "The Night Song."[246] It is precisely the same issue that we had presented in the image of the one who "lives in his own light" (*PN*, 218),[247] who drinks back into himself only his own flames, who lives in the present discussion, and finds in things only what he has put there.

We might wonder then, what Nietzsche has in mind in the same passage when, having said that, he goes on then to speak about the strangest of all things, that is, proved most near. What is that strangest of all things that is proved most near? Presumably it is that being can't be proved. In other words, what is most nearly proved is an utterly self-destructive skepticism. What is most nearly proved is skepticism: that being can't be proved.

(3) That strangest of all things is only nearly proved and not quite proved. And it is not quite proved because there is still one thing that does not speak. There is one instance in which being can be induced to speak and even, Nietzsche insists, to speak honestly.

What is that one instance? What is that one thing that does speak? What is that one thing that can be induced to speak of its being? It is, of course, [the] self, the ego. Only the being of subjectivity speaks: only the being of the subject makes itself manifest. All other beings are fictions that mirror subjectivity. To say the same in a more traditional way, all other being has its ground in subjectivity.

How does the ego speak?[248] Nietzsche goes on to say how it speaks. It speaks, he says, specifically in terms of its contradiction and confusion.[249] That is to say, it speaks in terms of its relation to itself. Again, it is the subject's relation to itself which is at issue. And when it speaks in this way, according to this passage, it proves then to be a creating, willing, valuing ego. That's how it speaks of itself.

I want to take from this passage a clue from this final character-ization; that is, that one thing that makes its being manifest, the ego, when it does so, it makes itself manifest, as creating, willing, valuing ego. I want to take this as our basic clue, our basic directive in order to try, from this, to develop with (deliberate) ‹ reference › most of all to *Zarathustra*, to try to get more systematic insight into Nietzsche's conception of subjectivity. Here we have a three-fold description of subjectivity. It is creating, willing, and valuing. So I want to consider each of these characterizations in turn, and through these to try to come to a somewhat more systematic view of Nietzsche's conception of subjectivity and in particular to our larger context, to try to see to what degree Nietzsche's conception of subjectivity is metaphysical, [to what degree it] remains precisely in the metaphysical. How far can we go in Nietzsche's conception of subjectivity, and still remain within that system? How much of a metaphysician can we make of Nietzsche?

First, let's take the characterization of the subject given there as willing. The ego is willing. The subject is willing. There are several things we need to note in that connection.

(a) We have seen already that one of the very common names that Nietzsche uses for subjectivity is the name "life"; life,[250] for Nietzsche, means subjectivity. It is especially in this connection, in speaking of life as subjectivity that Nietzsche describes the subject as will. And in fact, not only as will, but as will to power. To cite only two instances: in the section on "Self-overcoming" in Part II of *Thus Spoke Zarathustra,* Zarathustra says, "where I found the living, there I found will to power" (*PN,* 226).[251] And again, in the second passage in *Beyond Good and Evil,* Sec. 13, here Nietzsche is even more explicit. He says, "life itself is will to power" (*BW,* 211).[252]

(b) Secondly, in relation to the subject as willing, I want to suggest that in describing subjectivity as willing, or more specifically as will to power, there is among other things a kind of negativity. That is, in describing subjectivity as will to power, Nietzsche is also wanting to deny that subjectivity is certain other things. I might say, rather special other things: other things that subjectivity was said to be in the course of the philosophical tradition. Now one such denial, one such negative attempt here, is already evident, I think, in the passage that we were discussing in the section "On the Afterworldly." Zarathustra says there that the ego speaks most honestly of its being. Ego is the one thing that speaks, makes itself manifest as being. Then he adds a further statement and says, "and this most honest being, the ego, speaks of the body" (*PN,* 144).[253] That speaking in which it makes its being manifest is a speech in which it speaks of the body. The ego makes itself manifest then, as having a bodily character. Subjectivity is bodily.

And this bodily character of the subject is referred to most explicitly in the section which follows the one "On the Afterworldly," the section "On the Despisers of the Body." It is there that Zarathustra distinguishes quite explicitly between what he calls, on the one hand, the "great reason" [*grosse Vernunft*], which he identifies as the body or even as the self, and on the other hand, what he calls the "little reason" [*kleine Vernunft*], the spirit. And he says in that

80

connection, "beneath your thoughts and feelings, my brother, there stands a mighty ruler, an unknown sage—whose name is self. In your body he dwells; he is your body" (*PN*, 146).[254]

In negative terms, then, this means that subjectivity is not identical with consciousness for Nietzsche. Consciousness is, rather, as he often says, only a surface. And in fact, in *The Gay Science*, he says, that the greater part of our intellectual activity goes on unconsciously, i.e., beneath that surface.

I think we have to be very careful of what he says here, that the whole relation of subjectivity to the body is the denial that subjectivity is consciousness. Let me point to some of the things that we need especially to keep in mind. First of all, to say that subjectivity is not identical with consciousness, to say that the subject is body, is not simply to resort to a kind of simple materialism. It is not merely to take up a kind of simple materialism that would make man just a thing among other things. The body is not a mere thing. To make subjectivity bodily is not to make subjectivity a thing because the body is not a mere thing. The body for Nietzsche is not a mere chunk of matter. Because after all, if it were, how could Nietzsche ever say, as he does, that there is more reason in your body than in your best wisdom? How could he call the body the great reason, if the body were a mere thing?

I would like to suggest, then, rather than wanting to make man— i.e., to make subjectivity—into a mere thing, that Nietzsche's point in saying that consciousness is only a surface is that there is much in the subject that is beneath the surface. This is what he wants to say. More specifically, he wants to say that there is much in the subject, there is a wealth: an abundance within the subject that remains concealed from the subject, intrinsically concealed from the subject. Or, to put it in a more traditional way, Nietzsche wants to say that the subject is not transparent to itself. The subject is not totally transparent to itself.

In this connection, in this denial of total transparency to itself Nietzsche repeatedly launches an attack against the kind of traditional assertion of the self's transparency, which is to say, against the Cartesian 'cogito.' He attacks the belief in the possibility that one can grasp oneself fully, that one can grasp oneself adequately

PART II

in an act of thinking. He attacks the belief that, in reflection, the subject has an immediate certainty of itself.

Let me cite for you his critique of the 'cogito,' given in *Beyond Good and Evil*, section 16. Nietzsche says,

> [W]hen I analyze the process which is expressed in the sentence, 'I think,' I find a whole series of daring assertions that would be difficult, perhaps impossible to prove. For example, that it is *I* who thinks; that there must necessarily be something that thinks; that thinking is an activity, an operation on the part of a being who is thought as the cause; that there is an 'ego'; and finally, that it is already determined what is to be designated by thinking—that I [notice the curiously Platonic argument, R.S.] *know* what thinking is (*BW*, 213).[255]

And then he continues,

> For if I had not already decided within myself what it is, by what standard could I determine whether that which is just happening is not, perhaps, 'willing'—or 'feeling'? In short, the assertion, 'I think,' assumes that I *compare* my state at the present moment with other states in myself which I know in order to determine what it is. On account of this retrospective connection [notice how he is temporalizing, R.S.] with further 'knowledge,' it has, at any rate, no 'immediate certainty' for me (ibid.).[256]

So then, without going into the details of that,[257] we can say, at the very least, you see, that the presumed kind of "immediate certainty" of oneself as a thinking being is something which has its roots beneath the level of consciousness; something is already taken for granted by the 'cogito.' The very presumption of having this kind of transparency, this kind of reflective self-possession already takes for granted something that is not transparent. So that this certainty of oneself has its roots beneath presumed certainty, beneath the level of consciousness.

Let me refer here to another issue. In light of this critique of the 'cogito,' we might ask: given Nietzsche's radical attempt to deny the self-transparency of subjectivity, and of consciousness, how on the positive side, does Nietzsche understand self-consciousness? Certainly, in placing the possibilities of the self-consciousness

82

under this kind of limitation, as we just saw here, he nevertheless clearly is not just wanting to deny the fact of self-consciousness. So we might ask how, on the positive side, does he understand self-consciousness? To what extent can man, whatever the limitations, become conscious of himself?

Let me refer just to one or two things. First of all, in section 354 of *The Gay Science* I think we find the most explicit discussion of this question. There Nietzsche suggests that there is a relationship between, on the one hand, the development of self-consciousness, self-awareness and, on the other hand, the necessity for communication. In other words, he suggests here that it is only as a social animal that man learns to become conscious of himself. He makes the same point in the *Genealogy of Morals*. It is only as a social animal that man learns to be conscious of himself. And man's self-consciousness is something tied to communication within the social complex. And by being tied to communication, it is also tied to speech, tied to language. Self-consciousness is tied essentially to man's social dimension and to language. Self consciousness develops in the framework of society and language. I think you can see here that Nietzsche is strikingly close to Hegel in the first of these.

From this general discussion then, in which Nietzsche tries to see self-consciousness coming about within the social and linguistic context, he goes on to draw a most interesting conclusion on this same passage in the *The Gay Science*. The conclusion is this: "Consequently, each of us, in spite of the best intention of *understanding* himself as individually as possible, and of 'knowing himself,' will always just call into consciousness the non-individual in him, namely, his 'averageness'" (*GS*, 299)[258]—a most interesting passage and, I might say, most decisive eventually, for our whole question. In spite of the best intention of understanding the self as individually as possible, and of 'knowing' [the] self as best he can, ‹ he › will always call into consciousness ‹ the › *non-individual* in him, his *averageness*.

So to sum up, first of all Nietzsche wants to deny the identity of subjectivity with consciousness; he wants to speak of the dimension beneath the surface that is consciousness, to speak of a non-transparency; a radical non-transparency of the subject.

Part II

The other principal denial that I suggest is involved in Nietzsche's description of subjectivity as will to power is his denial (bearing very importantly now, in relation to the tradition) that the subject is to be understood in terms of the traditional concept of substance. In other words, the denial is that Nietzsche wants to say that the subject *is not*; subjectivity is not a kind of thing; a kind of substance (to use a technical word) behind our actions, behind our thoughts, our decisions. The subject, in other words, he wants to say, is not a kind of agent behind the scenes causing what happens on the scene of action. Or, as he likes to say, the subject is not a free subject. The subject is not a free subject in the sense that the subject is not able to remain aloof, to remain untouched, unaffected, uncompromised by activity. Nietzsche radically rejects the notion of freedom, of causality; I refer you here especially to his *Twilight of the Idols*.

In this connection there is an example Nietzsche repeats in several places but which he elaborates most carefully in the *Genealogy of Morals* to illustrate this point, i.e., the rejection of the understanding of the subject as a thing behind the act, as a kind of substance. Now, the example which he gives in the *Genealogy* is the example of lightning, which we express in the phrase, "lightning flashes" (*BW*, 481).[259] He says, just as in that case, we tend (because we are seduced by language, by grammar) to separate the lightning from its flash; we tend by the very structure of language to say the lightning flashes. Language causes us to tend to separate. We say 'here is the action' and 'here is the thing behind the scene which causes what happens on the scene.' So, Nietzsche says, precisely in the same way we tend to separate man from his action, we tend to place man behind the act, as a kind of cause, a kind of aloof uncompromised (one is almost tempted to say—noumenal) cause of the act.

And then to cite just his conclusion to that discussion, he says (in the ‹ *GM* › First Essay, section 13) "But there is no such substratum, there is no such 'being' behind doing, effecting, becoming; 'the doer' is merely a fiction added to the deed—the deed is everything" (ibid.).[260]

The same issue is discussed in the *Nachlass*, in section 671 [of *The Will to Power*] (*WP*, 354). Nietzsche refers to this issue and here he speaks specifically of the will as understood as such a substantial agent, as a substantial act behind the act causing ‹ it › in the same

THE ONTOLOGICAL TURN IN THE PHILOSOPHY OF THE WILL

way that the sentence, 'the lightning flashes' causes. In that connection he makes a most remarkable statement. Having spoken of the will so regarded, as a kind of substantial agent, Nietzsche then makes this statement: "There is *no* such thing as '*will*'" (ibid).[261] The will is not a thing, a being.

We have here, I would suggest, a kind of first test of Nietzsche's relation to metaphysics. What about this notion? What about his attack on the substantial conception itself? Is this a point at which we could regard Nietzsche as already escaping from the modern metaphysical tradition? Or can we take what he was saying here as [still remaining within] a metaphysical tradition?

I would suggest that at this point, Nietzsche is still very much a metaphysician. I would suggest even that Nietzsche is *only* reiterating the critique of the concept of substance that was initiated by Kant and that was developed in German Idealism. Nietzsche, in other words, in denying that the subject is some kind of substance behind the scene, yet on the contrary, understanding the subject in terms of, as he says, in terms of its contradiction and contrast, in other words, in terms of its relation to itself, in doing this, I would suggest, he is saying the same thing as Fichte says, that is, that 'being is a derivative concept' and the positive concept is activity. Being is derivative and what is positive is activity. To this point, at any rate, we may say that Nietzsche remains within metaphysics.[262]/[263]

With that by way of preface, let's go then to our inquiry regarding these three fundamental characterizations of the subject that are given to us in *Zarathustra*. The second of these descriptions of subjectivity is that the subject is a creating. One sense of this creating is suggested, I think, in the section in Part I., "On the Despisers of the Body": "Always the self listens and seeks. It compares, overpowers, conquers, destroys; it controls, and it is in control, of the Ego too" (*PN*, 146).[264]

So then, the subject compares, overpowers, conquers, destroys, and Zarathustra, I would suggest, sums up all these things, activities, when he says that the self controls. The self's creating is a *control*. The creating that belongs to the self, that fundamentally characterizes the self, is a control; or to take a word he uses more commonly, it is a *commanding*.[265]

85

PART II

This is made explicit in section 19 of *Beyond Good and Evil*, where Nietzsche says that the will is "above all an *affect*, and specifically the affect of the command" (*BW*, 215).[266] So then, we can say that the subject is the commanding. Or, to extend this, the subject is a mastering. The subject is a gaining power over. (I deliberately put all of these, of course, as Nietzsche does, in the verbal form, in order to insist on the distinction between subjectivity and traditional substance.) So the subject is a commanding, a mastering, a gaining power over.

In section 230 of *Beyond Good and Evil*, Nietzsche speaks of the will as "the will from multiplicity to simplicity. A will that ties up, tames, and is domineering and truly masterful" (*BW*, 349).[267] And again, he says of the will, "its power to appropriate the foreign stands revealed in its inclination to assimilate the new to the old," (and then in a remarkably Kantian phrase), "to simplify the manifold" (ibid., 350).[268] So then, willing, subjectivity, is an appropriating. It appropriates. Its creating is an appropriating, a commanding, a taking into its power, an ordering of chaos, a gaining of mastery, a gaining of power. And it is in this connection, you see, that Nietzsche calls it precisely will to power. In other words, you see, power is not just some kind of object after which the will strives. Power is not something, which, as it were, is outside the will and toward which the will strives. It is not some kind of thing at which the will is directed, in the way that desire, for instance, might be directed to a particular thing.[269] The point is, rather, you see, power expresses the very nature of willing. To say will to power is to say no more than will. To say will to power is simply to explain how the word will is to be taken. All of these say the same for Nietzsche. Or, to use the word which he uses most frequently, especially in *Thus Spoke Zarathustra*, will to power is will as overcoming. The character of appropriating, of overcoming. It is not something added on to the will, as it were, as a kind of characteristic of it, but rather what defines the very essence of the will.

Now if we characterize the will thus, as overpowering, gaining mastery over, or overcoming, the obvious question then is: what does it overcome? What does it gain mastery over? And the answer is given already in the very title of one section of *Thus Spoke Zarathustra*, the section entitled "On Self-Overcoming" (*PN*, 225). Zarathustra says, "And life itself confided this secret to me. 'Behold,' it said, 'I am *that which must always overcome itself*" (ibid. 227).[270]

What will to power overcomes by its very essence as will is itself. Its willing, in other words, is a willing beyond itself, a creating beyond itself. Will to power and self-overcoming are the same thing. This is made even more explicit in *Beyond Good and Evil*, that is, that the overcoming is a self-overcoming; that will to power is essentially the overcoming of itself. For instance, in section 19, which is perhaps the most important section in the entire work, Nietzsche writes:

> A man who *wills* commands something within himself that renders obedience, or that he believes renders obedience. But now let us notice what is strangest about the will—this manifold thing for which people have but one word [..., R.S.]. We are at the same time, the commanding *and* the obeying parties (*BW*, 216).[271]

That is to say, both that which overcomes and that which is overcome.

We need to ask then, what is the structure of this manifold thing? What kind of structures are involved in this process which is self-overcoming? What kind of articulation can we find that would render this intelligible? Well, the structure of will to power is elaborated in many places. For instance, in *Beyond Good and Evil* section 19 (to which I just referred), Nietzsche stresses that will to power involves a basic duality. That its structure is basically a dual structure. And there he expresses the relevant duality by speaking of that away from which one wills and that toward which one wills.

So this manifold thing, will to power, self-overcoming, gaining mastery over self, has a fundamentally dual structure. The character of the duality, away from which and towards which, is perhaps must clearly elaborated in *Thus Spoke Zarathustra* itself. I refer you specifically to the section, "On the Tarantulas" (*PN*, 211). Zarathustra says in a most remarkable statement, "life must overcome itself again and again." And then he continues: "Life wants to build itself up into the heights with pillars and steps; it wants to look into vast distances and out toward stirring beauties: *therefore* it requires [..., R.S.] steps and contradiction among the steps and the climbers."

And then the final statement is, "life wants to climb and to overcome itself in the climbing" (*PN*, 213).[272]

So then this says that life requires passage (according to the metaphor here) into the heights; requires a passing, a move, an overcoming which takes it beyond itself. This expresses one side of the essential duality of the will to power. A movement beyond itself: an overcoming, a transcendence. This element, this side, as it were, of the will to power, is what Nietzsche, especially in the *Nachlass*, but also elsewhere, designates by the German word, *Steigerung*, which we might translate as something like enhancement.

But the passage which I just read says that not only must there be a move, a transcending move, a movement beyond itself, but it also stresses especially that precisely in order that there be such a movement from the heights there must be steps on which one ascends to the heights. In other words, the movement toward the heights, to use Nietzsche's metaphor here, the overcoming movement requires that there be some kind of basis from which one ascends and by means of which one ascends. The movement of transcendence, the movement of the self beyond itself, requires some kind of established basis on which it can move upwards, even though indeed the outcome is to overcome such steps. Life overcomes itself climbing, you see. So one side of the duality is the movement itself, the movement beyond, the transcendence. But on the other side, we have the need for a basis, as it were, to be established on which and from which the transcending move can be made. And this is the other side of the duality that makes up the structure of the will.

The steps, the established basis from which the movement can be made, that is the second side of the duality. This second element then, Nietzsche normally designates by the German word *Erhaltung*, which we can perhaps translate as something like *preservation*. The idea being that something has to be established. Something has to be preserved, as it were, instituted as a basis from which the overcoming proceeds, even though the very effect of the overcoming is to disrupt what previously was the base of the movement. Again, life wants to overcome itself by climbing.

I want to suggest, then, that here we have the most fundamental structuration of the theory of the will to power. To summarize what I have been saying:

Will to power means commanding, gaining mastery over, and specifically over oneself. Hence, will to power means self-overcoming.

And in that overcoming, there is this fundamental duality, the movement of transcendence itself, and the basis which has to be, as it were, established, preserved, for the possibility of such a movement. So that we can say that the structure, will to power, is the dynamically inner-working duality of *Erhaltung* and *Steigerung*. This is the basic structure of will to power.

A student asked if the interaction of these two sides of the structure is a metaphysics. Answer: what I want to try to show is that, in the way in which Nietzsche brings these two together, he is catapulted out of metaphysics. I have still to do that. Somewhere in the *Nachlass,* Nietzsche says that metaphysics has projected the conditions of man's well being as being itself. That's a paraphrase of what he says. I want to try to show that the very question of metaphysics represents one way of taking this essential duality. We will see as we go on that *Erhaltung* has a fundamental reference to truth, and to knowledge; and *Steigerung* has a fundamental reference to art.

Let's go now to the third major description. Taking our cue from a description of subjectivity as will to power and as creating and in each case, trying to unfold a number of senses thereby involved— let us go now to the third description, namely that subjectivity is a valuing. In order to see what is really at issue in this description of subjectivity as valuing, I think it would perhaps be helpful if we take as our point of departure a section of the *Twilight of the Idols* to which I have referred repeatedly in previous lectures, namely, the section entitled, "How the 'True World' Finally Became a Fable," in which, if you recall, in little more than a page, Nietzsche traces the history of metaphysics.

You recall that in this remarkable section Nietzsche traces out six steps, the first being, of course, Platonism, and then down through the history of metaphysics, always interrogating throughout man's relation to the metaphysical, the supersensible, until finally he comes to the sixth and last stage, which incidentally, is the stage at which he says Zarathustra begins, and this last stage is, in effect, the stage of the death of God: the stage of nihilism.

Here's how he describes that last stage in the history of metaphysics, that is, the present stage, the stage from which Zarathustra begins. He says, "the true world" (that means of course the metaphysical; being in itself) "we have abolished. What world has remained? The apparent one, perhaps? But no! *With the true world, we have also abolished the apparent one*" (*PN*, 486).[273] The point is that once the true world, that is to say, being in itself, the metaphysical, the supersensible, once the true world has collapsed, then the apparent world, the sensible world, the empirical world, can no longer be understood as it has been through the tradition in reference to the supersensible. Once the supersensible, once the metaphysical has collapsed, then it is no longer possible to understand the physical, the sensible, the empirical world in reference to a metaphysical or supersensible reality. Hence it is no longer an apparent world at all, that is, a world understood as an appearance of something else. The sensible can no longer be understood as a mere image, to use the Platonic term, of the meta-physical.

If it can no longer be understood in this fashion—no longer an apparent world understood as an image of something else—the problem Nietzsche then confronts, right here at this point where Zarathustra begins, is how this world is to be understood? How is what was previously taken as the apparent world, as the mere appearance of being in itself, of the metaphysical, now to be understood, once the metaphysical has collapsed?

It's here that we come to the notion of values in Nietzsche. In a very important section of the *Nachlass*, in the volume entitled *The Will to Power*, section 567, Nietzsche gives this answer to the question of how the apparent world is to be understood after the death of God. Here is his answer: he writes, "the apparent world, that is, a world viewed according to values, ordered, selected according to values, i.e., in this case according to the viewpoint of utility in regard to the preservation (*Erhaltung*) and enhancement [*Steigerung*] of the power of a certain species of animal" (*WP*, 305).[274]

How, then, is the world of appearance to be understood? The world of appearance is a world viewed according to values; ordered, shaped, formed, according to values. And furthermore, the passage suggests, values somehow are related to the needs, to the conditions, of preservation and enhancement—*Erhaltung* and *Steigerung*. Values are somehow related back to the conditions, needs (he speaks here of utility) in supplying, providing what is essential to life.

The problem, then, of understanding the world of appearance, the only world which is left after the collapse of the metaphysical, becomes simply the problem of values. We need, then, to try briefly to see what the main issues are in this question of values. What does Nietzsche mean by values? Let me warn you in advance that what he means is not at all the same thing that we mean in our ordinary talk about values, though it has its very definite relation. He uses the word in a sense which he himself, I might say, shapes and forms. So let's try to see what he means by values or, in the active sense, what he means by valuing, evaluating.

The first point we need to make in that connection is that valuing or evaluating is not just one of the various activities in which man is involved. This valuing or evaluating is not something which man can choose either to do or not to do. It is not, as it were, a kind of accidental activity. Rather, valuing, evaluating, Nietzsche wants to say, is something that belongs fundamentally to life. It is something which belongs fundamentally to the will to power.

He puts this very straightforwardly in the section in *Thus Spoke Zarathustra* "On the Thousand and One Goals." He says, "No people can live without first evaluating" (*PN*, 170).[275] In other words, no evaluating, no life, no will to power.

Secondly, however, we need to note that when Nietzsche speaks of evaluating, valuing, that this does not mean for him simply to estimate or to judge things in terms of some kind of presupposed set of values or standards. In other words, when he speaks about evaluating, he does not mean the kind of thing we do when, for instance, we see a person performing some act and we judge in terms of some values that we already have at hand, that it is a good act or a bad one. So evaluating, valuing, does not mean making a judgment and estimating in terms of some already at hand set of values. But rather, when Nietzsche speaks about evaluating, what he means, basically, is the positing of these values, these standards themselves. Valuing, evaluating does not mean taking a certain unquestioned set of standards and judging things in terms of those standards. It does not mean looking at a work of art and judging that work of art to be beautiful in terms of some standard of beauty that one had already. What Nietzsche wants to speak about when he talks of valuing or evaluating is the very positing of the standards, of the values, in terms of which then one is subsequently able to interpret things. (So valuing refers to the prior, the fundamental process of setting up the standards of evaluation in the first place).

In the section, "On the Thousand and One Goals," this is made quite clear. Zarathustra says here:

> Verily, men gave themselves all their good and evil. Verily, they did not take it, they did not find it, nor did it come to them as a voice from heaven. Only man placed values in things to preserve himself—he alone created a meaning for things, a human meaning (*PN*, 171).[276]

To evaluate, Zarathustra says, is to create. And then he adds: "Through evaluating alone is there value, and without evaluating the nut of existence would be hollow" (ibid.).[277]

The point is that values presuppose evaluating. Values presuppose the creative activity in which those values are posited. It is the creative positing of values which Nietzsche wants to designate as evaluating. Values are presupposed in valuing, rather than being presupposed by it.[278]

The third point: for Nietzsche, values are posited by will to power. They are not something found, taken, something that comes as a voice from heaven as Zarathustra puts it, but something posited. Values are creatively put forth, posited, by will to power. But then, as posited, as something posited by a subject, a subject which posits them, after all, from out of a certain life situation; these values that are posited are always posited from some standpoint, from some viewpoint. If values are posited, not by some absolute being, but rather by a concrete subject immersed in a life situation, then values are always correlative of some viewpoint, always relative to a perspective, to the life perspective from which they are posited. So we have to speak, then, not of the values only but, in order really to understand the values, we have always to talk about the perspective, the life situation, the conjuring of needs, from out of which the values are posited.

Now, if we grant that values are posited by concrete human beings out of a certain life situation—perspective—then I think you can see that this has a most important consequence. Because after all, it is in terms of values, if you recall how we first raised this problematic, it is in terms of values that the world is viewed. What is the world of appearance? It is a world shaped, formed, ordered by values. It is values that determine the appearance which the world is, that determine the face the world has for us. They determine the character which the world has for us. So if values determine, as it were, the character of the empirical world, and if values in turn are always relative to the life perspective from which they are posited, then the character of the world is always relative to a perspective. What the world appears as being, is always relative to a viewpoint, to a perspective. This is Nietzsche's much celebrated notion of perspective. This is Nietzsche's perspectivism.

There are many passages where Nietzsche speaks of this. To cite one, in *The Will to Power* section 481, he says that the world has "no meaning behind it, but countless meanings." And then his problematic dash—and then he writes: "perspectivism" (*WP*, 267).[279] The world has no meaning behind it, but it has countless meanings, meanings which it has by virtue of being shaped and formed by different values; that is, by values posited out of different life perspectives.

We need to ask then, to follow this up, in the way in which the world appears formed and shaped by values relative to a perspective from which those values were posited—we need to ask then, what is the character of these perspectives, these viewpoints from which values are posited and in relation to which the meaning, the appearance of the world is determined? What defines the perspective? And how is the perspective related to the values that are formed from that perspective? How is the perspective related to values?

Part of this question is answered in *The Will to Power* section 481 where, with remarkable gravity, Nietzsche says, "it is our needs *that interpret the world*" (ibid.).[280] Or again, to cite just one other passage in *Beyond Good and Evil*, section 268, he says: "The values of a human being betray something of the *structure* of its soul, and where it finds its conditions of life, its true need" (*BW*, 407).[281] We might say then, that the viewpoint, the perspective, in relation to which values are posited, and to which values, and thereby, the very way in which the world makes its appearance, by which these are determined, we might say that the viewpoint is defined, fundamentally, in terms of the needs and the conditions of life.

We see the kind of regress we are making.

We begin with the apparent world, a world shaped by values.

Values in turn are posited by a perspective.

The perspective is defined by the needs, the conditions of which have to be fulfilled by that positing subject, in order for it to be what it is.

Okay. We need to ask, then, what kind of needs, to carry our regression even further. What kind of needs, what kind of conditions define the perspective? What is the character of those needs which basically determine the perspective, hence determining the character of the values posited, hence determining the very way in which the world is formed? Nietzsche is very explicit as to what kind of conditions are relevant here, about the character of these conditions.

In *The Will to Power*, section 715, he writes a most important statement. He says, "the viewpoint of 'value' is the viewpoint of the *conditions of preservation and enhancement* for complex forms of relative life-duration within the flux of becoming" (*WP*, 380).[282] This says that the conditions which determine the perspective, which determine the viewpoint from which values are posited, thereby determine the very character of the values posited, and ultimately, even the very way of appearing that the world has. These conditions are the conditions necessary for preservation and enhancement (*Erhaltung* and *Steigerung*). The needs, as it were, that define the perspective as the perspective of a value-positing, are the needs and the conditions necessary for preservation and enhancement. It is these conditions, then, it is the conditions of *Erhaltung* and *Steigerung*, which determine the perspective, and which consequently determine values, which consequently determine the way in which the only world there is after the collapse of the metaphysical is shaped and formed, the way in which this world appears.

In *The Will to Power*, section 507, Nietzsche says, "In *valuations* are expressed *conditions of preservation* and *enhancement*" (*WP*, 275).[283] This is a very straightforward statement.

To sum up, the positing of values is simply the way in which these needs are satisfied. The positing of values which takes place in the function of the conditions, the needs pertaining to values. And the positing of values is the way in which the will to power supplies its most basic needs. The positing of values is the way in which will to power guarantees the fulfillment of those basic conditions without which, we might say, it could not exist as will to power.

To use the expression from *The Birth of Tragedy*, the positing of values is the means by which life secures its own continuation.

This idea, that there are two fundamental types of needs or conditions in life for which we now see the positing of values has become a means of satisfaction, this is not something arbitrarily and suddenly introduced in the *Nachlass* or even in *Thus Spoke Zarathustra*. This idea that there are two fundamental kinds of needs or conditions that must be satisfied if life is to secure its own continuation is an idea which I would suggest is present almost from the very beginning of Nietzsche's thought. It does not come first in the *Nachlass* in 1887 and 1888. It comes already in 1872, almost from the beginning of Nietzsche's writings, though perhaps, it is never so explicit there.

At any rate, I think it is very much this same duality of needs that is expressed already at the end of that early unpublished essay, *On Truth and Lie in an Extra Moral Sense*. And in fact, the only fundamental difference we might say, is that in the early essay Nietzsche formulates the distinction between these two types of conditions, preservation and enhancement, as a distinction between two types of men rather than as a distinction between two conditions within every man.

You recall in that essay, that on the one hand Nietzsche speaks there about what he calls the rational man. The rational man there is the man who is engaged in constructing, as Nietzsche says, a framework of ideas. He is a man who constructs a kind of framework that gives stability, permanence and order to life, that gives something like the steps on which life might choose to ascend, to carry Nietzsche's metaphor along. And then, you remember, also at the end of that essay, Nietzsche goes on to contrast the rational man who gives a framework of stability and so on with what he there calls the intuitive man, or the artist. And you remember that in drawing the contrast, he says that the artist is the one who throws the metaphors into confusion. The artist is the one who shifts the boundary stone, as he says, he is the one who throws out of gear the framework of ideas that the rational man has set up. You recall seeing Nietzsche do something remotely like that in *Zarathustra*. Also, he says there, not only that the artist throws the framework out of order, out of joint, but also he says that the artist uses this order provided by the rational man, but he uses it only as a scaffolding for a movement beyond, for an overcoming. So I think you can see from that brief comparison, how we have to do here with the same duality that Nietzsche in an early work presented as a distinction between two kinds of men. Now he introduces it as a fundamental duality within every man, within will to power itself.

Furthermore, we can push our regression. We can go back even further than the essay *On Truth and Lie*, can we not? Because the contrast we find there between the rational man and the artist is in turn a development of the contrast that we found already in *The Birth of Tragedy*. And I am thinking, of course, of the contrast between Socrates and Dionysus. The distinction between the rational man and the artist is only a distinction between science and tragedy, between Socrates and Dionysus. Knowledge, Truth, preservation, conditions, order, stability, on the one hand; art, enhancement, overcoming, on the other.

3. Heidegger[284]

a. Protest against "busy-ness"

> In busy-ness the project of the object-region
> is primordially built into entities.[285]
> Heidegger, "The Age of the World Picture"[286]

The two anarchic displacements that I have traced, the practical negation of goals and the transmutation of responsibility, impair the smooth functioning of what Heidegger calls "busy-ness" [*der Betrieb*].[287] How, one must wonder, could a society *function* if Meister Eckhart's 'life without why,' Nietzsche's 'eternal return of the same,' and Heidegger's 'call of the difference' were allowed to subvert the project of objectivation? The word "busy-ness" is meant to indicate that this project, while legitimate in its own region (and legitimated by the Existential Analytic), is today extended to the totality of entities. Technology is the factor that renders it so primordial. The action Heidegger urges as the practical condition for responding and corresponding to today's constellation of the difference entails a certain dis-articulation of that project which has made and still makes the technocratic universe. If the 'atomic' economy is effectively—actually and efficaciously—bi-frontal, if it is a threshold economy, its mere situation calls into question the pertinence of the Aristotelian inquiry into the *function* of man. By its historical locus alone, technology simultaneously pushes the referential features of the economies to their extreme and hampers them, corrupting the interest in the ordered functioning of communities, an interest that is perhaps the most evenly distributed commodity in the world. Located on the boundary of possible closure, technology as the last 'stamp' both produces and transgresses "uncanny" functioning.[288]

The concept of *Betrieb*, busy-ness, in Heidegger designates first of all the decontextualization of artworks:[289] even "if we visit the temple in Paestum at its site and the Bamberg cathedral on its square, the world of these works, henceforth objectively present, has perished." To say that their world no longer is, and that in the contemporary era they are rendered objectively present, is to say the same thing twice. Object is opposed to work. "The object-being of the works [..., R.S] is not their work-being." What is the criterion for that disjunction? A work institutes a world that is its own, while an object, constituted by the mathematical project—the project of generalized calculability and accountability—lacks a world of its own. A work rests in its world, but an object results from an entirely different project: the subject's scheme of placing everything at its own disposal. A work that becomes an object is thereby torn out of its context, and that decontextualization is irreparable. "World-withdrawal and world-decay can never be undone."[290] The work has changed into one item among others in the isomorphic universe of calculation. 'Busy-ness' is the consequence of the project of objectification.[291] [Transformation into busy-ness] affects everything present in the contemporary economy. This is the critical charge pressed by Heidegger here. It can be spelled out by tracing the original and the originary origins of busy-ness.

Originally, busy-ness is that modern scheme of transformation through which 'things' lose their 'world' by becoming 'objects.' This scheme is imposing itself today on all entities as such, without exception. The logic of technology consists in building object-being into them. The logic of *mathēsis* and the (transcendental subjectivist) logic of object constitution have prevailed beyond Descartes' and Kant's fondest dreams, as the way of being 'objectively present' or 'given for handling' (*vorhanden*) gets built into everything, including the subject. This is a logic of implacable violence.[292] "In busy-ness the project of the object-region gets primordially built into entities."[293] [O]nly the empirically verifiable is present.[294] Furthermore, if modernity originates with (although not from) experimental science, then the endless *et cetera* of hypotheses and their verification through experiment, yielding new hypotheses, is the original busy-ness. Under this concept, then, Heidegger exhibits one of the basic traits of science, namely, that the results of previous research prescribe the ways and means to be adhered to in new research. "This need to adapt itself to its own results as the ways and means of advancing its procedure is the essence of busy-ness as a feature of research." Busy-ness designates the process through which experimental sciences perpetuate themselves by feeding on their own products. But from the start the experimental sciences have been in the service of practical mastery over nature, not vice versa. Technology, the contemporary figure of that mastery, a figure "whose essence is identical with the essence of modern metaphysics,"[295] equally progresses and even maintains itself only on the condition of eating its own children, like Kronos. The "priority of procedure over entities (Nature and History)" means "science as research has, in itself, the character of busy-ness."[296] In the bustle of scientific research the omnivorous essence of technology shows forth, which in turn finally reveals the violence inherent in the fundamental position of metaphysics' boundary epoch.

Heidegger contests busy-ness as the ultimate and totalitarian shape of objectivation simply by asking what it is originarily, what its essence is. As with Socrates, raising the question of essence already means calling into question and protesting (except that the Athenian Senate perceived the danger in such essential questioning better than the German Chancelleries following 1935). Unlike

Socrates, however, Heidegger raises the question of essence in historical terms. Essence is always a mode of unconcealment. That is why it is reached, not by an act of intuition, but by deconstructing the economies that it structures. *Betrieb* comes from *treiben*, to drive. I have said that this translates the cogito, as *co-agitatio*. But that original drive toward mastery has as its originary condition the 'drift' (*die Trift*) in presencing, i.e., the way being is time for modernity. A certain directionality of time, toward solid presence, is the essence of busy-ness. To so deconstruct our fundamental position and to retrieve the truth of its temporal essence is neither to condemn nor to countenance it. Busy-ness is no more a matter of condemnation for Heidegger than technology in general. Neither the modern drift in presencing nor the sequence of economies it has produced, leading up to the atomic age, harbor anything fatal: "I do not see the situation of man in the world of global technology as an inextricable and inescapable fate."[297] But if the essential questioning of busy-ness is—like 'thinking' in general—a doing, it definitely counteracts it by a practice impossible to co-opt.[298]

To begin with, the thinking proper to busy-ness, a thinking that poses and disposes, has its corollary practice: imposing the project of objectivation on entities in their totality. 'The other thinking,' the one that questions and calls into question, also has its corollary practice. It is non-attachment, *Abgeschiedenheit*. That attitude alone, Heidegger argues, opens us to a new ply in the history of economies by making us comply with it.[299] To take leave, *Abschied nehmen*, is what those detached always do. They are *abgeschieden*, departed. Non-attachment is the practical protest that may bear to term a breed detached from the ontological difference. *Abgeschiedenheit*, then, is the one praxis capable of undoing the principles that have run the age of ontological difference.[300] The way of calling busy-ness and its essence into question is to be unattached to the epochal principles. Non-attachment contests the global technological enterprise just as 'the other thinking' contests the project of total objectivation. Both denature the epoch of calculation and by the same stroke denaturalize those who inhabit that epoch.

Several commentators have drawn attention to the protest against objectivation and calculative thinking as one of the rare "political elements" in Heidegger.[301] Still, the conditions on which such protest

PART II

can be staged make it peculiar. Heidegger does not attempt to redress alienation. He does not come to the rescue of total man. If he indicts—both declares publicly or denounces (in Latin, *indicere*) and gives evidence against (*indicare*)—the conditions for indictment are provided by our economy of presence. Indeed, no polemic can be drawn from the temporal difference unless this difference first declares itself publicly in the evidence of an epochal break. The original locus of the polemics Heidegger engages, the locus of the original *polemos*, is the contemporary economy of presence. It is the confrontation of the principial constellation with the anarchic. Meditative thinking does not combat calculative thinking— nor non-attachment, busy-ness—in the way Don Quixote tilts at windmills.[302] That 'the sciences do not think' does not amount to opposing thought to science as the negation to a position. Thought and science are not contraries within one genus. If the call to thinking in Heidegger meant, as has often been claimed, an escape from the technological age and a return to the Greek 'dawn,' then the call would be ideological. But: "Never have I spoken against technology, nor against the so-called demonic[303] in technology. Rather, I try to understand the *essence*[304] of technology."[305] It is well known which ideology,[306] at least in Europe, expresses itself today— and certainly not fortuitously—through the slogan of a return to Greece.[307] Heidegger, on the other hand, observes that we lack all models. "The renunciation of historically fabricated models—ages, styles, tendencies, situations, ideas—is the sign of the extreme distress we and those to come have to endure." Even if we wished, "that initial thinking cannot be 'renewed,' nor even erected as a 'model.'"[308] Lines such as these should put an end, once and for all, to the conservative readings of Heidegger which hold that for him thinking is a matter of preserving the "ever so few authentic things" bequeathed by our ancestors[309] from being levelled by busyness. Inquiring into the essence of technology is neither a conservative nor a progressive undertaking. It is a search for the categories according to which presence has spelled itself out since the time of those figures known as the Presocratic philosophers. A quest for historical categories is hardly an ideological return to the Greeks.

Non-attachment to busy-ness is not an option placed before our free will. Heidegger distorts the tradition from which he takes the word *Abgeschiedenheit* by treating it as designating an economic possibility. As such, it points to a practical potential in the current era, the power "to bring an issue where it belongs and henceforth to leave it there."[310] Which issue? The one that, at the moment of economic transgression, most amply provides food for thought, *das Bedenklichste*, and is most worthy of question, *das Fragwürdigste*. Anything, then, insofar as it appears to the gaze of the anticipatory incidences of the transitional categories: any 'thing' in its relation to its 'world.' It remains for us to prepare the thinking capable of such non-attachment. If that word indeed designates a potential to be set free—the relation to things through which they are "left" to their world—then non-attachment amounts as clearly to a doing as does thinking. Essential thinking and unattached acting are inseverable as the *practical* reply to the *economic* ply in which the principles wither. That practice and that economy together form the condition for the transition toward *ontological* anarchy, pliant being.

In this way protest gets distorted, too. Heidegger does not directly *protest against* technology and the atomic age, but he *protests* directly the economy that produced them: he testifies to it. Quite as Nietzsche protested the innocence of becoming, Heidegger protests the possibility for thinking to become essential and for acting to become non-attached. 'Protestation' thereby recovers its primary sense, which is to declare, to attest to a truth. The way to challenge busy-ness is to protest non-attachment. The latter, in turn, by its very possibility attests to an economy without principle, to essentially anarchic presencing.

After the practical negation of goals and the transmutation of responsibility, non-attachment provides a clue for verifying which path is aberrant and which is viable in the contemporary bi-frontal order. The point of impact of Heideggerian dissent is situated neither behind nor ahead of us, it is a dissent out of neither nostalgia nor utopia. Its impact is on today's course as affected by a possible, thoroughly contingent declination. Even preparatory thinking—preparatory for 'the other thinking' which Heidegger hopes will become "efficacious" after all, perhaps 300 years from now[311]—first constitutes a challenge to the current hold of busyness. Non-attachment is necessary so that things may enter a mode of interdependence unattached to principles. Contingent pliancy in

PART II

presencing must be affirmed *as contingent* for an entirely contingent aletheiological constellation to arise. Stated in Trakl's words: the hold of busy-ness is to be unloosened through non-attachment for a breed severed from ultimate grounds to be borne to term.

b. Transmutation of "destiny"

> By 'destiny' one usually understands what
> has been determined and imposed by fate:
> a sad, an inauspicious, a beneficial destiny.
> This sense is derivative. Indeed, originarily
> to 'destine' means to prepare, order, bring
> everything where it belongs.
> *Der Satz vom Grund*[312]

These lines describe the transmutation to which Heidegger subjects the notion of destiny. Commonly humanist or 'existentialist,' it turns economic and topological.[313]

To fashion one's destiny or acquiesce to it, to assume and carry it out or to meet it: such human doing is not the horizon in which these lines inscribe *Geschick*. Once the modalities of presencing have been recognized as the very issue of phenomenology, destiny can no longer designate an individual's or a collectivity's appointed lot and its reception. It designates, rather, the way the modalities address us, as if they were emitted. To be 'destined' or bound for a particular place is to have committed oneself to it. To commit, emit, transmit all imply a sending, *schicken. Geschick* has therefore been translated as "mittence."[314] At stake are the ceaseless arrangements and rearrangements in phenomenal interconnectedness that "bring everything where it belongs." To speak of destiny is, then, to speak of places and of placing.

In this transmutation two consequences must be seen which make it clear that humanity's lot is not what holds Heidegger's closest attention. The first is nothing new: destiny so understood—no longer as man's vocation, but as each thing's allocation to its locus, as its situation in its site—only instantiates the methodic anti-humanism that characterizes this phenomenology in its entirety.

102

The second consequence is more incisive. It points to one result of the turning toward the anarchic economy. The arrangement of phenomena committed or 'sent' to us with that turn, situates us differently. The specific *mittence* of the moment of metaphysical closure enacts a change of place, a displacement. The end of metaphysics is a concrete possibility as the modalities of presencing—destiny—begin to place us otherwise and elsewhere. On that threshold Heidegger's generally anti-humanist notion of destiny becomes specified as anti-principial.

The economic tenor of *situation* only appears in the writings subsequent to *Being and Time*. In *Being and Time* Heidegger wrote: "By 'destiny' (*Geschick*), we understand the coming-to-pass (*Geschehen*) of being-there in being-with-others." He thus understood destiny as a collective process. Furthermore, it was understood as exhibiting the sense of being, its threefold ecstatic directionality: destiny is grounded in "the anticipatory act of translating oneself into the 'there' of the moment."[315] We are bearers of destiny to the extent that future, past and present are united, not in individual *Dasein*, but in "the coming-to-pass of the community, the people." Destiny engages being-there ecstatically, "in and with its 'generation'."[316] It ties us to our heritage and becomes explicitly our own when we repeat, or retrieve, that heritage for the sake of new possibilities ahead of us. In *Being and Time* destiny designates man's lot, the allotment that befalls him due to his historical and social constitution. It is man's lot to have to suffer his past, his link to ancestors and contemporaries, and to assume the tradition into which he is born even as he fashions his future.

With his discovery of the epochal essence of situation, Heidegger's understanding of destiny shifts. That discovery—namely, that presencing itself has a history and concretely has had the history of metaphysics—makes it necessary for him to give up whatever words may evoke the philosophy of meaning with its attendant philosophy of the 'existent' for whom his lot has or does not have meaning. The move away from the search for a meaningful destiny is a move toward "the truth, the *alētheia*, of being." Truth so understood "is historical in its essence, not because to be human is to run through the temporal flow, but because mankind remains positioned (sent) in metaphysics, which alone is capable of grounding an epoch." The new understanding of destiny, after the turn, results from the fundamental positions whose genealogy Heidegger then traces. For us Westerners, to have a destiny means to be placed in a history of forgetfulness, under "the destiny of the default of Being in its truth."[317] Paradoxically, the dehumanization of destiny in the later Heidegger is thus coupled with a new emphasis on history. But man is not the agent of that history.[318] If in this second period Heidegger displays some preoccupation with the future which, given the accumulated heritage of concealment, will be ours, he can hardly counsel more than to wait and see: "Each time, being lets powers arise for a while, but it also lets them sink with their impotencies into the inessential."[319] There is nothing mythical in this way of speaking about being since it is not itself treated as some superpower. It does not 'make' the powers that be. No one nor anything—neither man nor being—has power over history. The 'destiny of being' re-issues neither God's Providence nor capital's 'invisible hand.' It is the most ordinary phenomenon known to everyone who says 'things are no longer as before,' 'this is going to change,' 'the time is not right,' etc. Destiny is the ever moving order of presencing-absencing, the aletheiological constellation as it situates and re-situates everything in time.

What the later Heidegger calls destiny can best be described in terms of place or site. Tracing "the destiny of the default of being," he discovers the possibility of another destiny. The technological constellation may assign us to a site that is radically new, although at first imperceptibly so. That destinal break cannot be described in categories such as 'unconcealment,' which address only the recapitulatory incidence of the transition. Having outlined *alētheia*'s history, Heidegger can draft a topology. The *topoi* of being are of two kinds: ruled by principles and ruled only by the event of presencing. The new site would differ from all received positions as nomadic differs from sedentary life. To speak of the end of epochal history and of the entry into the locus called event is strictly to speak about the same matter twice—of the boundary where one economy expires and another sets in, where an entire culture finds itself *displaced* and where "another destiny of being is released,"[320] "a different destiny, yet veiled."[321] With that break in its destiny, Western culture takes the shape of a heritage bequeathed without directions for use. "Our heritage is preceded by no testament" (René Char).[322] The displacement of culture felt by so many of Heidegger's contemporaries has perhaps been expressed best by Nietzsche's phrase 'God is dead.' For the topology, 'God' stands for all supreme ontic principles in metaphysics, for all archic *topoi*. Since Heidegger extends the impact of this phrase of Nietzsche's to the whole of epochal economies, the new, anarchic, *topos* has been in the making since the Greeks: "This phrase of Nietzsche's names the destiny of two millennia of Western history."[323]

The destiny of metaphysics is, throughout, the destiny in which principles wither away, and not episodically but essentially. That destiny of withering comes to completion with technology, "the last epoch of metaphysics."[324] But does this hypothesis of a new *topos* then not smack of reconciling us with what has been estranged, of humanity restored in its autonomy, liberated from the representations of the first entities under which it has been humiliated? Does Heidegger not re-issue Feuerbach's critique of religion and urge man to recapture the goods alienated for too long in heaven? Is the displacement beyond epochal destiny not a highly interesting thought, interesting man above all? Does Heidegger's thinking, then, not exhibit the utmost concern about a better future for mankind? And does he not go as far as to compare the overcoming of metaphysics to "what happens when one gets over grief or pain"?[325] Do not texts that proclaim a new era—and Heidegger's role in preluding it—abound? But what is the status of those texts? When he hints at a possible mutation in destiny, does Heidegger speak, like Nietzsche, in the capacity of a physician of culture? Is the future for him, as it was for Nietzsche, a curative, medicinal art?[326] Few misreadings of Heidegger would be more unsound. The diagnostic art of highlighting[327] the contours of a closure has nothing to do with the therapeutic art of stemming a malady in order to recover from it.

> All mere chasing after the future so as to compute its picture by extending what is present, although half-thought, into what is to come, although now veiled, itself still moves within the attitude of technological, calculating representation.[328]

To want to close metaphysics in order to depart from it—to want to deconstruct it in order to construct the future—would amount to implanting oneself more firmly than ever in the attitude that counts and discounts, that takes into account rather than into custody. The displacement "cannot be fabricated and even less forced."[329] The constructions of History entirely miss both the practical a priori required for anarchic displacement and its destinal nature, which is impossible to reckon up.

A certain disinterest in mankind's future is evident not only in this conception of place, but also in the conception of time required for understanding today's context as potentially anarchic. An anarchic economy would be one in which thinking and acting espouse the fluctuations in the modalities of presencing. It would be an economy in which the only standard for everything doable is the event of mutual appropriation among entities. It follows that the temporality of that event is no longer to be understood—can no longer be understood—from man's viewpoint. As a place, Ereignis[330] is as irreducible to epochal stamps (Heidegger's second period) as it is to man's projected world (first period). As time, it is as irreducible to aletheiological history (second period) as it is to ecstatic temporality (first period). If 'destiny' is to designate no more than the epochal determination by retrospective categories—if, in other words, destiny is eschatological[331]—then the event itself has neither history nor destiny. It is "a-historical (*ungeschichtlich*), or better, without destiny (*geschicklos*)."[332] Not that the event is atemporal: its temporality is the coming-about of any constellation of thing and world. In such coming-about the preeminence of the future that characterizes ecstatic time as well as aletheiological-historical time is preserved (event as advent). But it is obvious that this originary coming-about of any relation between thing and world differs from the original coming-about of an age just as the 'soundless' play 'without consequences' differs from any inaugural founding deed. These are but two ways of stating the temporal difference between the event as condition and all economies as the conditioned. When Heidegger envisages an 'entry into the event,' i.e., a post-modern economy whose only time structure[333] is the originary, he trusts that the event could become our sole temporal condition, one without principial overdeterminations. The crisis he tries to think is not, then, a founding one. Today's destinal break is rather a disseminating crisis. In this sense, the temporality of the event puts an end to the effort to know and decide what the principles of the forthcoming human world on earth should be.

From the locus of the one to that of the many,[334] the displacement in economy can only occur in a 'leap.' No progression, no evolution, links one destiny to the other. Summer does not 'become' autumn. Suddenly it is autumn, the eighties, old age. Suddenly there is another way of thinking ("From the moment the question 'What is metaphysics?' is asked, the interrogation proceeds already from another question domain"[335]). Suddenly the anarchic economy is ours. "The turning of the danger occurs and appropriates [us, R.S.] suddenly. *Die Kehre der Gefahr ereignet sich jäh.*"[336] Clearly the leap which Heidegger says separates thinking, *Denken,* from the understanding, *Verstand,*[337] refers to mental activities only secondarily. Primarily, that leap comes to pass as a break between economies of presence. Such disjunctive ruptures are in no way spectacular. They may go unnoticed for a long time. They are nevertheless sudden inflexions in the fundamental disposition of presence. To become thinkable, they demand of us an equally *decisive* leap. Western history appears as a closed destiny from the moment thinking risks placing itself resolutely where it is already situated, namely, outside the principles whose downfall technology consummates. "What is called 'destiny of being' characterizes the history of Western thinking so far, inasmuch as we look back upon and into that history from out of the leap."[338] A closed destiny makes for a closed thinking. In order to risk oneself beyond that enclosure, courage is not enough. Two conditions must be fulfilled, each of which, from its own angle of transgression, has priority over the other: priority of the economic break over the leap in thinking, but also a priority of the leap in thinking over the economic break. The turn toward an essentially new mode of presencing—"the reversal in our fundamental position in relation to being"—is the *economic a priori* for entering the *topos* or place of a new thinking: for entering the "essentially other realm of essential thinking."[339] But conversely, that other thinking is the *practical a priori* for bearing to term the other fundamental position already in place around us and in us. The leap freezes the understanding so as to unfreeze thinking.[340]

The issue for the understanding is whatever is first in an order of foundation; the issue for thinking is being. Therefore the leap "sets out from the principle of reason as a proposition about entities over to the utterance of being qua being."[341]

It is first of all the modality of presencing that frees itself from epochal principles. Only then can thinking and uttering be freed from the proposition 'nothing is without reason.' Conversely, however, if we are already situated, be it inceptively, in another destiny, thinking and acting must first become 'without reason' so that our world may be freed from principial vestiges and idols.[342]

PART III

Legislation and Transgression[343]

1. Kant: From the good will to the legislative will: the three formulae of the categorical imperative

In this third and last section about the modern "triumph of the will," we will study another strategy in philosophy from Kant to Heidegger: the link between legislation and transgression. My thesis is that the act of legislating is identically, formally, an act of transgressing the law that is so declared. The model where this formal identity between transgression and legislation is most easily seen is Nietzsche's concept of will to power. You remember the formulation, which reads like a definition, that the will to power is that which seeks "preservation and enhancement." The will to power declares and erects obstacles so as to transcend them. The creation of obstacles, e.g. laws, is for the sake of their transgression. The very act of creating a law is already the act of "*Steigerung*," enhancement of the will itself, through transgressing the obstacle that it has set before itself. For this very Nietzschean thought, the pattern or model lies again in Kant. It is not as explicitly stated in Kant, of course. Nevertheless, the subject legislating for itself, in that very act of legislating, is both the giver and the receiver of law. As receiver, to put it bluntly, he obeys; as giver he is beyond the law as the origin is prior to what is originated. This I call the formal act of transgression. I think it can best be shown by looking at the main formulations that Kant gives of the categorical imperative in the *Groundwork*. These formulations show indeed a progression from *receiving* the moral law to *directing* it, to *legislating* it—a progression from the good will as 'subject' to the law, to the idea of 'end,' to that of the autonomy of the will.

It is obvious that we cannot treat here the most important questions concerning the moral imperative, according to Kant: how is something like the categorical imperative possible, etc.? For this, you will have to rely on courses on Kant's moral philosophy. I

109

merely look at the formulations of that imperative in the second section of the *Groundwork*. It is also advisable to read Lewis White Beck, *A Commentary on Kant's* Critique of Practical Reason.

The second section[344] is entitled "Passage from Popular Moral Philosophy to a Metaphysic of Morals." Just one remark on this: the popular moral philosophy that Kant condemns again and again, is not the moral knowledge of popular reason. Indeed, we heard that popular consciousness is never wrong in moral matters. Only popular philosophers are wrong—those that base morality for instance on the calculus of the greater good, or on the social conditions in a given society, or on power, etc., all extrinsic, empirical factors. The most extreme version of this "popular moral philosophy" is Jeremy Bentham, whom Marx will again deride later as "that Great Accountant of moral deeds."[345] The Kantian critique of popular moral philosophy brings us to the heart of the matter of legislation: he condemns these utilitarian and other speculation because it assumes that morality can be drawn from facts of experience. Hence the necessity of grounding popular moral 'consciousness.' Such grounding can only be achieved by what Kant calls 'metaphysics.' I said that metaphysics means, for him here, 'pure of any empirical element.' Now what is so pure of any empirical mixture? Only the rational representation of the moral law itself. This is the core of Kant's moral teaching: morality consists in representing the law itself in its rigor, in its authority, and in making this representation of the law into the principle that determines the will.

Here[346] is the first formula of the categorical imperative:[347] "*Act only on that maxim through which you can at the same time will that it should become a universal law*" (*GMM*, 88).[348] This formula deals with our actions. It is a subjective principle of action. Example: The German chancellor Adenauer was asked whether one may lie in politics. Answer: "Yes, but you have to have a good memory." That is a maxim: in politics I may tell a lie as long as I remain able to control the situation and cannot be caught.

The categorical imperative tests maxims. More precisely: it commands the conformity of our maxims to the moral law. We saw[349] that this conformity is established through non-contradiction. Adenauer's maxim is in fact self-contradictory: I cannot will a lie as my own maxim, because I cannot will it as everyone's maxim. If every-

110

one were allowed to lie—as I claim that I am—then a lie would cease to be a lie. If everyone could tell anything about anything, it would be impossible to talk at all; particularly it would be impossible to lie. Thus an immoral maxim is self-defeating.

The categorical imperative contains only the criterion for conforming our personal maxims to a universal law. It is in fact a law for the will: I am told to act only according to that maxim through which *I can will* that it should become a universal law.

From this first formula—which is like the matrix-formula from which all others arise—Kant immediately develops a second:[350] "*Act as if the maxim of your action were to become through your will a universal law of nature*" (*GMM*, 89).[351] This is a test of the will.[352] Indeed, we can fully well act against duty. We can even will to act against our duty, i.e., we can follow a totally subjective maxim. But we can never will that this maxim should become a universal law. This universalization would be self-contradictory. It would negate our very project—for instance, of getting through politics by telling lies.

In terms of the will: any evil will is self-contradictory. That does not make it impossible, but it makes it irrational. This is our capacity to act according to the representation of rules, I said. You also see that this second formula—which is the first daughter-formula from the mother-formula—adds nothing to the first except the concept of nature.[353] We are asked to act in such a way that we can will our maxims to become laws of nature. Is this so strange? Are laws of nature not gravity and causality, etc., i.e., cosmological? And if Kant intends to speak rather of human nature, does he not contradict his earlier statement about the pure—not empirical—origin of the moral law? Human nature, one would then say, is weak; let us base morality on it and have a calculus of weaknesses, or interests, or 'compassion'...

The concept of nature that Kant deals with here is the same as in the *Critique of Pure Reason.* It is determined, not empirically, but a priori. It is a system of functions obeying universal and necessary laws. Thus nature derives from laws, and not laws from nature. Empirical nature—i.e. so-called human nature—is full of shortcomings: we are not sure even, he says, that in the entirety of human history one single act has ever been performed 'out of' the moral law. Thus the conformity that the second formula speaks of is an ideal: it is regulative.

The two first formulations of the categorical imperative thus deal with the law and the necessity to conform our maxims to the general moral law. Then he adds: "The will is conceived as a power of determining oneself to action *in accordance with the idea of certain laws*" (*GMM*, 95).[354] The term "idea" makes it clear that no empirical correspondent can ever be found with certainty for the categorical imperative.[355] This line also shows that practical reason is essentially self-affection, self-imposition of a law. This will be very important as we proceed.

Kant then specifies what it is that determines the will as moral: "Now what serves the will as an objective ground for its self-determination is an *end*" (ibid.).[356] One remark about the text. The translator (Paton) substitutes—"perhaps rashly,"—"subjective' for "objective." This is a serious mistake. Paton writes: "'An objective ground'—if it could mean anything here—would have to mean 'a ground in objects'" (ibid.).[357] This is short-sighted. Kant frequently uses the term 'objective' as more or less synonymous with "universal and necessary." When Kant says—and this goes to the heart of the topic—that the end is objective and as objective determines our action, this is not to say that an empirical goal—an object in the sense of something given to our sense—should determine our action. Such a theory is precisely what he always rejects; it is the empirical moral theory, that of the popular moral philosophers à la Bentham. Here 'objective' means: conform to the objectivity as determined by reason. 'Objective' means 'rational'—the exact contrary of what Paton thinks it to mean.

We now have to see the role of 'end' in relation to the 'law.' We maintain that "objective end" means "end in itself," or as established by reason, universally and necessarily.

The point here is that formal principles do not eliminate finality altogether, they eliminate only subjective or material finality: the goals that we may choose or may not choose. What, now, is that end of the will that is not subjective, not material, not extrinsic, not sensible, not dependent on a hypothetical imperative?

Suppose there were something *whose existence* has *in itself* an absolute value, something which as *an end in itself* could be a ground of determinate laws; then in it, and in it alone, would there be the ground for a possible categorical imperative—that is, of a practical law (*GMM*, 95).[358]

Clearly, there can be only one such end. And since it is immanent to reason it cannot be anything else than reason—but reason from a certain point of view: "Now I maintain, that man, and in general every rational being, exists as an end in itself" (ibid.).[359]

Only man is an end in itself.[360] Man, however, from what point of view? The allusion to 'existence' indicates that Kant wishes to speak of men not merely as pure rational beings, but *as they exist*. This emphasis is still stronger in what we now have to call the second derivative formula of the categorical imperative:[361] "*Act in such a way that you always treat humanity, whether in your own person or in the person of any other, never simply as a means, but always at the same time as an end*" (*GMM*, 96).[362]

The difficult words are "merely," *bloss*, and "at the same time," *zugleich*. They indicate that man as he exists will always have to be dealt with as a means, too. There would be no commerce, no public life, no type of any interaction if the other were not a means towards an extrinsic end and at the same time an end in himself.

The meaning of 'end' is here another than in the context of the hypothetical imperatives.[363] In hypothetical imperatives the principles of action are deduced from the end: given X as an end to reach, Y is the necessary means. Here one cannot say that the imperative commands 'so as to' achieve an end. The end is merely the respect for man: the imperative posits the end, and not the other way around.

Thus the end is not an end to be achieved, it is an end to be respected. In Kant's terms again: it is not an end 'of' the will but an end 'for' the will, or even 'before' the will. And yet, the end is posited by the will, i.e. by practical reason— it *is* the will.

Humanity, "whether in your own person or in the person of any other" is to be treated as an end. By humanity is thus meant the practical side of reason, i.e. the will. The will here appears as an end to itself—not yet as the "will to will" (Nietzsche), but as indeed both active and passive; as 'subject' of its act as well as 'object.'

The first formula exhibited the will 'under' the law.[364] The second shows it as both 'giver' of the law and 'recipient.' This is not to say that the will is ever above the law. No will is, for Kant...not even the "holy will." The second formula simply adds that the will is subject to the law, not from outside, but from within itself. If the will is submitted merely passively to the moral law, it would not be an end in itself.

As to the second formula, if this were taken by itself it would make us believe that the law is a mere means towards an extrinsic end. It is thus necessary to show the identity of the two formulae: this is what the third achieves, which enunciates the autonomy of the will.

Here[365] is how Kant formulates this principle:

> From this there follows our third practical principle for the will—as the supreme condition of the will's conformity with the universal practical reason—namely the Idea *of the will of every rational being as the will which makes universal law*" (*GMM*, 98).[366]

What we have to understand immediately is that the will is now no longer seen as merely subject to law: it is the law-maker. The will is "Urheber," or author of the law. Kant formulates the paradoxical situation of the will with regard to the law—both receiving and giving it—in respect to 'interest': "A will which is subject to law may be bound to this law by some interest; nevertheless, a will which is itself the supreme lawgiver cannot possibly as such depend on any interest" (*GMM*, 99).[367]

In the short section entitled "Autonomy of the Will as the Supreme Principle of Morality," Kant states the double-sidedness of the will most clearly: "Autonomy of the will is the property the will has of being a law to itself" (*GMM*, 108).[368] The principle of autonomy is the most important of the three. It shows that the categorical imperative expresses the fundamental self-determination of the will. For Kant, this self-determination is important to display the disinterested essence of the moral law; but reading him retrospectively from Nietzsche, we can see that the self-determination of the will places the will in fact above the law that it creates. It thus transgresses what it creates, in the very act of legislation.

For Kant,[369] autonomy means that the moral law is found nowhere else than in man: "not in heaven, not on earth" (*GMM*, 93),[370] as he says a little later. That is, he dismisses both religion and naturalism as a possible source of morality.[371]

APPENDIX

The Time of the Mind and the History of Freedom

Review of Hannah Arendt, *The Life of the Mind* [372]

"I do not believe in a world, be it a past world or a future world, in which man's mind, equipped for withdrawing from the world of appearances, could or should ever be comfortably at home" (II, 158]).[373] In these lines Hannah Arendt states the radical paradox that permeates the phenomenon called "the life of the mind" as well as the two-volume work that bears this title (vol. I: *Thinking*, vol. II: *Willing*. Notes for a projected vol. III: *Judging*, have been appended by the editor to the second volume).[374] The phenomenon of mental life is paradoxical in that its chief trait appears to be withdrawal from the world, while there is no place to which to withdraw. As to the posthumously published opus, it is paradoxical in that the author, whom the *Encyclopaedia Britannica* lists as a "political scientist," should have left behind as the weightiest of her works this philosophy of what she herself calls the *vita contemplativa* as opposed to the *vita activa*, the active life in the world of appearances.

The project is ambitious. It consists in nothing less than taking up the Kantian tripartite division of mental activities—thinking (as distinct from knowing), willing, judging—freed from the transcendental construction which prevented Kant from recognizing their *historical* nature. Hannah Arendt shows how, from antiquity to the present, the activities of the mind have prevented philosophers from being comfortably at home in the world. She admirably depicts how the homelessness of the mind has led them to answer, ever anew, such questions about ourselves as: What makes us think? Where are we when we think? But Hannah Arendt does not want merely to trace the history of these faculties. Her aim is to show how the mind affects itself, "regardless of outside events, thus creating a kind of *life* of the mind" (II, 38), how from Plato to Heidegger the "soundless dialogue of me and myself" constitutes its own realm of action, an "entirely inner 'action'" (II, 185). (Regarding several

117

of the philosophers considered, one cannot resist objecting to the presentation she gives. In particular, the chapters on Duns Scotus, Nietzsche, and Heidegger in my opinion should be read more to learn what Hannah Arendt has to say than these authors have to say.)

For a technological age, these volumes are therapy. To what others have called the performance principles, Arendt opposes an entire domain of experiences from which achievement, calculus, production, and even cognition are absent. At first sight, then, the life of the mind equals inwardness. The philosopher's real home is within himself: "The philosopher takes leave of the world given to our senses and does a turnabout to the life of the mind" (I, 23). Such a turnabout is nothing extraordinary; it is rather the most ordinary event in daily life. When it happens—when we stop being busy in order to think for a moment, to "turn our mind to ourselves"—we look a little stupid, actually absent-minded. It is this absence from the world of appearances, Hannah Arendt claims, that has given rise to the most celebrated speculative constructs, which she calls "metaphysical fallacies." Philosophers, instead of giving a phenomenal account of such moments of interruption in which we consult ourselves and dialogue with ourselves, have hypostatized this place into which we withdraw. From the inconspicuous experience of pondering within themselves, they have built such rather conspicuous doctrines as the Platonist 'two-world theory,' the Scholastic theory of the 'standing now' or the 'now of eternity,' theories 'Void,' of 'Spirit,' of 'Being.' The most exciting pages in the two volumes are perhaps the ones in which Hannah Arendt deconstructs these theories, not without some naughty contentment: "I have clearly joined the ranks of those who for some time now have been attempting to dismantle metaphysics" (I, 212). Dismantling metaphysics is the great chance for thinking provided by the historical situation in which we find ourselves today. Only through such dismantling, and not through some intuition of essences, can we hope to learn something of the life of the mind: "The metaphysical fallacies contain the only clues we have to what thinking means to those who engage in it" (I, 12).

In Hannah Arendt's attitude toward the metaphysical tradition the presence of her two mentors, Karl Jaspers and Martin Heidegger, is ever so obvious. It is perhaps regrettable that in her attempt to dismantle the history of philosophy, she should remain more loyal to the former's notion of existential exchange among philosophers than to the latter's notion of phenomenological destruction. Indeed, in spite of her insistence on history, philosophy is no more a historical phenomenon for Hannah Arendt than for Karl Jaspers. Why, for instance, a Duns Scotus—although called the *doctor subtilis*—could not write a critique of pure reason, nor a Kant, a genealogy of morals, remains simply unintelligible as long as we believe that despite the distance in time we can somehow enter into a direct dialogue with past authors. The great rupture brought about by the discovery of historical consciousness has placed all past authors at our disposal, at equal distance for direct consultation. For Hannah Arendt, as for Jaspers, the philosophers are there (on our shelves) to speak with. It is the advantage of our situation, she maintains, to be so cut off from the continuous effective-history. Had she followed Heidegger's approach, on the other hand, she could not have quoted with such fondness these lines from the French poet René Char: "Notre héritage n'est précédé d'aucun testament" (Our inheritance comes to us by no will-and-testament) (I,12). A hermeneutician could never claim, as she does, that the demise of metaphysics allows us to look at the past "unburdened and unguided by any traditions [...] without being bound to any prescriptions as to how to deal with these treasures" (I, 12). This is her teacher Karl Jaspers at his worst. It should be clear, furthermore, that such an antihermeneutical approach to the tradition fits quite smoothly with the praise of inwardness: homeless in the world of appearances, we find companions in past philosophers among whom we move at ease. One instance of this unhermeneutical procedure is the use of quotes, in which Hannah Arendt excels. Whether from Cato or Valery, pertinent quotes express something which is 'right' or 'wrong,' that is, which either agrees with one's own experience of inner dialogue or not. Under the semblance of historicity, the life of the mind is thus once again rendered a-historical.

At second sight, however, the life of the mind can no longer simply be equated with inwardness. The immediate impulse to write these volumes, Arendt tells us, came from her attending the Eichmann trial in Jerusalem. In the personality of Adolf Eichmann "there was no sign of firm ideological convictions or of specific

APPENDIX

evil motives." The only notable characteristic was *thoughtlessness* (I, 4). The hypothesis of her work now sounds quite different than the praise of inwardness: "If there is anything in thinking that can prevent men from doing evil, it must be some property inherent in the activity itself, regardless of its objects" (I, 180). The life of the mind thus reveals itself to be far from wordless, and the inquiry into it far from unworthy of a political scientist.

As Hannah Arendt understands them, political deeds do not have their origin in the mere calculus of the feasible, measured against the profitable or the desirable. The way we act, that is, intervene in public, depends essentially upon the way we think. This is precisely not to say that in thinking we sight a goal beforehand and then look for the means to attain it, but quite the contrary: "All questions concerning the aim or purpose of thinking are as unanswerable as questions about the aim or purpose of life" (I, 197). And yet, the root of the most unspeakable evil committed in our times was thoughtlessness. Thinking is goalless, but when we are mistaken in our goals, the source of the mistake lies in the absence of thought— not in ignorance, which is the negation of knowledge, but in the absence of thought, which is the negation of meaning. Underlying this new paradox (Hannah Arendt was not afraid of paradoxes; she cherished them!) is the theory that political action is not a matter of knowledge, but of belief, persuasion, of 'shining' in public so as to convince. What can prevent men from doing evil things is "thinking, the quest for meaning—as opposed to the thirst for knowledge" (I, 78). One understands her debt to Kant: "Crucial for our enterprise is Kant's distinction between *Vernunft* and *Verstand*, 'reason' and 'intellect'" (I, 13). The activities arising from these two faculties are altogether different: *thinking* is concerned with meaning and therefore with rational belief, but *knowing* is concerned with truth and therefore with cognition. Truth is compelling, meaning is not. Truth and knowledge are opposed to meaning and thought, just as causal explanation is opposed to purposeless "being alive," as sight is opposed to speech, or—again in Kantian terms—as nature and man's empirical character are opposed to freedom and man's intelligible character. A spectator of political deeds can only *believe* that the meaning an actor grasps in *belief* may appear in history, that in the public arena we may encounter "signs" of "conviction." This

120

THE TIME OF THE MIND AND THE HISTORY OF FREEDOM

double precariousness of what makes political sense indicates that "thinking is out of order because the quest for meaning produces no end result that will survive the activity, that will make sense after the activity has come to its end" (I, 121–123). The problem with Arendt's notion of thinking as related to the public realm is, as many commentators have observed, that public action can no longer be measured by any yardstick other than convictions, and these always come in the plural. Rather than pursuing the difficulties that arise from such a reformulation of the problem of theory and practice, however, I return to another issue that seems philosophically debatable to me and that has received little attention from commentators: her treatment of time and history.

Hannah Arendt very appropriately indicates that the faculties of willing and judging are generated from the temporalization of the mind. To think is to 'ob-ject': the time dimension is [the] present. To will is to 'pro-ject': the time dimension is the future. To judge is to 're-flect': the time dimension is the past. The time concept of antiquity, as she sees it, is entirely centered on the first of these three dimensions, the present. Hence, there was a "curious lacuna in Greek philosophy," the absence of a philosophy of will and of freedom. It is Augustine who "discovers the will," in much the same way as later it is Kant who "discovers judgment." Only with the mind so temporalized does the role that history plays in the philosophies of the nineteenth and twentieth centuries become understandable. Only with the mind so temporalized can the will move to the fore as it does in the age of modernity. For nearly two centuries, philosophers have ascribed some form of ultimacy to the will in their accounts of reality. To Hannah Arendt, this modern preeminence of the will—and hence of the quest for mastery over nature—is but a consequence of the mental preeminence of the future: "That there exists such a thing as the life of the mind is due to the mind's organ for the future and its resulting 'restlessness'" (II, 44). One wonders: if the mind comes to life because of its directedness toward the future, toward death, how can this *essentially* anticipatory constitution of the mind be held to account for the particular features of one *epoch*, modernity? If the Augustinian *inquietum cor* [restless heart] reveals the temporal condition or the temporal essence of the mind, how does the will come to be the particular stamp of one age,

121

APPENDIX

technology? On this latter point, Arendt certainly follows Heidegger: "Technology's very nature is the will to will" (II, 178).

Hannah Arendt traces what one would have to call the *ecstatic* (temporal) determination of our mind and, in a parallel way, the epochal (historical) determination of our culture. She does not use these terms, however, and with good reason. She shows both how present-future-past derives from thinking-willing-judging and how the basic features of our age derive from the will, from futurity, from freedom, from the priority of the potential over the actual. She brilliantly emphasizes the historical unfolding of these faculties. She points out the thinkers and the ages when they were discovered, and still more decisively she shows how the faculty of willing today has come to put its mark on an entire age. But the two tracks of her reflection—the genesis of time from our three faculties and the development of history out of the epochal character of what is held to be ultimate—raise a question that concerns more than the problem of coherence in an argument: How does one of the three temporal dimensions of mental life, the future (and with it, the will), come to characterize one particular age? To what prior understanding of time and history can technology appear as the age of the will? There is no ground in these volumes to consistently construe a transition from what I just called ecstatic temporality to epochal temporality. I know, however, how Hannah Arendt would reply to objections like this: "Professional thinkers [...] have not been 'pleased with freedom' [...] Let us put them aside therefore" (II, 198).

The point is that despite her insistence on the temporal and historical dimensions of the life of the mind, her inquiry remains an inquiry into thinking, willing, and judging as faculties. Kant thus provides her with more than the architectonic for her three areas of investigation. He provides her with the presupposition of a mind whose structure remains unaffected by history. When it becomes apparent that to solve 'the problem of the new' a determinate concept of history is needed, she slips back into her guise of a political scientist: in order to justify the possibility of 'beginnings' in a given civilization, "we turn from the notion of philosophical freedom to political liberty" (II, 198). As a philosopher, she can account for the temporalization of the life of the mind, but not for its historicization. As a political scientist, she accounts for the latter, but in a

THE TIME OF THE MIND AND THE HISTORY OF FREEDOM

way that only superficially agrees with the former. Indeed, what is political as opposed to philosophical freedom? "Political freedom is distinct from philosophic freedom in being clearly a quality of the I-can and not of the I-will. It is possessed by the citizen rather than by man in general" (II, 200). The moments of beginnings that structure history turn out to be rare, great junctures in which people act in concert, in which new institutions of liberty are founded, and in which 'freedom' comes to be almost synonymous with 'power.' These are moments of direct democracy: the town meetings in the American Revolution, the people's societies in the French Revolution, the workers' and soldiers' councils in the Russian Revolution, the 1968 student rebellion. Political freedom, which is not a quality of the will, becomes determinate at certain junctures— once or twice in a century. It is obvious that this way of politically determining history in no way rests on the temporal determinations of the life of the mind. Her concept of history does not need her concept of time. It relies on premises that are of an altogether different order than the correlation between thinking-willing-judging and present-future-past. In fact, her understanding of history flatly contradicts her understanding of time. The transition from ecstatic time to epochal history does not succeed because Arendt roots the former in the faculties of the mind rather than in constitutive acts of existence and because she roots the latter in her paradigm of political liberty, the Greek polis, rather than in any notion of time at all. I can find no conceptual bridge between her phenomenological discourse on time and her political discourse on history.

The same heterogeneity between the time of the mind and the history of freedom can finally be shown from Arendt's remarks on judging. The 'faculty of judging' is not a cognitive faculty. It deals, not with universals, but with particulars. Judgment is performed, not by the actors in history, but by the spectators. One reaches a judgment literally in retro-spect, in looking back. Once the Revolution has begun in France, Kant, in his own words, watches it with "a wishful participation that borders closely on enthusiasm." At the same time, he adds: "While the Revolution lasted, each person who openly or covertly shared in it would have justly incurred punishment" (II, 259). From the standpoint of practical reason, of the will, of morals, a revolution is "at all times unjust." But from the standpoint of judgment, of the faculty of taste, of aesthetics, it generates "inactive delight." Following Kant, Hannah Arendt thus distinguishes between willing and judging as between the principle according to which one acts and the principle according to which one reckons, assesses, appreciates. It is this other realm, composed of critics and spectators and not of actors and makers, which she calls the "public realm." The representational capacity of the mind—its power to make something present again and thus to evaluate it—is then clearly seen as temporal. We are able to judge an occurrence, any occurrence, because we are able to bring it back into the present, to recall it. But again it is not this time-dimension of the mind that generates history. Our faculty of rendering present what is past remains disconnected from our capacity of entering the public realm. Hannah Arendt works out precise and commendable concepts of the threefold dimension of our mental faculties as well as of what Karl Jaspers called the "axial times."[375] But she refuses to ground history so understood as political, in time so understood as mental. One may take a further step: her notion of history is bound to remain 'axial' instead of 'epochal' *because* her notion of time remains 'mental' instead of 'ecstatic.' The discoverers of the faculties of willing and judging, Augustine and Kant, could not reach an understanding of history as constitutive of man's existence because of their very metaphysics of the mind in which time can only be defined in relation to the soul. Hannah Arendt by no means abandons that metaphysical presupposition. And yet, for her, history is to penetrate to the core of the human condition. Given her mentalist presupposition, such an advance can be achieved conceptually only by calling in a type of history that is not construed out of the freedom in the life of the mind, but out of political freedom. (This is not the place, of course, to indicate how an ecstatic notion of time would yield an epochal notion of history). In the end, it is due to her distinction between *vita activa* and *vita contemplativa,* despite the deep modifications that she has these terms undergo, that Hannah Arendt proves to be a 'metaphysical' thinker. She is all ready to dismantle all "metaphysical fallacies"[376] except the one according to which the mind is something, according to which it is distinct from appearance and the public realm, and according to which it has a vitality of its own, the life of the mind.

Notes

1 { ‹ " that they tend to be wrong " › }
2 { *ex fide* legislation }
3 Ric[œur] dans *Enclycl[opédie]* *Univ[erselle.* Schürmann is referring to Paul Ricœur's entry "Volonté" (Will) in *Encyclopedia Universalis, XVI* (Paris: Encyclopedia Universalis France, 1973), 943–948, (II.A.296). The headings of the three historical introductory sections here dedicated to Aristotle, Augustine, and Descartes, are in clear reference to Ricœur's entry. Alongside an "Introduction" and a "Bibliography," Ricœur divides his account of the will into a series of 'contexts,' which contain the following sections:
   – Le contexte "éthique": Aristote [The 'ethical' context: Aristotle];
   – Le contexte "théologique": Augustin [The 'theological' context: Augustine];
   – Le contexte "épistémologique": Descartes [The epistemological context: Descartes];
   – Le contexte "critique": Kant [The 'critical context': Kant];
   – Le contexte "dialectique": Hegel [The 'dialectical' context: Hegel];
   – Le noyau phénoménologique. [The phenomenological core].]
4 { ‹ διάνοια › [diánoia] }
5 Aristotle, Nic[omachean] *Eth[ics]*, III, 3, 1112 a 30–33[: "βουλευόμεθα δὲ περὶ τῶν ἐφ᾽ ἡμῖν καὶ πρακτῶν [... R.S.]. αἰτίαι γὰρ δοκοῦσιν εἶναι φύσις καὶ ἀνάγκη καὶ τύχη, ἔτι δὲ νοῦς καὶ πᾶν τὸ δι᾽ ἀνθρώπου." Schürmann is quoting W. D. Ross's translation in Aristotle, *Nicomachean Ethics*, trans. W. D. Ross (Oxford: Clarendon Press, 1908), bk. 3, http://classics.mit.edu//Aristotle/nicomachaen.html]
6 { depending }
7 { ‹ "freedom from constraint and deliberate choice among alternatives. Such is" › }
8 { ≠ }
9 { [realm of the deliberate →]
   [realm of what we prefer →]   }
10 { ≠ }
11 [Cf. Hannah Arendt, *The Life of the Mind,* One Vol. Edition, 2. "Willing," section 10: "Augustine, the first philosopher of the Will" (New York & London: Harcourt Brace Jovanovich, 1978 (1971)), 84–110.]
12 { ‹ "(*malum est* [*enim*] *male uti bono*)" › }["evil is, in fact, the misuse of good," see Augustine of Hippo, *De Natura Boni, Contra Manichaeos, Liber I*, 36.]
13 [See G.W.F. Hegel, in *Werke: [in 20 Bänden]*, Band 7, *Grundlinien der Philosophie des Rechts oder Naturrecht und Staatswissenschaft im Grundrisse*, eds. E. Moldenhauer and K. M. Michel (Frankfurt am Main: Suhrkamp, 1986), §124, 233: *Das Recht der Besonderheit des Subjekts, sich befriedigt zu finden, oder, was dasselbe ist, das Recht der subjektiven Freiheit macht den Wende- und Mittelpunkt in dem Unterschiede des Altertums und der modernen Zeit. Dies Recht in seiner Unendlichkeit ist im Christentum ausgesprochen und zum allgemeinen wirklichen Prinzip einer neuen Form der Welt gemacht worden.*" Trans. by R.S., emphasis added by Eds. for coherence to German text.]

NOTES

14 [Cf. Arendt, *The Life of the Mind*, 2. "Willing," section 8: "The Apostle Paul and the impotence of the Will," 63–73 and section 10: "Augustine, the first philosopher of the will," 84–110.]

15 { i.e. ≠ body/mind -- = x2 will }

16 [Here Schürmann adds the following parenthetical remark: "(See lecture notes of Augustine course at the library)." The reference is to his course *Augustine's Philosophy of Mind*, [1975/'79/'84/'91] in *Reiner Schürmann papers*, NA.0006.01, box 5, folder 4 (New York: The New School Archives and Special Collections). See especially p. 49–80, in which "mind's ternary structure" is discussed in detail. For example: "[T]he mind, one in number, [...] possesses three fundamental forms of activity which follow from the single nature of the mind and which are distinguished by relative otherness" (65); "[A]ll powers of the soul are driven by the will; it is the agent in all their impulses" (78).]

17 [See, e.g., Sophocles, *Oedipus at Colonus*, 521–523: "ἤνεγκ᾿ οὖν κακότατ᾿, ὦ ξένοι, ἤνεγκ᾿ ἀέκων μέν,/ θεὸς ἴστω,/ τούτων δ᾿ αὐθαίρετον οὐδέν" ("I have suffered the greatest misery, strangers—suffered it through unintended deeds—/may the god know it!/No part was of my own choice." Trans. by Sir Richard Claverouse Jebb (Cambridge: Cambridge University Press, 1889), available for research on Perseus Digital Library. In *Broken Hegemonies*, Oedipus serves as a paradigmatic figure for the tragic *differend* and the tragic knowing ensued from suffering—*pathei mathos*. See BH, 4 and passim.]

18 { ≠ }

19 [Trans. by R.S. See René Descartes, *Meditationes de Prima Philosophia*, IV "*De vero & falso*": "Nam per solum intellectum percipio tantùm ideas de quibus judicium ferre possum, nec ullus error proprie dictus in eo praecise sic spectato reperitur" (1641). The Duc de Luynes' French version, which was published with Descartes' approval—*Les méditations métaphysiques de René Descartes touchant la première philosophie, dans lesquelles l'existence de Dieu, et la distinction réelle entre l'âme et le corps de l'homme, sont démontrées* (1647)—reads as: "Car par l'entendement seul je n'assure ni ne nie aucune chose mais je conçois seulement les idées des choses, que je puis assurer ou nier. Or, en le considérant ainsi précisément, on peut dire qu'il ne se trouve jamais en lui aucune erreur, pourvu qu'on prenne le mot d'erreur en sa propre signification."]

20 [Ibid. trans. by R.S.: "quia [voluntas] tantùm in eo consistit, quòd idem vel facere vel non facere (hoc est affirmare vel negare, prosequi vel fugere) possimus, vel potius in eo tantùm, quòd ad id quod nobis ab intellectu proponitur affirmandum vel negandum, sive prosequendum vel fugiendum, ita feramur, ut a nullâ vi externâ nos ad id determinari sentiamus" / "Car elle [la volonté] consiste seulement en ce que nous pouvons faire une même chose ou ne la faire pas, c'est-à-dire affirmer ou nier, poursuivre ou fuir une même chose, ou plutôt elle consiste seulement en ce que, pour affirmer ou nier, poursuivre ou fuir les choses que l'entendement nous propose, nous agissons de telle sorte que nous ne sentons point qu'aucune force extérieure nous y contraigne."]

21 [Ibid., trans. by R.S.: "sed etiam ad illa [voluntate] quae non intelligo extendo; ad quae cùm sit indifferens, facile a vero & bono deflectit, [atque ita & fallor & pecco]" / "je l'étends [la volonté] aussi aux choses que je n'entends pas; auxquelles étant

NOTES

de soi indifférente, elle s'égare fort aisément, et choisit le faux pour le vrai[, et le mal pour le bien: ce qui fait que je me trompe et que je pèche.]"]

22 { we assert willfully }

23 { to the point, or too far }

24 [Schürmann is referring to Leni Riefenstahl's 1935 nazi propaganda film *Triumph des Willens* (Triumph of the Will).]

25 FA in CDU 5–6. [Cf. Ferdinand Alquié, *Leçons sur Kant: La morale de Kant*, (Paris: La Table Ronde, "La Petite Vermillon," 2005), re-ed. of *La morale de Kant*, (Paris: Centre de Documentation Universitaire (Les Cours de Sorbonne), 1957), 5–6. Abbreviated henceforth as *MK*. References to Alquié's course on Kant's moral philosophy appear in the margins all throughout the sections of *Modern Philosophies of the Will* on Kant (Part I, 1; and Part III, 1).]

26 [Schürmann provides the following parenthetical bibliographical reference: "Reicke, *Lose Blätter aus Kants Nachlaß*"—I. Kant, *Lose Blätter aus Kants Nachlaß*, mitgeteilt von Rudolf Reicke, Erstes Heft (Königsberg: F. Beyer, 1889)—which can also be found in *MK*, 5–6.]

27 { ‹ "Leibniz" › }[Schürmann crossed out "Leibniz" and hand-wrote "rationalism." However, "Leibniz" is kept throughout the whole paragraph.]

28 [Cf. Alquié, *MK*, 13].

29 [See Jean-Jacques Rousseau, "La Profession de foi du vicaire savoyard" in *Émile ou de l'éducation*, *Œuvres complètes*, 4 vols. (Paris: A. Houssiaux, 1852–53), vol. 2, 584: "*nous pouvons être hommes sans être savants.*"]

30 [Cf. Alquié, *MK*, 15f.]

31 [Cf. Alquié, *MK*, 9–12]

32 [The sentence has been rearranged for readability. Schürmann's typescript reads as: "In this text, reason appears as giving the form to morality, and the sentiment, matter."].

33 [Cf. Alquié, *MK*, 16–18.]

34 [*GMS*, BA 74; *AA* IV, 433: "*Der Begriff eines jeden vernünftigen Wesens, das sich durch alle Maximen seines Willens als allgemein gesetzgebend betrachten muß, um aus diesem Gesichtspunkte sich selbst und seine Handlungen zu beurteilen, [führt auf einen ihm anhängenden sehr fruchtbaren Begriff, nämlich den* eines Reichs der Zwecke.]"]

35 [*GMS*, BA viii; *AA* IV, 389: "*ob man nicht meine, daß es von der äußersten Nothwendigkeit sei, einmal eine reine Moralphilosophie zu bearbeiten, die von allem, was nur empirisch sein mag und zur Anthropologie gehört, völlig gesäubert wäre; denn, daß es eine solche geben müsse, leuchtet von selbst aus der gemeinen Idee der Pflicht und der sittlichen Gesetze ein.*" Trans. mod. by R.S.]

36 [*GMS*, BA ix; ibid.: "*ihnen Eingang in den Willen des Menschen* [...] *zu verschaffen*"]

37 [*GMS*, BA xii; *AA* IV, 390: "*Denn die Metaphysik der Sitten soll die Idee und die Prinzipien eines möglichen reinen Willens untersuchen, und nicht die Handlungen und Bedingungen des menschlichen Wollens überhaupt, welche größtentheils aus der Psychologie geschöpft werden*"]

38 { ≠ }

39 [*GMS*, BA xii–xiii; *AA* IV, 391: "*den Unterschied [ihrer] Quellen zu achten.*" Schürmann paraphrases and provides his own translation. Paton's translation

127

reads: "without taking into account differences in their [viz., universal concepts] origin."]
40 { ≠ }
41 [Cf. Alquié, MK, 20-22.]
42 { facere → factum }
43 [GMS, BA 1; AA IV, 393: "Es ist überall nichts in der Welt, ja überhaupt auch außer derselben zu denken möglich, was ohne Einschränkung für gut könnte gehalten werden, als allein ein *guter* Wille." Trans. mod. by R.S.]
44 { Δ }
45 [Cf. Alquié, MK, 31.]
46 [Cf. Alquié, MK, 34.]
47 [Cf. Alquié, MK, 35f.]
48 ["Übergang von der gemeinen sittlichen Vernunfterkenntnis zur philosophischen."]
49 [GMS, BA iii; AA, IV, 387: "Die alte griechische Philosophie theilte sich in drei Wissenschaften ab: die *Physik*, die *Ethik*, und die *Logik*. Diese Eintheilung ist der Natur der Sache vollkommen angemessen, und man hat an ihr nichts zu verbessern, als etwa nur das Prinzip derselben hinzu zu thun [...]." Trans. mod. by R.S.]
50 { KpV } [Cf. *Critique of Pure Reason*.]
51 [Schürmann corrects his own typescript by crossing out 'non-reason' and instead writing 'unreason.']
52 [GMS, BA 1; AA IV, 393: "Verstand, Witz, Urtheilskraft, und wie die *Talente* des Geistes sonst heißen mögen [...]."]
53 [Ibid.: "[...] Muth, Entschlossenheit, Beharrlichkeit im Vorsatze, als Eigenschaften des *Temperaments*, sind ohne Zweifel in mancher Absicht gut und wünschenswerth; aber sie können auch äußerst böse und schädlich werden, wenn der Wille, der von diesen Naturgaben Gebrauch machen soll [...] nicht gut ist."]
54 {   Aporia at beginning of Groundwork

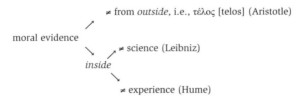

... discovery of *practical* (≠ theoretical) *reason* }
55 [GMS, BA 3; AA IV, 394: "Der gute Wille ist nicht durch das, was er bewirkt, oder ausrichtet, nicht durch seine Tauglichkeit zu Erreichung irgend eines vorgesetzten Zweckes, sondern allein durch das Wollen, d.i. an sich, gut [...]."]
56 [ἁπλῶς ἀγαθόν.]
57 [GMS, BA 3; AA IV, 394: "(freilich nicht etwa ein bloßer Wunsch, sondern als die Aufbietung aller Mittel, so weit sie in unserer Gewalt sind)." Trans. mod. by R.S.]
58 [Cf. Alquié, MK, 37-39.]

NOTES

59 { ≠ "will is reasonable" [//] = "reason is *volitional*," besides *Vern*[*unft?*] + *Verst*[*and?*] }
60 [*TI*, "How the 'True World' Finally Became a Fable." " "History of an error," 3; *eKGWB/GD*-Welt-Fabel, 3: "[...] (Die alte Sonne im Grunde, aber durch Nebel und Skepsis hindurch; die Idee sublim geworden, bleich, nordisch, königsbergisch.)"]
61 [Cf., for instance, J.-J. Rousseau's letter to Christophe de Beaumont, Archbishop of Paris—dated 11.18.1762—in Rousseau, *Œuvres complètes*, vol. 2, 439: "il n'y a point de perversité originelle dans le cœur humain" / "there in no original perversity in the human heart." Trans. by Eds.]
62 { ≠ classical 'torch' ‹ ill. › }
63 [*GMS*, BA 4; *AA* IV, 394–395: "Es liegt gleichwohl in dieser Idee von dem absoluten Werte des bloßen Willens [...] etwas so Befremdliches, daß, unerachtet aller Einstimmung selbst der gemeinen Vernunft mit derselben, dennoch ein Verdacht entspringen muß, daß vielleicht [...] die Natur in ihrer Absicht, warum sie unserm Willen Vernunft zur Regiererin beigelegt habe, falsch verstanden sein möge." Trans. mod. by R.S.]
64 [Cf. Alquié, *MK*, 40–44.]
65 [See *KrV*, B 29; *AA* III, 46, *Einleitung*, VII, *Idee und Einteilung einer besonderen Wissenschaft, unter dem Namen der Kritik der reinen Vernunft*: "zwei Stämme der menschlichen Erkenntniß."]
66 [Understanding and Reason.]
67 { *3rd?* source could only be *emotions* ... i.e. discarded because ≠ good *in itself* because *either?* *universal* or *particular* }
68 { (≠ kingdom of ends) }
69 { direct consequence of Copernican revolution: ultimacy of subject }.
70 [*GMS*, BA 4–5; *AA* IV, 395: "Wäre nun an einem Wesen, das Vernunft und einen Willen hat[, seine *Erhaltung*, sein *Wohlergehen*, mit einem Worte] seine *Glückseligkeit*, der eigentliche Zweck der Natur, so hätte sie ihre Veranstaltung dazu sehr schlecht getroffen, sich die Vernunft des Geschöpfs zur Ausrichterin dieser ihrer Absicht zu ersehen. Denn alle Handlungen, die es in dieser Absicht auszuüben hat, und die ganze Regel seines Verhaltens würden ihm weit genauer durch Instinkt vorgezeichnet [...]." Trans. mod. by R.S.]
71 [*GMS*, BA 7; *AA* IV, 396: "die Cultur der Vernunft." Trans. mod. by R.S.]
72 [Cf. Alquié, *MK*, 48–51.]
73 [*GMS*, BA 8; *AA* IV, 397: "de[r] Begriff der Pflicht [...], der den eines guten Willens, obzwar unter gewissen subjektiven Einschränkungen und Hindernissen, enthält."]
74 { *Willkür* vs. *Wille* } [Arbitrary will vs. rational will. In *DHB*, Schürmann himself translates these terms in Kant as "volonté arbitraire" [arbitrary will] and "volonté rationelle" [rational will] (541), then "libre arbitre" [free 'arbitrium'—Reginald Lilly in *BH*, 477, renders it as "free will"] and "volonté morale" [moral will] (549).]
75 [*GMS*, BA 39; *AA* IV, 414: "einen heiligen Willen."].
76 [*subsumption?*]
77 [*GMS*, BA 10; *AA* IV, 398: "pflichtmäßig" / "aus Pflicht."]
78 [Cf. Alquié, *MK*, 51–54.]
79 { ‹ ill. › *Ni[etzsche]?*? }

129

NOTES

80   [*GMS*, BA 15; *AA* IV, 401: "[es brauchte also dazu nicht] des Willens eines vernünftigen Wesens, worin gleichwohl das höchste und unbedingte Gute allein angetroffen werden kann." Trans. mod. by R.S.]

81   [The section 1 on Kant of Part 1 of the original typescript ends here. On p. 25, only the following handwritten annotation can be found: { *Wille* vs. *Willkür* }.]

82   { Kant: practical reason = will }

83   Hirsch II 375–87 [Cf. Johannes Hirschberger, *Geschichte der Philosophie*, 2 vols. (Freiburg: Herder, 1949–1952), vol. 2, 375–387 / Hirschberger, *The History of Philosophy*, 2 vols., trans. Anthony N. Fuerst (Milwaukee: Bruce, 1958–1959).]

84   [We were unable to locate the corresponding passage. Schürmann seems to be citing from memory, and is perhaps paraphrasing from the following sentence which, although often attributed to Schelling, is not found in the SW: "Die Natur schlägt im Menschen ihre Augen auf und bemerkt, daß sie da ist / Nature opens its eyes in the human being and observes that it is there." Trans. by Eds. It is fair to assume that Schürmann also had the following words by Meister Eckhart in mind: "Daz ouge, dâ inne ich got sihe, daz ist daz selbe ouge, dâ inne mich got sihet; mîn ouge und gotes ouge daz ist éin ouge und éin gesiht und éin bekennen und éin minnen" ("The eye in which I see God is the same eye in which God sees me; my eye and God's eye are one eye and one vision and one knowing and one loving," Pr. 12, "Qui audit me" in *Die deutschen Werke*, vol. I, ed. and trans. J. Quint, (Stuttgart: Kohlhammer, 1958), p. 201, lines 5–8, trans. by Eds.).]

85   [Schürmann has "impoverishing"]

86   [*SW*, I, 7, 333, trans. mod. by R.S.: "so wurde der Gegensatz von Natur und Geist billig zuerst von dieser Seite betrachtet. Der feste Glaube an eine bloß menschliche Vernunft, die Ueberzeugung von der vollkommenen Subjektivität alles Denkens und Erkennens und der gänzlichen Vernunft- und Gedankenlosigkeit der Natur, sammt der überall herrschenden mechanischen Vorstellungsart, indem auch das durch Kant wiedergeweckte Dynamische wieder nur in ein höheres Mechanisches überging [...] Es ist Zeit, daß der höhere oder vielmehr der eigentliche Gegensatz hervortrete, der von Nothwendigkeit und Freiheit, mit welchem erst der innerste Mittelpunkt der Philosophie zur Betrachtung kommt." Schürmann here adds: "reference to vol. VII of the *Jubiläumsausgabe* in the margin of the tr[ans]l[ation]."]

87   [In the margins Schürmann refers to Hirschberger, *Geschichte der Philosophie*, vol. 2., 380f.]

88   { inorganic }

89   { ἐπιστροφή } [epistrophé]

90   { *falsche *Vernunft?*!* }

91   [*SW*, I, 3, 341, trans. by R.S.: "die sogenannte todte Natur aber überhaupt eine unreife Intelligenz, daher in ihren Phänomenen noch bewußtlos schon der intelligente Charakter durchblickt. – Das höchste Ziel, sich selbst ganz Objekt zu werden, erreicht die Natur erst durch die höchste und letzte Reflexion, welche nichts anderes als der Mensch, oder, allgemeiner, das ist, was wir Vernunft nennen, durch welche zuerst die Natur vollständig in sich selbst zurückkehrt, und wodurch offenbar wird, daß die Natur ursprünglich identisch ist mit dem, was in uns als Intelligentes und Bewußtes erkannt wird." Although Schürmann provides

NOTES

the following as bibliographical reference—*Project of a Philosophy of Nature*, p. 57—the passage is from *System des transscendentalen Idealismus*.]
92 { *KdU*! } [Cf. *Critique of Judgment!*]
93 { artistic errance of man (› Kant) }
94 [Schürmann substitutes "longing" for "desire."]
95 { it!! }
96 F.W.J. Schelling, *Clara oder über den Zusammenhang der Natur mit der Geisterwelt*. Aus dem *Nachlass*, hrsg. von K.F.A. Schelling (Stuttgart und Augsburg: J.G. Cotta Verlag, 1862), 178, trans. by R.S.; F.W.J. Schelling, *Clara, or, On Nature's Connection to the Spirit World*. trans., with an Introduction by Fiona Steinkamp, (Albany, NY: SUNY, 2002), 80: "Unserm Herzen genügt das bloße Geisterleben nicht. Es ist etwas in uns, das nach wesentlicher Realität verlangt [...] der Künstler nicht ruht im Gedanken seines Werkes, sondern nur in der körperlichen Darstellung [...] so ist das Ziel aller Sehnsucht das vollkommenen Leibliche als Gegenbild und Abglanz des vollkommenen Geistigen."]
97 [See *SW*, I, 2, 56: "Die Natur soll der sichtbare Geist, der Geist die unsichtbare Natur seyn."]
98 [Schürmann gives the following parenthetical reference: "(Vol. IV, p. 337f.)" It is reasonable to assume on the basis both of the preceding and the following references that he might be referring to Schelling's *Sämmtliche Werke*. However, no corresponding passage is found in *SW*, I, 4, 337f. Nonetheless, the belonging together, the unity of the subjective and the objective as well as of the real and the ideal, is clearly stated by Schelling in other places, e.g., in *SW*, I, 6, 168: "die ewige Einheit alles Subjektiven und Objektiven, alles Idealen und Realen / the eternal oneness of everything subjective and objective, of everything ideal and real" (transl. by Eds.) or "die ganze absolute Identität von Realem und Idealem, von Subjektivem und Objektivem / the whole absolute Identity of the real and the ideal, the subjective and the objective" (transl. by Eds.).]
99 { The One has to be *dramatic* to multiply—therefore *will* (› Aug[ustine]: will divided) }
100 [In the margins Schürmann refers to J. Hirschberger, *Geschichte der Philosophie*, vol. 2., 388f.]
101 { "particular" }
102 [*SW*, I, 7, 370f: "Dieses Wesen [das Positive, Eds.] zu erkennen, ist der dogmatischen Philosophie unmöglich, weil sie keinen Begriff der Persönlichkeit, d.h. der zur Geistigkeit erhobenen Selbstheit, sondern nur die abgezogenen Begriffe des Endlichen und des Unendlichen hat." Trans. mod. by R.S.]
103 [Ibid.: "[...] bedarf es etwas Positives, welches sonach im Bösen nothwendig angenommen werden muß, aber so lange unerklärbar bleiben wird, als nicht eine Wurzel der Freiheit in dem unabhängigen Grunde der Natur erkannt ist." Trans. mod. by R.S.]
104 [*Ibid.*: "Jenen [Die Vorstellungen unseres Zeitalters, Eds.] zufolge liegt der einzige Grund des Bösen in der Sinnlichkeit, oder in der Animalität [...] Diese Vorstellung ist eine natürliche Folge der Lehre, nach welcher die Freiheit in der bloßen Herrschaft des intelligenten Princips über die sinnlichen Begierden und

131

NOTES

Neigungen besteht, und das Gute aus reiner Vernunft kommt, wonach es begreif-
licherweise für das Böse keine Freiheit gibt [...]."]
105 [SW, I, 7, 352: "Der reale und lebendige Begriff [der Freiheit, Eds.] aber ist, daß
sie ein Vermögen des Guten und des Bösen sey." Trans. mod. by R.S.]
106 [SW, I, 7, 381f.: "Dieser allgemeinen Nothwendigkeit ohnerachtet bleibt das Böse
immer die eigne Wahl des Menschen; das Böse, als solches, kann der Grund nicht
machen, und jede Creatur fällt durch ihre eigne Schuld." Trans. mod. by R.S.
Gutman translates "basis" instead of "ground."]
107 [SW, I, 7, 350: "Es gibt in der letzten und höchsten Instanz gar kein anderes Seyn
als Wollen. Wollen ist Urseyn, und auf dieses allein passen alle Prädicate desselben: Grundlosigkeit, Ewigkeit, Unabhängigkeit von der Zeit, Selbstbejahung.
Die ganze Philosophie strebt nur dahin, diesen höchsten Ausdruck zu finden."
Trans. mod. by R.S.]
108 [SW, I, 7, 359n.: "[...] der einzig rechte Dualismus, nämlich der, welcher zugleich
eine Einheit zuläßt."]
109 { [*Plotinus?*]: νοῦς [noûs] = absolute }
110 [SW, I, 7, 358: "Dieser Grund seiner Existenz, den Gott in sich hat, ist nicht Gott
absolut betrachtet, d.h. sofern er existirt [...]." Trans. mod. by R.S. (emphasis
added.) Interestingly, Schürmann omits "God" from the citation in his transcript.
Gutman's text reads: "This ground of his existence, which God contains within
himself, is not *God* viewed as absolute, that is insofar as he exists."]
111 { Schelling: ground = *individual!* }
112 [SW, I, 7, 359: "[...] die Dinge ihren Grund in dem haben, was in Gott selbst
nicht, *Er Selbst ist*, d.h. in dem, was Grund seiner Existenz ist. Wollen wir uns
dieses Wesen menschlich näher bringen, so können wir sagen: es sey die Sehnsucht, die das ewige Eine empfindet, sich selbst zu gebären." Trans. mod.]
113 { principle of individuation }
114 [Ibid.: "Sie [die Sehnsucht, Eds.] will Gott, d.h. die unergründliche Einheit, gebären [...]."]
115 [Ibid.: "Sie ist daher für sich betrachtet auch Wille; aber Wille, in dem kein Verstand ist, und darum auch nicht selbständiger und vollkommener Wille [...]."]
116 [Ibid.: "[...] der Verstand eigentlich der Wille in dem Willen ist."]
117 [Ibid.: "[...] nicht ein bewußter, sondern ein ahndender Wille, dessen Ahndung
der Verstand ist."]
118 { N[ietzsche]: Apollo + Dionysos}
119 [Ibid., 359f.: "Nach der ewigen That der Selbstoffenbarung ist nämlich in der
Welt, wie wir sie jetzt erblicken, alles Regel, Ordnung und Form; aber immer liegt
noch im Grunde das Regellose, als könnte es einmal wieder durchbrechen, und
nirgends scheint es, als wären Ordnung und Form das Ursprüngliche, sondern
als wäre ein anfänglich Regelloses zur Ordnung gebracht worden. Dieses ist an
den Dingen die unergreifliche Basis der Realität, der nie aufgehende Rest, das,
was sich [mit der größten Anstrengung] nicht in Verstand auflösen läßt[, sondern
ewig im Grunde bleibt." Trans. mod.]
120 { M[eister] E[ckhart]: Eigenschaft }
121 [SW, I, 7, 381, trans. mod. by R.S.]

NOTES

122 { N[ietzsche]'s thesis: in moral philosophy reason has functioned as our organ for an ideal. }

123 [eKGWB/NF, 1880,7[64]: "Christenthum und Judenthum: das Ideal außer uns gesetzt, mit höchster Macht und befehlend! [...] [Und *wie wenig willkürlich* wird ihm das Bild von sich erscheinen müssen!] Darf er sich als dessen Schöpfer fühlen?! Kaum!" Trans. by R.S.]

124 [*WzM*, § 204; *eKGWB/NF*-1887,10[157]: "der Idealist' (—Ideal-Castrat) auch aus einer ganz *bestimmten* Wirklichkeit heraus geht [...] Der Castratist formulirt eine Summe von neuen Erhaltungsbedingungen für Menschen einer ganz bestimmten Species."]

125 [*BGE*, "Preface"; *eKGWB/JGB*-Vorrede: "Platonismus für's 'Volk.'"]

126 [*WzM*, § 95; : *eKGWB/NF*-1887,9[178]: "Phantast des Pflichtbegriffs."]

127 [See above n. 60.]

128 [*TI*, How the 'True World' Became a Fable." "History of an Error"; *eKGWB/GD*-Welt-Fabel, 4: "Die wahre Welt [...] *unbekannt*. Folglich auch nicht tröstend, erlösend, verpflichtend: wozu könnte uns etwas Unbekanntes verpflichten? ... (Grauer Morgen. Erstes Gähnen der Vernunft. Hahnenschrei des Positivismus)." Trans. mod. by R.S.]

129 [*eKGWB/NF*-1884,25[436]: "*Wollen* d < als ist > *befehlen*: befehlen aber ist ein bestimmter Affekt (dieser Affekt ist eine *plötzliche Kraftexplosion*)—gespannt, klar, ausschließlich Eins im Auge, innerste Überzeugung von der Überlegenheit, Sicherheit, daß gehorcht wird—'Freiheit des Willens' ist das 'Überlegenheits-Gefühl des Befehlenden' in Hinsicht auf den Gehorchenden: '*ich* bin frei, und *Jener* muß *gehorchen*.'" Trans. by R.S.]

130 { against K[ant] }

131 { *rationality*: more *terrible* form of commanding because *inescapable* }

132 { with K[ant] }

133 [*eKGWB/NF-1872*,19[104]/[105]: "Ganz wahrhaftig zu sein [...] Das ist das *tragische Problem Kants*! Jetzt bekommt die Kunst eine ganz *neue* Würde. [...] *Wahrhaftigkeit der Kunst*: sie ist allein jetzt ehrlich."]

134 { *tragic*: rational will — legislates — subjects itself }

135 [*TI*, "'Reason' in Philosophy", 6; *eKGWB/GD*-Vernunft-6: "*ein [...] hinterlistige[r] Christ zu guterletzt.*"]

136 { i.e. self-subjection }

137 [*WzM*, § 578; *eKGWB/NF*-1887,9[160]: "die transscendente Welt erfunden, *damit* ein Platz bleibt für 'moralische Freiheit.'"]

138 [*TI*, How the 'True World' Became a Fable." "History of an Error"; *eKGWB/GD*-Welt-Fabel, 5: "Die 'wahre Welt' — eine Idee, die zu Nichts mehr nütz ist, nicht einmal mehr verpflichtend [...] (Heller Tag; Frühstück; Rückkehr des bon sens und der Heiterkeit; Schamröthe Plato's; Teufelslärm aller freien Geister.)."]

139 [*WzM*, § 671; *eKGWB/NF*-1883,24[32]/[34]: "Unfreiheit oder Freiheit des Willens? Es giebt *keinen Willen*.[... Es giebt keinen 'Willen':] das ist nur eine vereinfachende Conception des Verstandes, wie 'Materie.'"]

140 [*WzM*, § 46; *eKGWB/NF*-1888,14[219]: "Schwäche des Willens: das ist ein Gleichniß, das irreführen kann. Denn es giebt keinen Willen, und folglich weder einen starken, noch schwachen Willen. Die Vielheit und Disgregation der Antriebe, der

NOTES

Mangel an System unter ihnen resultirt als 'schwacher Wille'; die Coordination derselben unter der Vorherrschaft eines einzelnen resultirt als 'starker Wille' [...]."]

141 [WzM, § 488; eKGWB/NF-1887,9[98]: "'Subjekt': von uns aus interpretirt, so daß das Ich als Substanz gilt, als Ursache alles Thuns, als *Thäter*. [...] der Glaube an Substanz, Accidens, Attribut usw. hat seine Überzeugungskraft in der Gewohnheit, all unser Thun als Folge unseres Willens zu betrachten:—so daß das Ich, als Substanz, nicht eingeht in die Vielheit der Veränderung.—*Aber es giebt keinen Willen.*—"]

142 [See WzM, § 485; eKGWB/NF-1887,10[19]: "'Subjekt' ist die Fiktion."]

143 [Schürmann here renders "disintegration" instead of "disgregation."]

144 [WzM, § 549; eKGWB/NF-1885,36[26]: "'Subjekt' 'Objekt' 'Prädikat' — diese Trennungen sind *gemacht.*" Trans. mod. by R.S.]

145 [WzM, § 715; eKGWB/NF-1887,11[73]: "[...] *Erhaltungs-Steigerungs-Bedingungen* in Hinsicht auf complexe Gebilde von relativer Dauer des Lebens innerhalb des Werdens."]

146 [Ibid.: "'Herrschafts-Gebilde'; die Sphäre des Beherrschenden fortwährend wachsend oder periodisch abnehmend, zunehmend; oder, unter der Gunst und Ungunst der Umstände (der Ernährung —)."]

147 [Ibid.: "*es giebt keinen Willen*: es giebt Willens-Punktationen, die beständig ihre Macht mehren oder verlieren."]

148 [Schürmann here crossed out the verb referring to "the factor that integrates [impulses]," and replaces it with "results from integrated [impulses,]" thus turning the active clause into a passive one.]

149 [WzM, § 529; eKGWB/NF-1888,14[146]: "[Die ungeheuren Fehlgriffe: 1)] die unsinnige Überschätzung des Bewußtseins, aus ihm eine Einheit gemacht, ein Wesen gemacht, 'der Geist,' 'die Seele,' etwas, das fühlt, denkt, will—"]

150 [Ibid: "2) der Geist als *Ursache*, namentlich überall wo Zweckmäßigkeit, System, Coordination erscheinen."]

151 [Ibid: "3) das Bewußtsein als höchste erreichbare Form, als oberste Art Sein, als 'Gott.'"]

152 [Ibid: "4) der Wille überall eingetragen, wo es Wirkung giebt."]

153 [eKGWB/NF-1886,7[34]: "Der Causalismus. Dieses 'Aufeinander' bedarf immer noch der *Auslegung*: 'Naturgesetz' ist eine Auslegung usw. 'Ursache und Wirkung' geht zurück auf den Begriff '*Thun* und *Thäter.*' *Diese* Scheidung woher?" Trans. by R.S.]

154 [eKGWB/NF-1885,1[38]: "[NB.] Der Glaube an Causalität geht zurück auf den Glauben, daß ich es bin, der wirkt, auf die Scheidung der 'Seele' von ihrer *Thätigkeit*. Also ein uralter Aberglaube!" Trans. by R.S.]

155 [WzM, § 657; eKGWB/NF-1886,5[64]: "Was ist 'passiv'? widerstehen und reagiren. *Gehemmt* sein in der vorwärtsgreifenden Bewegung: also ein Handeln des Widerstandes und der Reaktion. Was ist 'aktiv'? nach Macht ausgreifend."]

156 [See above n. 140.]

157 { will = time }

158 [WzM, § 462; eKGWB/NF-1887,9[8]: "An Stelle der 'Sociologie' eine *Lehre von den Herrschaftsgebilden.*"]

NOTES

159 [*WzM*, § 630; *eKGWB/NF*-1885,36[18]: "Ich hüte mich, von chemischen '*Gesetzen*' zu sprechen: das hat einen moralischen Beigeschmack. Es handelt sich vielmehr um eine absolute Feststellung von Machtverhältnissen: das Stärkere wird über das Schwächere Herr [...]." Trans. mod. by R.S.]

160 [*WzM*, § 1, 5; *eKGWB/NF*-1885,2[127]: "Seit Copernikus rollt der Mensch aus dem Centrum ins x."]

161 [*eKGWB/GM*-III-25: "Ist nicht gerade die Selbstverkleinerung des Menschen, sein *Wille* zur Selbstverkleinerung seit Kopernikus in einem unaufhaltsamen Fortschritte? [...] Seit Kopernikus scheint der Mensch auf eine schiefe Ebene gerathen,—er rollt immer schneller nunmehr aus dem Mittelpunkte weg—wohin? in's Nichts?"]

162 [*WzM*, § 649; *eKGWB/NF*-1886,7[44]: "das *Mehrgefühl*, das Gefühl des *Stärker-Werdens* [...]."]

163 [*WzM*, § 293; *eKGWB/NF*-1888,14[31]: "Wenn das Werden ein großer Ring ist, so ist Jegliches gleich werth, ewig, nothwendig ... In allen Correlationen von Ja und Nein, von Vorziehen und Abweisen, Lieben und Hassen drückt sich nur eine Perspektive, ein Interesse bestimmter Typen des Lebens aus: an sich redet Alles, was ist, das Ja."]

164 [See above n. 124.]

165 [The corresponding passage could not be located. Schürmann offers only the following parenthetical as reference "(Unschuld des W[erdens])." Cf. *eKGWB/NF*-1882,5[1]-227: "Man muß vergehen wollen, um wieder entstehen zu können—von einem Tage zum anderen. *Verwandlung* durch hundert Seelen—das sei dein Leben, dein Schicksal: Und dann zuletzt: diese ganze Reihe noch einmal wollen! / One must will to pass away for being able to rise again—from one day to the other. *Metamorphosis* through a hundred souls—that be your life, your fate: and then at last: to will the whole series once again!" Trans. by Eds.]

166 [*TSZ*, III, "On the Vision and the Riddle," 1; *eKGWB/Za*-III-Gesicht-1: "War *das* das Leben? Wohlan! Noch Ein Mal!"]

167 [*WzM*, § 940; *eKGWB/NF*-1884, 25[351]: "'Du sollst'—unbedingter Gehorsam bei Stoikern, in den Orden des Christenthums und der Araber, in der Philosophie Kant's (es ist gleichgültig, ob einem Oberen oder einem Begriff). Höher als 'du sollst' steht 'ich will' (die Heroen); höher als 'ich will' steht 'ich bin' (die Götter der Griechen)."]

168 [*eKGWB/NF*-1881,11[163]: "Meine Lehre sagt: *so* leben, daß du *wünschen* mußt, wieder zu leben ist die Aufgabe—du wirst es *jedenfalls*!" Trans. by R.S.]

169 [In Schürmann's typescript this section is numbered '3.' Since it follows Part 1, section 3, and precedes Part II, "The Ontological Turn in the Philosophy of the Will," the section has been numbered '4.']

170 [From *HBA*, §41, "The Problem of the Will," 245–250, trans. mod.]

171 *Wm*, 145[/*GA* 9, 313: "Wir bedenken das Wesen des Handelns noch lange nicht entschieden genug."]/*BWr*, 193, trans. mod. and emphasis added [by R.S.]

172 "Being-there can comport itself unwillingly [*unwillentlich*, R.S.] toward its possibilities; it can be inauthentic; and factically it is that way, proximally and for the most part" (*SZ*, 193/*BT*, 237[: "[...] *kann* sich das Dasein zu seinen

135

NOTES

Möglichkeiten auch *unwillentlich* verhalten, es *kann* uneigentlich sein und ist faktisch zunächst und zumeist in dieser Weise."]).

173 { reason }

174 'Decisionism' is opposed to 'normativism' in legal and moral philosophy. In this sense, although the concept dates from the twentieth century, Thomas Hobbes's principle "Autoritas, non veritas, facit legem" [authority, not truth, makes the law], is the most succinct formulation of that doctrine. Karl Löwith, here again the champion of the 'existentialist' reading of Heidegger, labelled the content of *BT* a "philosophy of resolute existence," which satisfied all criteria of "decisionism." As Löwith uses the term, decisionism is the doctrine that "destroys" the transmitted normative systems in order to exalt "the pathos of decision in the name of pure resolution" ([Karl Löwith,] *Gesammelte Abhandlungen*, (Stuttgart: Kohlhammer, 1960), 93f.).

175 *Rc*, 97[*GA* 55, 55: "das ekstatische Sicheinlassen des existierenden Menschen in die Unverborgenheit des Seins."]/*PLT*, 84 (65).

176 *Hw*, 55[/*GA* 5, 55: "Die in 'Sein und Zeit' gedachte Ent-schlossenheit ist nicht die decidierte Aktion [eines Subjekts ...."]/*PLT*, 67 (65). In other words, he is saying that *thesis—setzen* or *feststellen*, positing or establishing—is to be understood as "letting [something, R.S.] lie forth in its radiance and presencing," not in its fixity as a fact (*Rc*, 96[/*GA* 5, 71: "Vorliegenlassen in seinem Scheinen und Anwesen"]/*PLT*, 83 (82); cf. *Wm*, 159/*BWr*, 207 and *Gel*, 61/*DTh*, 81).

177 Jarava L. Mehta, *Martin Heidegger: The Way and the Vision* (Honolulu: University of Hawaii Press, 1976), 337; cf ibid., 33, 74 and 352. Hannah Arendt, in her chapter "Heidegger's Will-not-to-will," *The Life of the Mind*, 172–194, relies largely on Mehta, especially when she describes "letting-be" as an "alternative" opposed to the "destructiveness" of the will. She adds: "it is against that destructiveness that Heidegger's original reversal pits itself" (178). One of her very premises in the two volumes, entitled respectively *Thinking* and *Willing*, is precisely that thinking and willing are "opposites" (ibid., 179).

On decisionism, in addition to Karl Löwith, see Ernst Tugendhat, *Der Wahrheitsbegriff bei Husserl und Heidegger* (Berlin: De Gruyter, 1967), 361 and 380, as well as Christian Graf von Krockow, *Die Entscheidung: Eine Untersuchung über Ernst Jünger, Carl Schmitt, Martin Heidegger* (Stuttgart: F. Enke, 1958), 68–81 and 116–128. Herbert Marcuse takes up this common opinion about Heideggerian decisionism: in Heidegger, "the social-empirical context of the decision and of its consequences is 'bracketed.' The main thing is to decide and to act according to your decision. Whether or not the decision is in itself, in its goal, morally and humanly positive, is of minor importance," "Heidegger's Politics: An Interview," in *Graduate Faculty Philosophy Journal*, VI, 1 (1977), 35. See, in the same sense, Karsten Harries's article "Heidegger as a Political Thinker," Review of Metaphysics XXIX (June, 1976), 642–669, repr. in *Heidegger and Modern Philosophy*, ed. Michael Murray (New Haven and London: Yale University Press, 1978), 304–328.

In the same spirit, Wiplinger [Fridolin Wiplinger, *Wahrheit und Geschichtlichkeit. Eine Untersuchung uber die Frage nach dem Wesen der Wahrheit im Denken Martin Heideggers* (Freiburg: Verlag Karl Alber, 1961)], 270, calls attention to the

136

NOTES

"proportion" in *BT*: "The more authentically Dasein resolves [decides, R.S.] itself [...] the more unequivocally and unfortuitously does it choose and find the possibility of its existence" (*SZ*, 384[: "Je eigentlicher sich das Dasein entschließt, [...] um so eindeutiger und unzufälliger ist das wählende Finden der Möglichkeit seiner Existenz."]/*BT*, 435). This quotation illustrates Marcuse's position according to which I must at all costs reach 'my' decision and then, without equivocation but necessarily, I will find my ownmost possibility of existence.

All these interpretations of resoluteness or resolve, of deciding and willing, are antithetical to the reading given by Birault: "Letting-be is what *Being and Time* called *die Entschlossenheit* and what the more recent writings call *Gelassenheit* [...] The 'resolute decision' of *Sein und Zeit* does not have the 'heroic' meaning that was thought to be attributable to it, nor does Gelassenheit have the 'quietist' meaning that some wish to confer on it [...] *Entschlossenheit* [Here Schürmann adds in the margin: "*Ent-/Er*-schlossenheit"] must not be thought of in terms of the traditional forms of willing; on the contrary, one must think of those forms themselves in terms of *Entschlossenheit* so as to elaborate a *non-voluntarist theory of the will*" [Henri Birault, *Heidegger et l'expérience de la pensée* (Paris: Gallimard, 1978), 519f.]. Even Gabriel Marcel, in a text otherwise crammed with untenable epithets (the most massive concerning the "substantivization of being" in Heidegger), writes: "Human decision can intervene only on a level where [...] the decisive initiatives do not issue from man," "Ma relation avec Heidegger," in *Presence de Gabriel Marcel* I (Paris: Aubier, 1979), 31.

178 [This paragraph title is not found in *HBA*.]

179 {   I° *will* set loose |

 α) *B[eing and] T[ime]*   Entscheidung
    ↓ *letting* open-up |

 β) *ontological* turn in the philosophy of will → *epochal* decisions}

180 { Scheidung → *Kehre*

    |

  [*Heidegger*?] }

181 *N* II, 293[/*GA* 6.2, 293: "Das Denken ist noch nicht entstanden aus der Scheidung der metaphysischen Seinsfrage nach dem Sein des Seienden und derjenigen Frage, die anfänglicher, nämlich nach der Wahrheit des Seins, fragt [...]." Trans. by R.S.

182 { threshold: *intermittence* between two mittences }

183 *Hw*, 37[/*GA* 5, 35: "Die Welt ist die sich öffnende Offenheit der weiten Bahnen der einfachen und wesentlichen Entscheidungen im Geschick eines geschichtlichen Volkes."]/*PLT*, 48 [(47), trans. mod. by R.S. Schürmann here adds: "Origin of the Work of Art."]

184 [Schürmann crossed out the word "économiques" and hand-wrote "epochal." In *HBA*, 246, one reads instead "economic."]

185 [Schürmann crossed out the word "économique" and hand-wrote "epochal." In *HBA*, ibid., one reads instead "economic."]

186 *Hw*, 43f.[/*GA* 5, 42: "[...] ist die Welt die Lichtung der Bahnen der wesentlichen Weisungen, in die sich alles Entscheiden fügt. Jede Entscheidung aber gründet sich auf ein Nichtbewältigtes, Verborgenes, Beirrendes, sonst wäre sie nie

137

NOTES

Entscheidung."]/*PLT*, 55 [(53), trans. mod. by R.S. Schürmann hand-wrote his own translation of the French text. He renders: "éclaircie / clearing," "orbites / channels."]

187 {   ⌐ ‹ ill. ›
    rationality of   makes my *willing* finite
             ∟ technology   }

188 In the essay on "The Origin of the Work of Art," from which all these passages are taken, Heidegger can therefore ask: "Is it art still, or is it no longer, an essential and necessary way in which that truth happens which is decisive for our historical being-there?" (*Hw*, 67[/*GA* 5, 68: "Ist die Kunst noch eine wesentliche und eine notwendige Weise, in der die für unser geschichtliches Dasein entscheidende Wahrheit geschieht, oder ist die Kunst dies nicht mehr?"]/*PLT*, 80 (78), trans. mod. by R.S.). Perhaps art no longer functions as a decisive variable or 'track' for our existence. Religion, too, after having served as the conveyer of the essential injunctions throughout the ages, now has forfeited that role: ours "is the state of indecision toward God and the gods" (*Hw*, 70[/*GA* 5, 76: "[...] der Zustand der Entscheidungslosigkeit über den Gott und die Götter."]/*QCT*, 117, trans. mod. by R.S.). Indeed, "whether the god lives or remains dead is not *decided* by the religiosity of men [..., R.S.]. Whether or not God is God comes to pass from the constellation of being and within that constellation" (*TK*, 46[/*GA* 79, 77: "Ob der Gott lebt oder tot bleibt, entscheidet sich nicht durch die Religiosität der Menschen [...] Ob Gott Gott ist, ereignet sich aus der Konstellation des Seins und innerhalb ihrer."]/*QCT*, 49, emphasis added).

189 [Schürmann crossed out the word "économique" and hand-wrote "epochal." *HBA*, 246, has "systemic."]

190 *N* I, 168f.[/*GA*, 6.1, 144: "solche Grundworte wie Wahrheit, Schönheit, Sein, Kunst, Erkenntnis, Geschichte, Freiheit [...]."]/*N* i, 143, trans. mod. by R.S.

191 *FD*, 38[/*GA* 41, 49: "eine gewandelte Grundstellung"]/*WTh*, 50.

192 Constructive thinking must "constantly *de-cide* the sizes and heights [of its edifices] and consequently *ex-cise* [previous measures ..., R.S.]. Construction goes through decisions" (*N* I, 641[/*GA* 47, 255: "[Das Bauen als Er-richten ...] muß stets *ent-scheiden* über Maße und Höhen und demzufolge *aus-scheiden* [...]. Das Bauen geht durch Entscheidungen hindurch." Trans. by R.S.]).

193 From that thought "spring the possibilities of decision and separation [*Entscheidung und Scheidung*, R.S.] in regard to the being-there of man in general" (*N* I, 393[/*GA*, 6.1, 352: "ergeben sich Möglichkeiten der Entscheidung und Scheidung hinsichtlich des Daseins des Menschen überhaupt"]).

194 { volitional |
            decisionism
    disjunctive | }

195 { cf. Kant's 'Copernican Revolution' }

196 *VS*, 132[/*GA* 15, 394: "Für Marx ist im vorhinein entschieden, daß der Mensch und einzig der Mensch (und nichts anderes) die Sache ist. Woher ist das entschieden? Auf welche Weise? Mit welchem Recht? Durch welche Autorität? Auf diese Fragen kann man nur antworten, indem man auf die Geschichte der Metaphysik zurückgeht." (Trans. and emphasis added by R.S.)]

138

NOTES

197 Hannah Arendt, "Home to Roost," New York Review of Books (June 26, 1975), 5 (emphasis added).
198 [Schürmann crossed out the word "principes" and hand-wrote "theticism."]
199 [Schürmann crossed out the word "agir" and hand-wrote "willing."]
200 { will not to will }
201 *Hw*, 65[/*GA* 5, 66: "Sind wir in unserem Dasein geschichtlich am Ursprung?"]/ *PLT*, 78 (76).
202 Ibid.: "[...] Entweder-Oder und seine Entscheidung [...]."]
203 *N* I, 415[/*GA* 6.1, 372: "Der Gedanke muß nicht nur jeweils aus dem schaffenden Augenblick der Entscheidung des Einzelnen gedacht werden, sondern er ist als zum Leben selbst gehörig eine *geschichtliche Entscheidung* —eine *Krisis.*" Trans. by R.S.]
204 { i.e. hubris → the 'constant presence' of m[etaphysics] }
205 { vs. releasement}
206 { will not to will }
207 *Gel*, 32[/*GA* 13, 38: "ich will das Nicht-Wollen."]/*DTh*, 59, trans. mod. by R.S.
208 [Schürmann crossed out the word "principes" and hand-wrote "theticism."]
209 *Hw*, 328[/*GA* 5, 356: "Die Un-Fuge besteht darin, daß das Je-Weilige sich auf die Weile im Sinne des nur Beständigen zu versteifen sucht."]/*EGT*, 43[, trans. mod. by R.S.]. With regard to the "fourfold," Heidegger states that, on the contrary, "none of the four strives to persist" (*VA*, 178[/*GA* 7, 181: "Keines der Vier versteift sich auf sein gesondertes Besonderes."]/*PLT*, 179 (177), trans. mod. by R.S. Cf. Arendt, *Life of the Mind*, vol. II, 193f.
210 { theticism: bad insurrection }
211 Arendt, *Life of the Mind*, vol. I, 213.
212 One may presume that this interpretation of *adikia* in Heidegger depends directly on his view of contemporary technology. It is indeed technological man who "struts (*aufspreizen*) in the posture of lord of the earth" (*VA*, 34[/*GA* 7, 28: "[...] spreizt sich gerade der [...] Mensch in die Gestalt des Herrn der Erde auf."]/*QCT*, 27, trans. mod. by R.S.).
213 [Schürmann hand-wrote "time over" on "s'abandonnent."]
214 { reason — will
     | |
     thinking — releasing
               will not to will }
215 [The following sentences are crossed-out: However, the poet's craft yields greater lucidity than the thinker's. Unlike Hölderlin, Nietzsche "was not capable of discerning the historical rootedness of the metaphysical question concerning truth in general nor of his own decisions in particular" (*N* I, 633f.[/*GA* 47, 247: "[Nietzsche] die geschichtliche Verwurzelung der metaphysischen Wahrheitsfrage überhaupt und die seiner eigenen Entscheidungen im besonderen nicht zu durchschauen vermochte."]). Nietzsche's own decisions remain entirely, if unsuspectingly, inscribed within that other decision, the "decision not made by us but which, as the history of being, is made for our history by being itself." With Nietzsche, metaphysics "took a decisive turn toward the fulfillment of its essence" (*N* II, 98[/*GA* 6.2, 98: "eine entscheidende Wendung in die Vollendung

APPENDIX

ihres Wesens nahm."]/*N* iv, 59). This instantiates once more the poverty of the transitional thinkers: Nietzsche remained necessarily ignorant of the shift that articulated itself through him. But his [...].]

216 { 5 }

217 [Schürmann crossed out "principe" and hand-wrote "thesis."]

218 { rationality of technology *vs.* order of thinking }

219 [Schürmann crossed out "philosophie" and hand-wrote "technology."]

220 *Hw*, 33[/*GA* 5, 31: "Wo die wesenhaften Entscheidungen unserer Geschichte fallen, von uns übernommen und verlassen, verkannt und wieder erfragt werden, da weltet die Welt."]/*PLT*, 44f., trans. mod. by R.S.

221 *Gel*, 66[/*GA* 13, 68: "jenes Wollen[...], das, absagend dem Wollen, auf das sich eingelassen hat, was nicht ein Wille ist."]/*DTh*, 85, trans. mod. by R.S.

222 [Schürmann crossed out "principes" and hand-wrote "theticism."]

223 *Gel*, 59[/*GA* 13, 62: "Wenn wir uns auf die Gelassenheit zur Gegnet einlassen, wollen wir das Nicht-Wollen."]/*DTh*, 79, trans. mod. by R.S.

224 [Schürmann crossed out "principes" and hand-wrote "posits."]

225 *Gel*, 60[/*GA* 13, 63: "will wirken und will als sein Element die Wirklichkeit."]/ *DTh*, 80, trans. mod. by R.S.

226 [§41, The Problem of the Will from *HBA*, 245–250, trans. mod., has the following closing sentence: "Given our place at the end of epochal history, non-willing and releasement turn out to be more powerful than willing and hubris."]

227 [Chapter 1. "Schelling" of "Part II: The Ontological Turn in the Philosophy of the Will" is missing from the original typescript. On p. 59 of the latter—under the title "1. SCHELLING":—only the following hand-writing is found: { Hei: SAF!! [and] 12 [*Leibniz?*] ‹ ill. › }. By using the "SAF" abbreviation, Schürmann is here referencing M. Heidegger's *Schellings Abhandlung Über das Wesen der menschlichen Freiheit* (Tübingen: M. Niemeyer, 1971) / Heidegger, *Schelling's Treatise on Human Freedom (1809)*. Trans. Joan Stambaugh (Athens: Ohio University Press, 1985); [*GA*, 42, *Schelling: Vom Wesen der Menschlichen Freiheit* (Summer Semester 1936), ed. I. Schüssler (Frankfurt a.M.: V. Klostermann, 1988)]. This reference shows that it is reasonable to assume Chapter 1 most likely was to hinge on, or at least deal with, Heidegger's reading of Schelling.]

228 [In the margins, Schürmann offers the following reference: "Sallis, XVIII." Although the reference could not be located, it is certain that Schürmann not only reviewed John Sallis' famous work on Kant, *The Gathering of Reason* (see Schürmann, "Review of J. Sallis, *The Gathering of Reason*," *Journal of the History of Philosophy*, vol. 21, n. 2, 1983, 239–240), but also attentively engaged with his reading of Kant's 'strategies.' In "Legislation-Transgression: Strategies and Counter-Strategies in the Transcendental Justification of Norms," now re-ed. in Schürmann, *Tomorrow the Manifold. Essays on Foucault, Anarchy, and the Singularization to Come*, eds. Malte Fabian Rauch and Nicolas Schneider (Zürich-Berlin: diaphanes, 2019) Schürmann, while explicitly borrowing terminology from Sallis (i.e., by calling Kant's concept of being "subversive"), at the same time highlights the limits of the latter's reading, which he regards as "failing to trace the many 'forms of disunity' in the subject [...] to Kant's understanding of being" (82–83n.6) and as "miss[ing] the distinctive Kantian moment in

140

NOTES

ontology, namely, the incipient evidence that the metaphysics of full presence is cleft in its very positing of whatever happens to function as measure-giving First, the Good, God, or the subject" (94–95n.32). See also *BH*, 485 and 671n.145, in which Schürmann again quotes Sallis' *The Gathering of Reason*, (Athens: Ohio University Press, 1980), 166f.). In *Heidegger: On Being and Acting*, Schürmann refers to Sallis' essay, "Where Does Being and Time Begin?" (in F. Elliston, ed., *Heidegger's Existential Analytic* (The Hague: Mouton, 1978), 21–43) as a source to which his remarks on the "retrieval" in *Being and Time* are "indebted" (see *HBA*, 344n.76).]

229 [*TI*, "'Reason' in Philosophy", 3. *eKGWB/GD*-Vernunft-3: "das Sein eine leere Fiktion ist"; *WzM*, § 617, *eKGWB/NF*-1886,7[54]: "eine [solche] Welt des Seins erst erfunden war."]

230 [*WzM*, § 617, *eKGWB/NF*-1886,7[54]: "Dem Werden den Charakter des Seins *aufzuprägen*—das ist der höchste *Wille zur Macht*."]

231 [*TI*, "How the 'True World' Became a Fable." "History of an Error," last stage; *eKGWB/GD*-Welt-Fabel (6): "*mit der wahren Welt haben wir auch die scheinbare abgeschafft!*"]

232 { K[ant] — }

233 [Schürmann adds "ibid. 9" in the margin. The reference is to Sallis' work (see above note 227) but could not be located. However, in *The Gathering of Reason*, 165, the following paragraph seems to express the Kantian turn to the subject as ground in noticeably similar terms: "Kant's 'Copernican revolution' turns away from the intelligible ground, traditionally understood, to the subject as the ground of the objectivity of the object. In the new conception of the sensible, the constitutive opposition is not with the intelligible, traditionally understood, but rather with the grounding subject."]

234 { Sch[elling] — }

235 [*TSZ*, "On the Afterworldly"; *eKGWB/Za*-I-Hinterweltler: "Aber 'jene Welt' ist gut verborgen vor dem Menschen, jene entmenschte unmenschliche Welt, die ein himmlisches Nichts ist; und der Bauch des Seins redet gar nicht zum Menschen, es sei denn als Mensch."]

236 { ego ≠ *formal*
   = *living*, [*in Zen?*] }

237 [Ibid.: "[...] diess Ich und des Ich's Widerspruch und Wirrsal redet noch am redlichsten von seinem Sein, dieses schaffende, wollende, werthende Ich, welches das Maass und der Werth der Dinge ist."]

238 [Ibid.: "Einen neuen Stolz lehrte mich mein Ich, den lehre ich die Menschen: nicht mehr den Kopf in den Sand der himmlischen Dinge zu stecken, sondern frei ihn zu tragen, einen Erden-Kopf, der der Erde Sinn schafft! Einen neuen Willen lehre ich die Menschen: diesen Weg wollen, den blindlings der Mensch gegangen [...]." Trans. mod. by R.S.]

239 { no ‹ ill. › *after TSZ* }

240 [*WzM*, § 559; *eKGWB/NF*-1887,11[134]: "'Dinge, die eine Beschaffenheit an sich haben'—eine dogmatische Vorstellung, mit der man absolut brechen muß"]

241 { make N[ietzsche] speak as *m[etaphysi]cian of subjectivity*: [*after?*] world [*has slip[ped]?*] elsewhere (→ Herrschaftsgebilde }

APPENDIX

242 [*TSZ*, "On the Afterworldly"; *eKGWB/Za*-I-Hinterweltler: "Wahrlich, schwer zu beweisen ist alles Sein und schwer zum Reden zu bringen. Sagt mir, ihr Brüder, ist nicht das Wunderlichste aller Dinge noch am besten bewiesen?"]

243 { = determination }

244 [*TI*, "The Four Blunders," 3; "[Der Mensch] hat die 'Dinge' als 'seiend' gesetzt nach seinem Bilde, nach seinem Begriff des Ichs als Ursache. Was Wunder, dass er später in den Dingen immer nur wiederfand, *was er in sie gesteckt hatte?*" (emphasis added by R.S.)]

245 [Schürmann repeats the first clause of the last quote: "[Man] posited 'things' as 'being' in his image in accordance with his concept of the ego as a cause."]

246 [Schürmann's text reads as follows: "the issue is precisely the same as we dealt with *in the last lecture*, in the Night Song" (emphasis added by Eds.). However, in the typescript of *Modern Philosophies of the Will* there is no mention of *TSZ*, "The Night Song." It is reasonable to assume that Schürmann used the same notes for different courses. In fact, Schürmann refers to "The Night Song" in his course on the philosophy of Nietzsche (Schürmann, *The Philosophy of Nietzsche*, ed. F. Guercio (Zurich: diaphanes, 2020), 82), where he cites the notorious adage by Nietzsche: "the narrowest cleft is the hardest to be bridged (die kleinste Kluft ist am letzten zu überbrücken)." The very same passage from Nietzsche appears as an epigraph for Schürmann's essay on Meister Eckhart "Law of Nature and Pure Nature. Thought-Experience in Meister Eckhart" in *Krisis*, 5–6, 1986–87, 148–169.]

247 [See *TSZ*, "The Night Song": "But I live in my own light." *eKGWB/Za*-II-Nachtlied: "Aber ich lebe in meinem eignen Lichte."]

248 { multiple affirmation in body: Et[ernal] Rec[urrence] }

249 { Gestaltung, Ausgestaltung: des ewigen Sinnes … } [figuration, configuration: of the eternal sense …]

250 [Schürmann here adds: "as we were observing last time."]

251 [*TSZ*, "On Self-Overcoming"; *eKGWB/Za*-II-Überwindung: "Wo ich Lebendiges fand, da fand ich Willen zur Macht […]."]

252 [*BGE*, "On the Prejudices of Philosophers," 13; *eKGWB/JGB*-13: "Leben selbst ist Wille zur Macht […]."]

253 [*TSZ*, "On the Afterworldly"; *eKGWB/Za*-I-Hinterweltler: "Und diess redlichste Sein, das Ich—das redet vom Leibe […]."]

254 [*TSZ*, "On the Despisers of the Body"; *eKGWB/Za*-I-Veraechter: "Hinter deinen Gedanken und Gefühlen, mein Bruder, steht ein mächtiger Gebieter, ein unbekannter Weiser—der heisst Selbst. In deinem Leibe wohnt er, dein Leib ist er." Trans. mod. by R.S.]

255 [*BGE*, "On the Prejudices of Philosophers," 16; *eKGWB/JGB*-16: "wenn ich den Vorgang zerlege, der in dem Satz 'ich denke' ausgedrückt ist, so bekomme ich eine Reihe von verwegenen Behauptungen, deren Begründung schwer, vielleicht unmöglich ist,—zum Beispiel, dass *ich* es bin, der denkt, dass überhaupt ein Etwas es sein muss, das denkt, dass Denken eine Thätigkeit und Wirkung seitens eines Wesens ist, welches als Ursache gedacht wird, dass es ein 'Ich' giebt, endlich, dass es bereits fest steht, was mit Denken zu bezeichnen ist,—dass ich *weiss*, was Denken ist."]

NOTES

256 [Ibid.: "Denn wenn ich nicht darüber mich schon bei mir entschieden hätte, wonach sollte ich abmessen, dass, was eben geschieht, nicht vielleicht 'Wollen' oder 'Fühlen' sei? Genug, jenes 'ich denke' setzt voraus, dass ich meinen augenblicklichen Zustand mit anderen Zuständen, die ich an mir kenne, *vergleiche*, um so festzusetzen, was er ist: wegen dieser Rückbeziehung auf anderweitiges 'Wissen' hat er für mich jedenfalls keine unmittelbare 'Gewissheit.'" Schürmann also stresses the word "unmittelbare" (immediate)."]

257 [Schürmann adds the following parenthetical: "(it would be an interesting paper for someone to take that passage and really investigate each of these assertions about the 'cogito')"]

258 [*eKGWB/FW*-354: "[...] und dass folglich Jeder von uns, beim besten Willen, sich selbst so individuell wie möglich zu *verstehen*, 'sich selbst zu kennen,' doch immer nur gerade das Nicht-Individuelle an sich zum Bewusstsein bringen wird, sein 'Durchschnittliches' [...]." Trans. by R.S.]

259 [*eKGWB-GM*-I-13: "das Volk den Blitz von seinem Leuchten trennt / people separate the lightning from its flash [trans. mod. by Eds.]."]

260 [Ibid.: "Aber es giebt kein solches Substrat; es giebt kein 'Sein' hinter dem Thun, Wirken, Werden; 'der Thäter' ist zum Thun bloss hinzugedichtet,—das Thun ist Alles."]

261 [*eKGWB/NF*-1883,24[32]: "Es giebt *keinen Willen.*"]

262 [Schürmann here adds: "Due to a meeting of the Husserl Circle out of town, there will be no class next week."]

263 [The following paragraphs are crossed-out: I think what we see is that Nietzsche is denying this kind of depth dimension in the subject, not because he wants to dissolve the subject into its mere explicit activity, into its doing. But rather, he is denying the kind of conception of the depth of the subject as substance, only in order to insert another kind of depth dimension beneath the subject. He is denying the kind of depth dimension of subjectivity which is beneath the level of explicit activity, which is beneath the level of the 'doing' in his language; but he is doing that, not because he wants to deny any depth dimension in subjectivity, but rather because he is denying one kind of depth dimension, which would follow the traditional concept of substance, precisely in order to insert another depth dimension beneath subjectivity. After all, to say that the subject is not identical with consciousness means, as we saw, that consciousness is merely a surface. Nietzsche makes this statement again and again. Consciousness is merely a surface.

That is to say, there is something of which it is the surface then. That is to say, there is some kind of depth dimension to subjectivity, beneath the level of consciousness; beneath the level of explicit acts. There is, in other words, a kind of doer behind doing, but not a doer to be understood, you see, ontologically in terms of the concept of substance. But rather in quite a different way.

What is this raw depth dimension which Nietzsche is inserting, as it were, beneath the level of explicit activity? beneath consciousness which is on the surface? Well, in the first part of *Zarathustra*, he describes it as bodily, doesn't he? It is the body. As we continue, we will see that it has also some other names,

143

APPENDIX

perhaps even more interesting names. One such name is earth. Another is Dionysian.]

264 [*TSZ*, "On the Despisers of the Body"; *eKGWB/Za*-I-Veraechter: "Immer horcht das Selbst und sucht: es vergleicht, bezwingt, erobert, zerstört. Es herrscht und ist auch des Ich's Beherrscher."]

265 { Copernican Revolution }

266 [*BGE*, I, 19; *eKGWB/JGB*-19: "[…] ist der Wille […] vor Allem noch ein *Affekt*: und zwar jener Affekt des Commando's."]

267 [*BGE*, VII, 230; *eKGWB/JGB*-230: "[…] den Willen aus der Vielheit zur Einfachheit, einen zusammenschnürenden, bändigenden, herrschsüchtigen und wirklich herrschaftlichen Willen."]

268 [Ibid.: "Die Kraft [des Geistes], Fremdes sich anzueignen, offenbart sich in einem starken Hange, das Neue dem Alten anzuähnlichen, das Mannichfaltige zu vereinfachen […]." Although Nietzsche's text reads "spirit"—and not "will" as reported by R.S.—it is the *"Grundwillen des Geistes"* (basic will of the spirit) that is dealt with in this section.]

269 { power ≠ τέλος [telos] }

270 [*TSZ*, "On Self-Overcoming"; *eKGWB/Za*-II-Überwindung: "Und diess Geheimniss redete das Leben selber zu mir. 'Siehe,' sprach es, 'ich bin das, *was sich immer selber überwinden muss.'*"]

271 [*BGE*, I, 19; *eKGWB/JGB*-19: "Ein Mensch, der *will*—, befiehlt einem Etwas in sich, das gehorcht oder von dem er glaubt, dass es gehorcht. Nun aber beachte man, was das Wunderlichste am Willen ist,—an diesem so vielfachen Dinge, für welches das Volk nur Ein Wort hat: […] wir […] zugleich die Befehlenden *und* Gehorchenden sind […]."]

272 [*TSZ*, "On the Tarantulas"; *eKGWB/Za*-II-Taranteln: "das Leben sich immer wieder selber überwinden muss! In die Höhe will es sich bauen mit Pfeilern und Stufen, das Leben selber: in weite Fernen will es blicken und hinaus nach seligen Schönheiten,—*darum* braucht es […] Stufen und Widerspruch der Stufen und Steigenden! Steigen will das Leben und steigend sich überwinden."]

273 [*TI*, "How the 'True World' Became a Fable." "History of an Error," last stage; *eKGWB/GD*-Welt-Fabel, 6: "Die wahre Welt haben wir abgeschafft: welche Welt blieb übrig? die scheinbare vielleicht?… Aber nein! *mit der wahren Welt haben wir auch die scheinbare abgeschafft.*"]

274 [*WzM*, § 567; *eKGWB/NF*-1888,14[184]: "die scheinbare Welt d.h. eine Welt, nach Werthen angesehen, geordnet, ausgewählt nach Werthen d.h. in diesem Falle nach dem Nützlichkeits-Gesichtspunkt in Hinsicht auf die Erhaltung und Macht-Steigerung einer bestimmten Gattung von Animal."]

275 [*TSZ*, "On the Thousand and One Goals," trans. mod. by R.S. *eKGWB/Za*-I-Ziel: "Leben könnte kein Volk, das nicht erst schätzte […]".]

276 [Ibid.: "Wahrlich, die Menschen gaben sich alles ihr Gutes und Böses. Wahrlich, sie nahmen es nicht, sie fanden es nicht, nicht fiel es ihnen als Stimme vom Himmel. Werthe legte erst der Mensch in die Dinge, sich zu erhalten,—er schuf erst den Dingen Sinn, einen Menschen-Sinn!"]

277 [Ibid.: "Durch das Schätzen erst giebt es Werth: und ohne das Schätzen wäre die Nuss des Daseins hohl."]

144

NOTES

278 { *If this is metaphysical?* ‹ ill. › }

279 [*WzM*, § 481; *eKGWB/NF*-1886,7[60]:"[...] die Welt [...] hat keinen Sinn hinter sich, sondern unzählige Sinne 'Perspektivismus.'"]

280 [Ibid.: "Unsere Bedürfnisse sind es, *die die Welt auslegen* [...]."]

281 [*BGE*, IX, 268; *eKGWB/JGB*-268: "Die Wertschätzungen eines Menschen verrathen etwas vom *Aufbau* seiner Seele, und worin sie ihre Lebensbedingungen, ihre eigentliche Noth sieht." In his typescript, Schürmann reported Kaufmann's translation by writing "meanings" instead of "need," then he added "needs" without crossing out his first rendition.]

282 [*WzM*, § 715; *eKGWB/NF*-1887,11[73]: "Der Gesichtspunkt des 'Werths' ist der Gesichtspunkt von *Erhaltungs-Steigerungs-Bedingungen* in Hinsicht auf complexe Gebilde von relativer Dauer des Lebens innerhalb des Werdens." Trans. mod. by R.S.]

283 [*WzM*, § 507; *eKGWB/NF*-1887,9[38]: "in der *Werthschätzung* drücken sich *Erhaltungs-* und *Wachsthums-Bedingungen* aus." Schürmann modifies Kaufmann's translation which reads—instead of "enhancement"—"growth." Trans. mod. by R.S.]

284 [From *HBA*, §44. "Protest against 'Busy-ness,'" 265–268 and §45. "Transmutation of 'Destiny,'" 270–274, trans. mod.]

285 { *will* ontologized → }

286 *Hw*, 77[/*GA* 5, 84: "Im Betrieb wird der Entwurf des Gegenstandsbezirkes allererst in das Seiende eingebaut."]/*QCT*, 124, trans. mod. by R.S.

287 { ‹ ill. › "busy-ness"

Be - trieb

Co - agere

COGENCY [: Merriam-]Webster [Dictionary]: "having the power to compel or constrain"; "appealing forcibly to reason." CO-GITO }

288 "Everything functions. That is what is uncanny [*unheimlich*, R.S.], that it functions and that the functioning pushes ceaselessly further toward still more functioning" (*Sp* 206[/*GA* 16, 669f.: "Es funktioniert alles. Das ist gerade das Unheimliche, daß es funktioniert und daß das Funktionieren immer weiter treibt zu einem weiteren Funktionieren [...]."]/*ISp* 17).

289 { α }

290 [All these citations are taken from *Hw*, 30[/*GA* 5, 26f]/*PLT*, 40f. (39f.): "[...] indem wir z. B. den Tempel in Paestum an seinem Ort und den Bamberger Dom an seinem Platz aufsuchen, die Welt der vorhandenen Werke ist zerfallen"; "das Gegenstandsein der Werke [...] bildet nicht ihr Werksein"; "Weltentzug und Weltzerfall sind nie mehr rückgängig zu machen."]

291 [The following sentences are crossed-out: and bustle (*der Umtrieb*), the most glaring symptom of such transformation into busy-ness. Heidegger thus places such phenomena as the art market and the art industry within the scheme of universal *mathēsis*: "The whole art industry (*Kunstbetrieb*), even if carried to its zenith and busying itself entirely for the sake of the works themselves, reaches only the object-being of the works." (Note: [...] *Hw*, 30[/*GA* 5, 27: "Aller Kunstbetrieb, er mag aufs äußerste gesteigert werden und alles um der Werte selbst willen betreiben, reicht immer nur bis an das Gegenstandsein der Werte."]/*PLT*, 40f.

Cf. *Hw*, 56/*PLT* 69). The modern decontextualization of artworks has been described by Hans-Georg Gadamer, *Truth and Method*, trans. and ed. Garrett Bowden and John Cumming (New York: Seabury Press, 1975), 39–90.) Transformation into busy-ness extends, however, beyond the domain of artworks.]

292 { principle of the *will* }

293 [The following sentences are crossed-out: 'Region' does not refer to regional ontology, which is an a-historical phenomenology. If the object-region arises from the modern subject asserting itself, 'region' is a term of a historical ontology, of the history of being. What is primordial for modernity is that]

294 { β) science }

295 *Hw* 77 and 69[*GA* 5, 84: "Dieses Sicheinrichtenmüssen auf die eigenen Ergebnisse als die Wege und Mittel des fortschreitenden Verfahrens ist das Wesen des Betriebcharakters der Forschung." / *GA* 5, 75: "[das] Wesen[...] der neuzeitlichen Technik, das mit dem Wesen der neuzeitlichen Metaphysik identisch ist."]/ *QCT* 124 and 116.

296 *Hw* 77f.[/*GA* 5, 84: "[das Vorrang] des Verfahrens vor dem Seienden (Natur und Geschichte)" / "die Wissenschaft in sich als Forschung den Charakter des Betriebes hat."]/*QCT* 124f.; cf. *Hw* 90/*QCT* 138.

297 *Sp* 214[/*GA* 16, 677: "Ich sehe die Lage des Menschen in der Welt der planetarischen Technik nicht als ein unentwirrbares und unentrinnbares Verhängnis [...]."]/*ISp* 22.

298 { *SZ*:

inauthenticity		authenticity
↓		↓
technology:		Gelassenheit
principle of		
will }		

299 [The following sentences are crossed-out: He follows Georg Trakl in waiting for "a breed, not yet borne to term, whose stamp marks the future generation. The gathering power of non-attachment holds the unborn [stamp, R.S.] beyond the deceased, and saves it for the coming rebirth of mankind out of the dawn." (*US*, 67[/*GA* 12, 63: "Das Versammelnde der Abgeschiedenheit spart das Ungeborene über das Abgelebte hinweg in ein kommendes Auferstehen des Menschenschlages aus der Frühe."]/*OWL*, 185, trans. mod. by R.S.). This is a somewhat contorted way of linking, beyond deconstruction, the arrival of an age that bears the mark of the originary (presencing freed from the technological cathexis) to a return to the original dawn (ancient Greece). It is also a way of linking, beyond the epochs, the new stamp (economy, fundamental position) to a doing (the practical a priori). It is a way, in other words, of suggesting a transgression. The protest that hastens it does not act strategically, but rather through an apprenticeship in non-attachment. This erodes a boundary drawn since Parmenides. Heidegger describes that boundary as a certain conception of the "it is": its conception as ontological difference. (Note: "Then happens the farewell to all 'it is,'" *US*, 154 [/*GA* 12, 146: "Dann ereignet sich der Abschied von allem 'Es ist.'"]/*OWL*, 54, trans. mod. by R.S.) The allusion is to fragment 2 (Diels) from Parmenides and to

146

NOTES

the first "way of inquiry": "that of 'it is' and 'it cannot not-be.'" On the dismissal of the ontological difference see *HBA*, sec. 34, 209–214).]

300 { *Abgeschiedenheit?* : 1. *will not to will*; 2. the other modality of presence; 3. detaching *from* theticism (will) → "taking leave" from m[etaphysics] }

301 Otto Pöggeler, *Philosophie und Politik bei Heidegger* (Freiburg: Verlag Karl Alber, 1972), claims that Heidegger agrees with the "reform Marxists" on at least four points: "1. The critique of our time as that of great totalitarianisms [..., R.S.]. 2. The thesis that it is precisely 'reason,' as man's rise to mastery over nature, which has set in motion the process in which man himself is no more than object, a process to which Auschwitz belongs as well. 3. The critique of science and technology as an 'ideology' [..., R.S.]. 4. The characterization of their own thinking as a 'theory' [..., R.S.]." These four points would show Heidegger's and the reform Marxists' "common protest against the manipulated world" (40f.). I cannot help finding the first two to be truisms, and the last two, rather doubtful.

Karel Kosík, *Dialectics of the Concrete: A Study on Problems of Man and World* (Dordrecht, Holland and Boston: D. Reidel Publishing Company, 1976), seeks to establish "a fruitful dialogue between Marxism and existentialism" on the basis of their common denunciation of "manipulation" (ibid., 87). In the eyes of this Czech author, Heidegger described in *BT* only "the problems of the modern twentieth-century capitalist world" and not those of "the patriarchal world of backward Germany" (ibid., 86). "Care" would then designate "the subjectively transposed reality of man as an objective subject," as "manipulator and manipulated," caught "in a ready made and fixed reality." The philosophy of care in this way would denounce "mystified praxis," that is, "the manipulation of things and people" (ibid., 37–42). The price to be paid for this particular version of "dialogue" is obviously that the notion of care—to mention only this—comes to stand for the opposite of what it means in *BT*: not the originary being of man, but "a derived and reified form of praxis" (ibid., 86), alienated praxis.

Lucien Goldmann, *Lukács et Heidegger* (Paris: Denoël, 1973), has attempted to show that to a great extent, even if Heidegger never mentioned Lukács's name, *BT* consisted of a reply to the book by the early Lukács, *History and Class Consciousness* (1923). Aside from the extravagance of such a hypothesis, the two works perhaps share the same thrust against reification (*Verdinglichung, SZ,* 437/ *BT,* 487). The early Heidegger and the early Lukacs could be read as protesting against certain consequences of capitalist industrial civilization. To my mind, however, the parallel stops there. Goldmann, on the other hand, suggests an entire series of them: a parallel between the subject-object totality in Lukács and totality as the horizon of the existential project in Heidegger; the parallel between world-immanent meaning according to Lukács and Heideggerian being-in-the-world (*Lukács et Heidegger,* 65f.); between the "category" and the "existential" (ibid., 68); between reification as well as false consciousness in Lukács and *Vorhandenheit, das Man* and inauthenticity in Heidegger (ibid., 72), etc. To claim, as Goldmann does, that Heidegger offers an ontological complement to Lukács's more historical and social analyses (ibid., 76) is to recognize the systematic difference, beyond all resemblances, in their outlooks.

APPENDIX

Jean-Michel Palmier, *Les écrits politiques de Heidegger* (Paris: L'Herne, 1968), 213–93, is both more modest and bolder than Pöggeler, Kosik, and Goldmann. He makes no attempt to detect in Heidegger some collusion or complicity with the Marxist critique of capitalism. Heidegger's taking objectification and calculative thinking to task is linked by Palmier to the "figure of the worker" as the locus of the confrontation with technology. This allows Palmier to show—and there lies his boldness—that active protest against the technocratic universe is the necessary corollary to "overcoming metaphysics."

302 [The following paragraph is crossed-out: To raise the question of presencing and of the way a given constellation of presence differs from it is not to 'attack' the project of objectivation or its final shape, technology. Heidegger does not attack, but he asks where the type of deployment that he calls busy-ness comes from. This is, by the way, why there is not the slightest trace of an ideology in his writings, which have therefore resisted and confounded all partisan readings. His contestation puts into question, but does not take a position. 'Thinking' is not a position that one occupies like a fort and from which one launches out against the sciences and techniques.]

303 { demonical }

304 { theticism (*will*) }

305 *MHG*, 73[: "Ich habe nie *gegen* die Technik gesprochen, auch nicht gegen das sogenannte Dämonische der Technik. Sondern ich versuche, das *Wesen* der Technik zu verstehen."]/*IW*, 37. Contrast this with authors such as Wittgenstein and Simone Weil who do condemn science flatly: The atomic bomb offers "a prospect of the end, the destruction of a dreadful evil—our disgusting soapy water science," Ludwig Wittgenstein, *Culture and Value*, trans. Peter Winch (Chicago: University of Chicago Press, 1980; inexplicably, the translator leaves out the word "disgusting"), 49. "In the indifference which science since the Renaissance has shown for the spiritual life, there seems to be something diabolical," Simone Weil, *Intimations of Christianity Among the Ancient Greeks*, trans. Elizabeth Chase Geissbuhler (Boston: Beacon Press, 1957), 171.

306 { will to will / not to will [:] *incomparable* }

307 The French acronym GRECE (Greece) stands for *Groupement de Recherches et d'Études sur la Civilisation Européenne* (Research and Study Group on European Civilization), an influential right-wing organization in France.

308 *GA* 55, 68[: "[Der hier gewagte Versuch, Heraklits Wort zu erläutern,] rechnet keineswegs darauf, dieses anfängliche Denken wieder 'erneuern' oder auch nur als 'Vorbild' aufstellen zu können." Trans. by R.S.]

309 See *HBA*, sec. 20, n. 18, 353, the citations from Werner Marx. [Schürmann seems to translate directly from the German. See W. Marx, *Heidegger and the Tradition*, trans. T. Kisiel and M. Greene (Evanston: Northwestern University Press, 1971), 245: "only a very small number of 'genuine things'." On Schürmann's reading of Werner Marx's interpretation see, also, *HBA*, sec. 20, n. 2, 351).]

310 *WhD*, 159[/*GA* 8, 151: "die Sache dahin bringen und fortan dort lassen, wohin sie gehört."]/*WCT*, 146, trans. mod. by R.S.

311 *Sp*, 212[: "Es kann auch sein, daß [dieses Denken] 300 Jahre braucht, um zu 'wirken.'"]/*ISp*, 21.

148

NOTES

312 *SvG*, 108[*GA* 10, 90: "Gewöhnlich verstehen wir unter Geschick dasjenige, was durch das Schicksal bestimmt und verhängt worden ist: ein trauriges, ein böses, ein gutes Geschick. Diese Bedeutung ist eine abgeleitete. Denn 'schicken' besagt ursprünglich: bereiten, ordnen, jegliches dorthin bringen, wohin es gehört." Trans. by R.S.]

313 { *will* qua Being }

314 This term was coined by William Richardson, *Heidegger: Through Phenomenology to Thought* (The Hague: Martinus Nijhoff, 1963), 20f. and 435n.

315 *SZ*, 386[/*GA* 2, 510: "Das [...] liegende vorlaufende Sichüberliefern an das Da des Augenblicks [...]."]/*BT*, 438, trans. mod. by R.S.

316 Ibid., 384f.[/*GA* 2, 508: "in und mit seiner [des Daseins] 'Generation'."]/*BT*, 436.

317 *N* II, 257 and 397[: "Diese [der Wahrheit des Seienden] ist im Wesen geschichtlich, nicht weil das Menschsein in der Zeitfolge verläuft, sondern weil das Menschentum in die Metaphysik versetzt (geschickt) bleibt und, diese allein eine Epoche zu gründen vermag [...];" "das Geschick des Ausbleibens des Seins in seiner Wahrheit."]/ *N* iii, 187, trans. mod. by R.S.; *N* iv, 249.

318 { man = *willful ma[r]ker of history* → being '*wills*' [...] letting = essence of [*Being?*] }

319 *N* II 482[: "Das Sein läßt erst jeweils Mächte erstehen, läßt sie aber auch samt ihren Ohnmachten in das Wesenlose versinken."]/*EPh*, 76, trans. mod. by R.S. This issue of waiting may illustrate Heidegger's distance from those philosophers of his day who longed for a political leader capable of perfecting both man and the city. Whereas nostalgics of "classical" authority such as Leo Strauss vest their "hope and prayer" in a wise man to unite law and virtue, Heidegger awaits, not an extraordinary guide, but an ordinary economy to come. Leadership ceases to be an issue in his political thinking as the modes of presencing appear as what "lets power arise." He thereby breaks with the two ideals of Western conservatism, the Greek law-giver and the biblical messiah, and avoids the absurdity of expecting men to become "awake to the highest possible degree" through "the absolute rule of the wise" (Leo Strauss, *Natural Right and History* [Chicago: University of Chicago Press, 1953], 127 and 185). Heidegger's much-quoted advice, "We are to do nothing but wait" (*Gel* 37[/*GA* 13, 42: "Wir sollen nichts tun, sondern warten."/ D*Th* 62), occurs precisely in the context of one of his strongest statements on anti-humanism (see the epigraph to *HBA*, sec. 7, [44: "Should thinking, through an open resistance to "humanism," risk an impulse [..., R.S.]?" (*Wm*, 176[/*GA* 9, 346: "Oder soll das Denken versuchen, durch einen offenen Widerstand gegen den 'Humanismus' einen Anstoß zu wagen [...]."/*BWr*, 225)]). Leo Strauss, on the other hand, sides with Machiavelli, who wrote: "To found a new republic, or to reform entirely the old institutions of an existing one, must be the work of one man only" (*Discourses on Livy*, IX, 1). As to the phrase "being lets powers arise," it obviously gives a secularized version of the Christian doctrine of Providence (cf. Augustine, *The City of God*, bk. v, ch. 21, and bk. xviii, ch. 2, l)—deprived, however, of the phantasm of any agent governing the course of events.

320 *Hw*, 309[/*GA* 5, 335: "[der Anlaß], der ein anderes Geschick des Seins auslöst."]/ *EGT*, 25, trans. mod. by R.S.

149

APPENDIX

321 *Tk*, 37[/*GA* 79, 68: "[...] ein anderes, noch verhülltes Geschick wartet."]/*QCT*, 37, trans. mod. by R.S.

322 René Char, *Fureur et mystère*, (Paris: Gallimard, 1967 [1948]), 106, trans. by R.S.

323 *Hw*, 196f.[/*GA* 5, 213: "Das Wort Nietzsches nennt das Geschick von zwei Jahrtausenden abendländischer Geschichte."]/*QCT* 58, trans. mod. by R.S.

324 *Hw*, 234[/*GA* 5, 253: "die letzte Epoche der Metaphysik."]/*QCT*, 98, trans. mod. by R.S.

325 See *HBA*, Part II, ch. 5, n. 14[to "(The destruction is the positive appropriation of the tradition," 81): *SZ*, 23/*BT*, 44. Cf. *GA* 24, 31/*BPP*, 23. The positive appropriation of the tradition is indicated in the phrase "*Verwindung* of metaphysics" (e.g., *Wm*, 242[/*GA* 9, 414: "Verwindung der Metaphysik"]/*QB*, 87 and *VA*, 71 [/*GA* 7, 70: "die Überwindung der Metaphysik als Verwindung [...]"]/*EPh*, 84): not "overcoming" (Überwindung) (and certainly not "restoration"!) but disengagement, or perhaps "enucleation," extraction of the nucleus. We disengage ourselves from something only in grappling with it, as a neurosis is grappled with by Freudian "*durcharbeiten*," working-through. "One cannot shake off metaphysics as one shakes off an opinion. One can by no means set it behind oneself as a doctrine no longer believed and defended" (*VA*, 72[/*GA* 7, 69: "Die Metaphysik läßt sich nicht wie eine Ansicht abtun. Man kann sie keineswegs als eine nicht mehr geglaubte und vertretene Lehre hinter sich bringen."]/*EPh*, 85, trans. mod. by R.S.). To "*verwinden*" means first of all "getting over" suffering: "This gettingover is similar to what happens when, in the human realm, one gets over grief or pain" (*TK*, 38[/*GA* 79, 69: "Dieses Verwinden ist ähnlich dem, da geschieht, wenn im menschlichen Bereich ein Schmerz verwunden wird."]/*QCT*, 39, trans. mod. by R.S.).]

326 [*eKGWB/NF*-1888,15[20]: "Die *Heilkunst* der Zukunft / the *healing art* of the future," trans. by Eds.]

327 { 2 x will: *montrer* ['showing'] — *letting* }

328 *TK*, 45[/*GA* 79, 76: "Alle bloße Jagd auf die Zukunft, ihr Bild zu errechnen in der Weise, daß man halb gedachtes Gegenwärtiges in das verhüllte Kommende verlängert, bewegt sich selber noch in der Haltung des technisch-rechnenden Vorstellens."]/*QCT*, 48, trans. mod. by R.S.

329 "Standing in this reversal is something that can only be prepared historically in thinking, but it cannot be fabricated and even less forced" (*GA* 55, 103[: "Die Inständigkeit in diesem Wandel kann im Denken geschichtlich nur vorbereitet und weder gemacht noch gar erzwungen werden." Trans. by R.S.]).

330 { ≠ appropriation of [*my?*] world }

331 "Being itself, as destinal, is eschatological" (*Hw*, 302[/*GA* 5, 327: "Das Sein selbst ist als geschickliches in sich eschatologisch."]/*EGT*, 18).

332 *SD*, 44[/*GA* 14, 50: "[...] das Schickende als das Ereignis, ist selbst ungeschichtlich, besser geschicklos."]/*OTB*, 41, trans. mod. by R.S.

333 [While the English translation has "time structure," the original French reads "*marque*" ('stamp'). Schürmann uses *marque* in order to translate the Heideggerian term *Prägung*. On the crucial role played by the verb *marking* (*aufzuprägen*)—and its Nietzschean genealogy—in Schürmann's take on the will, see in this volume, 90n.230].

150

NOTES

334 { letting = *manifold* [≠] willing as marking = *totalitarian* }
335 *GA* 55, 98[: "In dem Augenblick, da gefragt wird 'Was ist Metaphysik?', wird schon aus einem anderen Fragebereich her gefragt." Trans. by R.S.]
336 *TK*, 43[/*GA* 79, 73]/*QCT*, 44, trans. mod. by R.S.
337 *GA* 55, 119.
338 *SvG*, 108[/*GA* 10, 90: "Was Geschick des Seins genannt wird, kennzeichnet die bisherige Geschichte des abendländischen Denkens, sofern wir auf sie und in sie aus dem Sprung her zurückblicken." Trans. by R.S.]
339 *GA* 55, 103 and 119[: "der Bereich des wesentlichen Denkens wesentlich [anders ist als der des gewöhnlichen]."
340 "It is only when 'normal' understanding stands still that the other, essential, thinking can perhaps be set in motion" (*GA* 55, 116[: "aber [...] doch 'normale' Verstand still steht, kann vielleicht das andere, wesentliche Denken in Gang kommen [...]").
341 The wordplay on "*Satz*," "proposition," but also "leap," is untranslatable: "Der Sprung ist der Satz aus dem Grundsatz vom Grund als einem Satz vom Seienden in das Sagen des Seins als Sein" (*SvG*, 108[/*GA* 10, 90. Trans. by R.S.]).
342 [In §45, "Transmutation of 'Destiny'" from *HBA*, 270–274, trans. mod., (274), this sentence ends with the words: "and so that we may pass from the era of Janus to that of Proteus." §45 itself ends with the following closing paragraph: At the end of the "slumber of being," [*SvG*, 97: "[der] Schlaf des Seins"] the *epechein*—that is, the destiny where presencing is granted only while also denied—can draw to its close. The new destiny renders possible and demands another way of thinking and uttering. It also renders possible and demands another way of acting. If Heidegger barely develops that 'other practice' which is to agree with 'the other thinking' and 'the other destiny,' it is because the three displacements are truly inseverable. That much at least he repeats unequivocally. The practice that would agree with the other thinking and the other destiny is action in compliance with the ever moving constellations of presencing, thus introducing a great fluidity into the public domain. But under the anarchy principle, as yet only on the threshold of closure, thinking remains merely preparatory and the other destiny, a potential. Similarly, preparatory acting must be distinguished from the 'other' acting. The only action capable of preparing an economy without principles is that which contests their vestiges in today's world and confines them to their site: as remnants of a closed destiny. In the final state of epochal destiny, the state that is ours, nothing can resuscitate those residua, "neither some patchwork of past fundamental metaphysical positions nor some flight into a reheated christianism." (*GA* 55, 84[: "irgendein Flickwerk bisheriger metaphysischer Grundstellungen und irgendeine Flucht in irgendein aufgewärmtes Christentum [nichts mehr vermag]." Trans. by R.S.). More precisely, then, what would 'the other acting be? That is to ask what the absence of systemic violence would be.]
343 [Part III—"Legislation and Transgression" (also titled "Will and Law" in the Bibliography provided by Schürmann—is missing most of its sections that were supposed to focus on "another strategy in philosophy from Kant to Heidegger," and to exhibit what Schürmann calls the "formal identity between transgression and legislation." Fortunately, the main theoretical moves informing Part III

APPENDIX

can be reasonably reconstructed from Schürmann's essay bearing the very same title—"*Legislation-Transgression: Strategies and Counter-Strategies in the Transcendental Justification of Norms*," now re-ed. in *Tomorrow the Manifold*, 77–120. Schürmann's thesis that "the act of legislating is identically, formally, an act of transgressing the law that is so declared" is a major tenet of his magnum opus *Broken Hegemonies*. See—especially regarding Kant—Schürmann, *BH*, vol. II, Part III, B. "The Regime of Spontaneous Consciousness: 'I, the Possessor of the World,'" 445–510.]

344 [Cf. Alquié, *MK*, 55–58.]

345 [In *Das Kapital*, vol. 1, Marx calls Jeremy Bentham "ein Genie in der bürgerlicher Dummheit / a genius of bourgeois stupidity," trans. by Eds. (See K. Marx, *Das Kapital. Kritik der politischen Ökonomie* (1867), in *Karl Marx/Friedrich Engels Gesamtausgabe*, Bd. II/5, (Berlin: 1983), 492.; I. Bd.: *Der Produktionsprozeß des Kapitals*, note 870). In *HBA*, 367 n. 21, Schürmann also recalls that Marx applied a similarly derisory epithet to Schelling, whom he called a "traveling salesman for all constructors / *Musterreiter aller Konstruktoren*." (See K. Marx, *The German Ideology*, trans. C. Dutt, W. Lough and C.P. Magill (Moscow: Progress Publishers, 1976), 146; trans. mod. by R.S.]

346 [Cf. Alquié, *MK*, 90.]

347 { 1 }

348 [*GMS*, BA 52; *AA* IV, 421: "*handle nur nach derjenigen Maxime, durch die du zugleich wollen kannst, daß sie ein allgemeines Gesetz werde.*"]

349 [Schürmann here adds: "at the beginning of the term."]

350 { 2 }

351 [*GMS*, BA 52; *AA* IV, 421: "*handle so, als ob die Maxime deiner Handlung durch deinen Willen zum allgemeinen Naturgesetze werden sollte.*"]

352 [Cf. Alquié, *MK*, 93.]

353 [Cf. Alquié, *MK*, 98–100.]

354 [*GMS*, BA 63; *AA* IV, 427: "Der Wille wird als ein Vermögen gedacht, *der Vorstellung gewisser Gesetze gemäß* sich selbst zum Handeln zu bestimmen."]

355 [Cf. Alquié, *MK*, 107–109.]

356 [*GMS*, BA 63; *AA* IV, 427: "Nun ist das, was dem Willen zum objectiven Grunde seiner Selbstbestimmung dient, *der Zweck* […]." Trans. mod. by R.S.]

357 [See Paton's note regarding his translation of the term "subjective" in B 63 (*GMM*, 140, 63n.2). The sentence preceding the one cited by Schürmann reads as follows: "I have here ventured—*perhaps rashly*—to substitute 'subjective' for 'objective'." (Emphasis added by Eds.). The "—*perhaps rashly*—" can only be found in the Routledge re-edition.]

358 [*GMS*, BA 64; *AA* IV, 428: "Gesetzt aber, es gäbe etwas, dessen Dasein an sich selbst einen absoluten Werth hat, was als Zweck an sich selbst ein Grund bestimmter Gesetze sein könnte, so würde in ihm und nur in ihm allein der Grund eines möglichen kategorischen Imperativs, d. i. praktischen Gesetzes, liegen." Trans. mod. by R.S.]

359 [Ibid.: "Nun sage ich: der Mensch und überhaupt jedes vernünftige Wesen existirt als Zweck an sich selbst […]." Trans. mod. by R.S.]

360 [CF. Alquié, *MK*, 110.]

NOTES

361 { 2¹ }

362 [*GMS*, BA 66f.; *AA* IV, 429: "*Handle so, daß du die Menschheit sowohl in deiner Person, als in der Person eines jeden andern jederzeit zugleich als Zweck, niemals bloß als Mittel brauchst.*"]

363 [Cf. Alquié, *MK*, 117.]

364 [Cf. Alquié, *MK*, 122.]

365 { 3 }

366 [*GMS*, BA 70; *AA* IV, 431: "hieraus folgt nun das dritte praktische Princip des Willens, als oberste Bedingung der Zusammenstimmung desselben mit der allgemeinen praktischen Vernunft, die Idee *des Willens jedes vernünftigen Wesens als eines allgemein gesetzgebenden Willens.*" Trans. mod. by R.S.]

367 [*GMS*, BA 72; *AA* IV, 432: "obgleich ein Wille, *der unter Gesetzen steht*, noch vermittelst eines Interesse an dieses Gesetz gebunden sein mag, dennoch ein Wille, der selbst zu oberst gesetzgebend ist, unmöglich so fern von irgend einem Interesse abhängen […]."]

368 [*GMS*, BA 87; *AA* IV, 440: "'Die Autonomie des Willens als oberstes Princip der Sittlichkeit'": "Autonomie des Willens ist die Beschaffenheit des Willens, dadurch derselbe ihm selbst […] ein Gesetz ist."]

369 [Cf. Alquié, *MK*, 125.]

370 [*GMS*, BA 60; *AA* IV, 425: "weder im Himmel, noch auf der Erde […]." Trans. mod. by R.S.]

371 [The typescript ends here. A single hand-written note is found on the last page: { — N! — }, which likely refers to a Nietzsche section that was to follow but is unfortunately missing.]

372 [First published in *Human Studies*, Vol. 3, No. 3 (July, 1980), 302–308, and, successively, in French as "*Le temps de l'esprit et l'histoire de la liberté*," in *Les Études philosophiques*, 3, 1983, 357–362.]

373 [See H. Arendt, *The Life of the Mind*, One-Vol. ed. (New York and London: Harcourt Brace Jovanovich, 1978 [1971]). This edition maintains the two-volume work pagination. In the review, all parentheticals are Schürmann's and the pagination expressed therein refers to the two-volume work.]

374 [Due to Arendt's death, Vol. Three, *Judging*, was never completed. Nonetheless, some excerpts of the latter have been published as an Appendix and can be found in the One-Vol. ed., *The Life of the Mind*, 255–272. Further reflections on judging can also be found in Arendt's *Lectures on Kant's Political Philosophy*, ed. Ronald Beiner (Chicago: University of Chicago Press, 1982).]

375 [Cf. K. Jaspers, *Vom Ursprung und Ziel der Geschichte* (Zürich: Piper Verlag, 1949).]

376 [Cf. H. Arendt, "On Hannah Arendt"(transcription of a debate held in Toronto in 1972), in *Hannah Arendt: The Recovery of Public Realm*, ed. M. A. Hill (New York, 1979), 306: "it's very easy to talk about the metaphysical fallacies, but these fallacies—which are indeed metaphysical fallacies—has [sic] each one of them its authentic root in some experience. That is, while we are throwing them out of the window as dogmas, we have got to know where they came from."]

153

Afterword

'The willing animal to whom nature must conform'

Kieran Aarons and Francesco Guercio

The aim of the present lecture course is to pinpoint a series of historical and philosophical turning points through which the problem of the *will* came to dominate the self-understanding of the subject, strengthening its claim to mastery over the world. Whether under the auspices of 'spirit,' the 'Overman,' or 'technology,' the subject of late modernity would come to understand itself as "the willing animal to whom nature must conform."[1] It is the hypothesis of the current lectures that the global reach of technology, which regulates our experience of phenomenality presently, must be understood as the "unbridled offspring of the transcendental turn in modern philosophy."[2]

At first glance, the accusation may appear paradoxical: did Kant's transcendental inventory of the subject not place new limitations on the rational subject? Did his synthesis of rationalism and empiricism not announce a movement away from the rationalism of his predecessors? However, as Reiner Schürmann explains, the effort to set limits on the rationalist project wound up producing an even more unlimited project in its wake. Having secured its basis in the Kantian system, the will in modern philosophy then swelled like a monstrous spider in a cartoon that pulls everything into its web, until it ultimately "triumphed." Moving from Aristotle and Augustine to German Idealism and Nietzsche, and finally to Heidegger's critique of technological voluntarism, *Modern Philosophies of the Will* retraces this sequence whereby the "will comes to determine primarily and at times exclusively the human subject."[3] Following

---

1 In this volume, 18.
2 Ibid., 17.
3 Ibid., 18. Cf. also Schürmann's unpublished lecture notes for the course *Philosophical Anthropology II: Its Contemporary Crisis*, in the Reiner Schürmann papers, NA.0006.01, box 4, folder 1–7 (New York: The New School Archives and Special

the example set by Paul Ricœur, Schürmann isolates a series of decisive conjunctures or "contexts"[4]—ethical, religious, epistemological, critical—until arriving, with Nietzsche and Heidegger, at the *fundamentum concussum*, that moment where "the long hidden crack bursts open."[5]

In a first moment, Schürmann shows how the grounds of the transcendental philosophy of the will were prepared by Aristotle, Augustine, and Descartes. Although the ancient Greeks have no precise word for 'will,' in its emphasis on freedom from constraint and choice among alternatives Aristotle's analysis in the *Nicomachean Ethics* of *proairesis*, or deliberated choice, forms a necessary starting point.[6] However, since the purview of deliberated choice is ethical rather than epistemological, its cosmological significance remains decisively bounded. It is only with Augustine that the "stage of the drama of the will,"[7] with its agonal simultaneity of *velle* and *nolle*, willing and nilling, is properly set. In Augustine, the will's power to turn either away from or toward God, as a "boundless either/or,"[8] endows it with a newfound capacity for evil. Infinite in its capacity for God, yet finite in its impurity, the will is lodged midway between desire and reason, divided against itself. Hence, the need for an *exercitatio animi*, an ascetic dressage of the will by which it becomes rational through submission to the mind's command. In this 'spiritualization,' the human has the pure will of God as its model and goal—a tension Kant will later

---

Collections), 32: "[the] human subject results from the *will* to submit all other forces to reason" (emphasis added).

4   Ricœur's reconstruction of the will for the *Encyclopedia Universalis* follows a similar sequence of "contexts." See P. Ricœur, "Volonté," in *Encyclopedia Universalis*, *XVI* (Paris: Encyclopedia Universalis France, 1973), 943–948 (II.A.296).

5   Schürmann, "Legislation-Transgression: Strategies and Counter-Strategies in the Transcendental Justification of Norms," in *Tomorrow the Manifold. Essays on Foucault, Anarchy, and the Singularization to Come*, eds. Malte Fabian Rauch and Nicolas Schneider (Zurich: Diaphanes, 2019), 96.

6   On the position of Aristotle's doctrine within the Greek context more generally, see Jean-Pierre Vernant, "Intimations of the Will in Greek Tragedy," in *Myth and Tragedy in Ancient Greece* (with Pierre Vidal-Naquet), trans. Janet Lloyd (New York: Zone Books, 1990).

7   In this volume, 22.

8   Ibid., 21.

interiorize. We thus see the scope of the will beginning to widen. It is against this backdrop that Descartes will introduce a new set of questions. In his *Meditations*, the will remains a central issue, as it was for Augustine; however, the problem to which the Cartesian strategy responds is no longer primarily ethical or psychological (since we do not 'experience' willing, only judgment's results), but epistemological. "Why is there anything else but truth?"—this is the question to which the will supplies an answer.[9] In this way, the exercise of the will is tethered no longer to the foundations of the good but to those of knowledge. As the "power of contraries"[10] which either affirms or negates the ideas of the understanding, the will appears to Descartes as an indifferent energy, innocent in itself yet not in its uses, since its misuse can push the mind beyond the limits of its understanding. Herein lies the possibility of error and deception (and only secondarily, of evil). In the Cartesian preoccupation with the correct usage of the will, a certain "megalomania"[11] of the latter advances to the fore in modern philosophy, in the form of an epochal decision to which all other *strategies* must respond, whether they be to extend, contain, or else dismantle it.[12]

'The will set loose'

The preceding three historical contexts paved the way for the critical or transcendental strategy. This strategy encompasses two fundamental turning points: a "subjectification" of the will, followed by a movement that displaces it beyond the narrow purview of the

---

9   Ibid., 25.

10   Ibid.

11   Ibid.

12   Schürmann's use of the term 'strategy' does not point to a subjective project or agenda, but to those modifications of thinking and acting brought about by mutations in the 'modalities' of presencing. Indissociable from an "interpretation," strategies belong neither on the side of heteronomy nor on that of autonomy, but play out at the intersection between thought and practice, cutting across and reconfiguring their configuration. Thinkers are less the agents than the 'site' in which strategies are epochally inscribed, invested and invited. On this point, see *HBA*, 299, and *Tomorrow the Manifold*, 78–80.

subject into the ground of the divine, or of being as such. Whereas the problem of the rational or irrational character of the will for Kant is still framed in terms of the relation between reason and its opposite, with Schelling and Nietzsche the 'critical' turn leaps over itself into a cosmological vision of unbridled illimitation.

While Schürmann tackles Kant's practical philosophy in greater depth elsewhere, the scope of his engagement in the present lecture course is somewhat more restricted, focusing on those works in which Kant deals directly with the relation between the will, reason, and desire.[13] Taking his cue from Ferdinand Alquié's *Leçons sur Kant*,[14] Schürmann observes that, already in the pre-Critical works, the will appears as an operator of harmony or unification between rational acts and irrational feelings, partaking in both. However, the ground of this harmony still remains subjectively bounded: so long as the will's 'intermediary' role depends upon an inner sense of peace in the subject, its 'unifying' agency can never be universalized. For instance, in *Dreams of a Spirit Seer*, the harmony afforded by "moral sense" is far more radical than that found among feelings, being rooted in our recognition of a rational community that demands the subordination of our individual will to its universal will. With each new phase in Kant's work, its unifying function will be expanded, as its rationality comes to be increasingly defined in terms of universal formal obligations, rather than material desire. In the final account, moral perfection will no longer be a public fact visible to others in the city, be it happiness or "objective excellence," but a purely formal disposition or intention—"purity of heart," as Rousseau put it. Kant thereby prepares what Schürmann calls the "subjectivation" of the will.

---

13 The most sustained treatment is found in *BH*, vol. II, Part I, B. "The Regime of Spontaneous Consciousness: 'I, the Possessor of the World,'" 445–510. Schürmann also taught a course entitled *Kant's Political Philosophy*, in which the "systematic unity of Kant's critical thinking" is analyzed following the guiding thread of 'autonomy' in its theoretical, moral, and political notions. See *Kant's Political Philosophy*, Reiner Schürmann papers, NA.0006.01, box 5, folder 1–22 (New York: The New School Archives and Special Collections), 4f.

14 Alquié's lectures at the Sorbonne on Kant's moral philosophy have been collected as Ferdinand Alquié, *Leçons sur Kant: La morale de Kant*, cited in this volume, 127.

By rejecting happiness as the *end* of the will (Aristotle) and science as its guide (Leibniz), Kant casts aside both the eudaimonism of classical antiquity and the utilitarian premises of his contemporaries. At the same time, if Rousseau was right to insist that "we can be humans without being scholars,"[15] then moral or practical reason must be separable from theoretical reason and, at the same time, irreducible to empirical knowledge. In other words, if practical reason is to overcome the traps laid for it by rationalism and empiricism, moral evidence must be distinguished from cognitive evidence. For all these reasons, a *pure* moral philosophy demands a new specification of the will and its relation to reason and sensibility.

The transcendental framework that responds to these imperatives will be consolidated in the *Groundwork*. As Schürmann observes, if the "critical point of view" can no longer be rooted in the empirical phenomenon of moral decision-making (the purview of psychology), it must seek instead to establish the "conditions of morality *within* ourselves."[16] In order for practical philosophy to liberate itself from its servility to science and desire, reason and sensibility, the will must operate independently. If the will is to be good, it must be so through its own willing (*Wollen*) alone. Its "autonomy," its capacity to become a "law to itself,"[17] offers the sole source of its moral goodness. As Kant famously argues, such goodness depends upon the universalization of individual maxims, or those rules that I give myself in acting, in accordance with a "categorical imperative."

By stripping moral quality of any reference to empirical goal-directed activities rooted in "inclination" or the "desire always to desire *something*,"[18] Kant strove to release practical philosophy from the "teleocratic" rule of ends. And yet, as Schürmann observes, the linkage between will and reason is never truly severed. Quite the contrary: although the goodness of the will is rendered independent from its capacity to achieve its ends, a different mode of subjection to archic command is reintroduced through Kant's insistence on

---

15 Rousseau,"La Profession de foi du vicaire savoyard," cited in this volume, 28.
16 In this volume, 32, emphasis added.
17 Kant, *GMM*, 108, cited in this volume, 114.
18 In this volume, 39, emphasis added.

"respect," that feeling of reverence for "reason *as the principle of action* and not for any content nor goal."[19] Naturally, such respect is something by which only a reasonable being can be affected: a being that is not only capable of representing the law to itself, but which stands prepared to render it present (to *re-present* it) at all times, so as to maintain it constantly before its eyes. What had initially appeared as an emancipated will, an autonomous, unifying and unified agency unwilling to subject itself to any law of which it cannot "regard itself as the author,"[20] now finds itself grounded instead on a respectful self-subjection. "Good will" is ultimately nothing but the will "subjected to reason alone."[21]

This representational character is key to understanding the triumph of the will in modern philosophy according to Schürmann. When Kant presents duty as "the necessitation of our subjective, individual will by reason"[22] *solely* out of respect for the rationality of the law, he does not merely reinscribe the subjection of will to the dictates of reason. By transposing it to the realm of the transcendental, he grounds 'representation' as the condition of the subject's mastery over itself and the world. This fundamental ambivalence, whereby the will is at once *subjected* and *subject*, attests to what Schürmann will refer to as the 'double bind of legislation-transgression.'[23]

This 'double bind' is a central feature of Schürmann's reading of the Western tradition, and of transcendental philosophy in particular. It is referenced in the title of Part III of *Modern Philosophies of the Will*, "Legislation and Transgression,"[24] of which only a few

---

19   Ibid., 41, emphasis added.

20   See Kant, *GMM*, 99; also, in this volume, 114.

21   In this volume, 38.

22   Ibid., 39.

23   Schürmann addresses the legislative-transgressive double bind in several writings: see "Legislation-Transgression: Strategies and Counter-Strategies in the Transcendental Justification of Norms," in *Tomorrow the Manifold*, 77–120; "Ultimate Double Binds," in ibid., 121–149; "On Judging and its Issue," in *The Public Realm: Essays on Discursive Types in Political Philosophy*, ed. R. Schürmann (Albany, NY: SUNY Press, 1989), 1–21; *BH*, vol. II, Part II, Ch. 7, "The Singularity to Come," 700–712 and passim.

24   At some point during the decade leading to the completion of *Broken Hegemonies*, Schürmann had considered "Legislation-Transgression" as a title for different parts of his magnum opus. He had also considered titling the latter *Le tragique légiférant* [*The*

dense pages on Kant have been preserved. In brief, what is at issue in the double bind is the tragic revelation, through suffering, that there is "no legislation without transgression immanent within it."[25] If the act of legislating is "identically, formally, an act of transgressing the law that is so declared,"[26] then beneath all archic acts of the will there is an an-archic undertow always already working to fatally "draw them toward their ruin."[27] It is this insight, above all else, that serves as the conducting thread between Schürmann's early major works and his posthumously published magnum opus, *Broken Hegemonies*. In the latter, the broken edifices of Western metaphysics are revealed to have been erected out of an attempt to legitimate human practice through *simple* nomothetic acts. To retrace the topology of their phantasmatic hegemonies is to grasp the work these edifices accomplished, namely, to blind us to the "fracture" on which they each rested.[28] Whereas *Broken Hegemonies* tracks these sites of (self)-blinding across the entire span of the West, highlighting those singular moments or cracks in which a blinded history came to *see itself as such*, it is in *Modern Philosophies of the Will* that the essentially principial role played by the will in this topological retrieval was first delineated.

Urgrund sive Ungrund

Kant transformed the will into a metaphysical operator: through its own self-imposition, a unified, nomothetic subject emerges as the site of any possible proper decision. However, as we saw above, Kant's effort to manage the legislative-transgressive double bind generates a fundamental ambivalence: the will is at once *subjected* and *subject*. The "ontologization" of the will by Schelling, as well

---

Lawmaking Tragic]. We would like to thank Ian Alexander Moore for this last piece of information.

25 *BH*, 134.
26 In this volume, 109.
27 *BH*, 3.
28 Ibid., 36.

as its historicization via the "ontology of the will to power"[29] by Nietzsche—both of which effectively dismantle it as a discreet faculty—will each be carried out as *reactions* to this subjection of will to representational reason. In this way, in spite of his efforts to enclose the will within the limits of reason and law, Kant inadvertently prepares the road to its triumphant expansion beyond both altogether.

While F.W.J. Schelling plays only a marginal role in Schürmann's published works, the "ontological turn" he introduces into the philosophy of the will stands at a decisive turning point in the present lecture course. In his dissatisfaction with the Kantian transcendental method, whose stark opposition between subject and object condemns us to a sterile and mechanistic view of nature, servile to the laws imposed upon it by the subject, Schelling will gradually extend the will all the way to the register of the absolute. In order for nature to recover its autonomous, organic form and spiritual life, spirit or reason must be understood as nothing other than nature "return[ing] completely upon itself,"[30] and vice-versa. What, then, is the common ground subtending and unifying the two realms? The ground of the identity between subject and object, spirit and nature, is precisely will. With this, Schelling not only ontologizes the will, he also provincializes reason. As the ground of the relation between freedom and necessity, mind and nature, the absolutized will is independent of the rational structures of subjectivity. Reason is merely *one* of its dimensions, but can no longer exhaust it.

However, Schelling's concern is not simply to unify the Kantian fracture between nature and spirit, but also to offer a positive account of the possibility of evil, an arduous task that will demand rescuing the individual or the singular as the "ultimate obstacle to reason."[31] Canonical theories of evil tend to return us to a basic aporia: either evil is located solely in the finite particularity of the senses (as opposed to infinity and reason), and is therefore not a consequence of our freedom; or else, if it finds its possibility in the

---

29 In this volume, 75.
30 Schelling, *SW*, I, 3, 341, trans. by R.S., cited in this volume, 44.
31 In this volume, 46. Schelling boasted he had announced the "the divinity of the singular" [*die Göttlichkeit des Einzelnen*]. Cf. Schelling, *SW*, I, 7, 143 (19).

latter, then we are obliged to trace it back to the ground of nature, that is to say, to God, whose goodness is thereby abolished. Evil is reduced either to a state of privation or to ignorance—negativity or unfreedom. In his effort to leap over these alternatives, Schelling commits a mad wager, introducing an element of irrationality into the divine, not in its being, but in its very *ground*. Evil, he boldly asserts, is something *positive*: it is the irrational freedom that forms the independent ground of nature, and which therefore must be traced all the way back to the will of the absolute.

With the will promoted to the rank of ultimate ground in which rationality and irrationality collide, the question still arises as to how to grasp the locus of this strife. As Schürmann is quick to highlight, Schelling's solution owes an important, albeit tacit, debt to Meister Eckhart.[32] Just as Eckhart distinguishes between Godhead and God, or God's (ineffable) nature and his (knowable) being, Schelling parses God's existence from his ground, or "the longing which the Eternal One feels to give birth to itself,"[33] aligning this distinction with his own unique association between freedom and evil. In this way, Schelling arrives at a framework for understanding both nature and history. God and his ground are now opposed in the absolute as one will to another: what appears outwardly as order, form, and organic rule henceforth can no longer be understood as primary, but as *orderings* of a "dark," unruly non-ground— "*Urgrund*, primordial ground, but also *Ungrund*, abyss."[34] Lawful nature, subjective reason are merely the dark will in the absolute that has been "*brought* to order."[35]

Schelling extends the illimitation of will to the absolute. In so doing, he radicalizes the transcendental legislative impulse, without ever escaping it. By projecting the Kantian tension between rational, universal will (*Wille*) and irrational, individual will (*Willkür*) beyond man into the Divine itself, Schelling displaces the human

---

32 Schürmann reminds his students of Schelling's Neoplatonic ascendency, via Plotinus, Eckhart, Nicholas of Cusa, Giordano Bruno, Jakob Böhme, Spinoza, and "many intermediary figures"; in this volume, 43, and passim.
33 Schelling, *HF*, 28, cited in this volume, 49.
34 In this volume, 50.
35 Schelling, *HF*, 28, cited in this volume, 50.

subject in the process: from now on, all efforts of rational universality to *appear* will be forever haunted by the disorderly and chaotic irrational abyss of its own freedom, which knows only singularity and individuality. Whence Schelling's 'Eckhartian' imperative, with which Schürmann closes his discussion: "Man must die to everything proper to him."[36]

It is only with Nietzsche's historicization of the will that the shattering of the 'facultative' analysis of the subject initiated by Schelling finally comes into its own. However, in order to bring into view the full stakes of Schürmann's excavation of this plurification of the *site* of the subject, and the epochal turn that announces itself through it, a bit of context may prove useful.

Mental, ecstatic, and epochal time

Schürmann taught *Modern Philosophies of the Will* three times: first in the fall of 1980, then again in the spring of 1987 and the spring of 1992. That the substance of his argument never substantially changed means that its referential bearings are rooted in the context of its initial composition, which was flanked by two major works: first, the posthumous appearance in 1977–1978 of Hannah Arendt's two-volume *Life of the Mind*; second, Schürmann's own *Le principe d'anarchie: Heidegger et la question de l'agir*, which would appear in French two years after *Modern Philosophies of the Will* (1982), and from which the current course incorporates several lengthy excerpts. Sandwiched between these two works, *Modern Philosophies of the Will* can be fruitfully read as Schürmann's attempt to trace an alternative philosophical archaeology of the will to that of Arendt, in the mode of an an-archaeology of the voluntarist subject understood as an epochal dispensation. This same methodology will then serve as the basis for his 'backward' interpretation of Heidegger's deconstruction of the West in *Le principe d'anarchie*, the English edition of which is significantly dedicated to Arendt's memory. If this is correct, then Schürmann's response to Arendt's

---

36   Ibid., 50, cited in this volume, 50.

thought supplies us with essential clues as to the critical requirements he applied to his own project in these lectures. For this reason, we deemed it important to include it in this volume.

In the spring of 1980, Schürmann founded a series of symposia at the New School for Social Research to commemorate the work of his late colleague, who had been a member of its philosophy faculty from 1967 until her death in 1975.[37] That summer, he published a strident review of *The Life of the Mind*, entitled "The Time of the Mind and the History of Freedom."[38] In it, he criticized Arendt for taking over the anti-hermeneutical and a-historical approach of her mentor Karl Jaspers, which relates to the tradition as if it were an open book accessible to unbiased scrutiny. Once the sediment of history offers no resistance or opacity, the compass for the thinker's exchange with the past naturally shifts inward, to be moved instead by the agreement or disagreement between the source material and "one's own experience of inner dialogue."[39] Philosophy thus appears less as a thoroughly historical phenomenon than as the exercise of mental faculties (thinking, willing, judging) whose relation to history is at best ambiguous.

At the same time, of course, Arendt was by no means content to remain in the sphere of subjective inwardness, and sought to draw broad conclusions about the source of the evil displayed by historical figures such as Adolf Eichmann, which she attributes not to ignorance or malice but to "thoughtlessness," the "negation of meaning."[40]

Herein lies the rub. According to Schürmann, not only do the two sides of Arendt's account of the will—mental and historical, *vita contemplativa* and *vita activa*—never quite come together, they even "flatly contradict one another."[41] Inner life as she por-

---

37 A selection of talks from the Hannah Arendt Memorial Symposia was edited by Reiner Schürmann and published as *The Public Realm: Essays On Discursive Types in Political Philosophy* (New York: SUNY Press, 1989).

38 See the Appendix to this volume, *"The Time of the Mind and the History of Freedom,"* 117–125. Schürmann's review was first published in *Human Studies*, vol. 3, no. 3, 1980, 302–308.

39 Schürmann, "The Time of the Mind," in this volume, 119.

40 Ibid.

41 Ibid.

trays it is riven between an apodictic account of the 'faculties' of mind and a political account of evil and freedom, and although the latter should have contextualized the mind's permutations from a historical-developmental perspective, the cleft between the two regimes of time is never ultimately bridged. It is never clear why Arendt believes she can explain an epochal mutation such as the ascendency in philosophy of the will in modernity by indexing it to the sudden "mental preeminence" of this or that mental faculty, e.g. the mind's "pro-jection" of the future, the essential nature of which remains unchanging. According to Schürmann, such a formalistic or "axial" approach to historical shifts, which implicitly relies on a fixed transcendental account of the faculties, ultimately fails short of explaining epochal change.[42] Although Arendt asks the right question—namely, how it is that the will comes "to be the particular stamp of one age, technology?"[43]—her methodology prevents her from offering a satisfactory answer, as it rests upon, and thus fails to deconstruct, the metaphysical distinction between *vita contemplativa* and *vita activa*.[44] In the final account, Arendt abides firmly within the Augustinian and Kantian legacy, operating with the "presupposition of a mind whose structure remains unaffected by history"; she is, in other words, "a 'metaphysical' thinker."[45]

The result is a methodological differend. The need for an alternative an-archaeology of the sort found in *Modern Philosophies of the Will* issues from the necessity of arriving at an "understanding of history as *constitutive* of man's existence."[46] It is a central tenet of Schürmann's reading that only a threefold temporality linking the *ecstatic* to the *epochal*, and the latter to the *evental*, can eventually yield such a "historical understanding." In his view, epochal mutations cannot be explained by referring them back either to a fixed transcendental account of mental operations, *or* to Dasein's ecstatic

---

42 As Schürmann asks, "if the mind comes to life because of its directedness toward the future, toward death, how can this *essentially* anticipatory constitution of the mind be held to account for the particular features of one *epoch*, modernity?" Schürmann, "The Time of the Mind," in this volume, 121.

43 Schürmann, "The Time of the Mind," in this volume, 121.

44 Ibid., in this volume, 124.

45 Ibid.

46 Ibid., 308, in this volume, 124, emphasis added.

temporality.[47] Such accounts must still answer a further question: "to what prior understanding of time and history can technology appear as the age of the will?"[48] For Schürmann, the installation of this "prior understanding" of time and history must be grasped not as rooted in pre-existing structures of subjectivity, but in "constitutive acts of existence."[49] Instead of taking a transcendental account of the subject as the point of departure, and only *later* historicizing its instantiations or configurations, Schürmann insists on the historicization of the subject's faculties themselves: the epochal, as the situating of the evental temporalization, must be the starting point to which ecstatic or transcendental strategies constitute a response. What, then, is the *site* of these acts of existence, if the latter cannot be positioned within transcendental subjectivity? And what happens to this site with Nietzsche and Heidegger, such that "the long hidden crack bursts open"?

A destiny of decline

A fundamental ambivalence surrounds the Nietzschean philosophy of the will. On the one hand, in its humanistic metaphysics of the artist, Nietzsche's thought represents a continuation and extension of the triumph of the transcendental legislative subject. On the other hand, in his conception of an a-telic, and a-subjectivistic will—the "will to power"—Nietzsche initiates the dismantling of this very same subject. In this, Nietzsche's site mirrors our own, he being both "still very much a metaphysician" and yet already "catapulted out of metaphysics."[50]

In what sense does Nietzsche's theory of the will to power as the "preservation and enhancement of complex forms of relative life-

---

47 "The 'ecstatic' opening cannot disown its antecedent, transcendental subjectivity." *HBA*, 126.

48 Schürmann, "The Time of the Mind," 306, in this volume, 122.

49 Ibid., in this volume, 123.

50 In this volume, 89.

duration within the flux of becoming"[51] allow us to glimpse the destitution of the voluntarist subject that readies itself within us today?

As we saw above, for Augustine as for Kant, "the will is the agent that unifies man."[52] Upon its joining activity depends the possibility not only of a harmony between inner and outer life—the possibility, that is, of a "spiritualized way of life"—but the very unity of the mind itself, as a ternary structure bound together by legislative determinations.[53] What came into view through the Nietzschean strategy was not solely the dependency of supposedly fixed transcendental forms upon formative acts of domination or primordial legislation, thereby demoting the lawgiving subject to merely "one among an infinite number of possible I-saying forces."[54] Of even greater importance was the disclosure of the epochal site of the subject as both the source *and* the result of these forces. This disclosure was itself only possible now that this site had itself become incapable of sustaining the illusion of full self-presence that had ensured the normative continuity between inner and outer life.

"All philosophers have seen a multiplicity in the human subject—multiplicity of 'parts' of the soul, or of 'soul and body,' or faculties of the mind."[55] The novelty of our time, Schürmann seems to say, lies not in the proliferation of difference, multiplicity, or fragmentation, whether inside or outside of the subject. What marks our site as an-archic is *the impossibility of producing any substantive unity through it*. This impossibility has at least two decisive aspects. It refers, first, to the impossibility of a system of enduring transcendental forms, all of which appear (after Nietzsche and Heidegger) as irreducibly *artificial*; secondly, to the recognition that this artificiality of principles has its origin within the subject itself. Once it no longer denotes "any subject as numerically one, the I ceases to be capable of instructing us about the legitimacy or illegitimacy

---

51 Nietzsche, *WP*, 380, cited in this volume, 56.

52 In this volume, 23.

53 Ibid.

54 Schürmann, "Legislation-Transgression: Strategies and Counter-Strategies in the Transcendental Justification of Norms," in *Tomorrow the Manifold*, 97.

55 In this volume, 56.

of norms."[56] If the subject is inherently multiple, if the systematic order of experience is not universal and necessary but a contingent achievement capable of greater or lesser coherence, then the normative referents that found their basis in the subject prove to be groundless.[57] In short, it is with Nietzsche that "'reason' as a faculty disintegrates together with the will," which sinks into the subject as into a fractured and dysfunctional ground.[58] It is this revelation that Schürmann has in mind when he asserts that the Nietzschean site reveals the *fundamentum concussum*: the moment where "the long hidden crack bursts open." If we must conclude, with Nietzsche, that "there is no such thing as the will," how was it that, at the same time, our site came to witness its supreme "triumph"?[59]

Following Heidegger, Schürmann identifies in our age a shattering of the *archai*, i.e., those binding representations or metaphysical Firsts that previously gathered words, actions, and things into a coherent historical regime of presence. This *kenōsis*, this emptying out of foundational referents, is at once historical and systematic in nature. As Nietzsche and Wittgenstein attest, our contemporary site is marked by a "dispersal" of those unique foci or ultimate grounds that once allowed us to peacefully live, construct, and govern ourselves (divine authority, reason, historical progress, etc.). Today the dispensation of presence is not referred back to *a simple principle* (as per the 'pros hen' referentiality) but refracted through a multiplicity of *Herrschaftsgebilde* (formations of domination), "constellations of will to power" or "language games and their grammars."[60] This systematic fragmentation brings to a close a certain historical cycle that begins with the Greeks, and whose defining feature lay in the vocation it assigns not only to the philosopher ("functionary"

---

56 Schürmann, "Legislation-Transgression: Strategies and Counter-strategies in the Transcendental Justification of Norms," in *Tomorrow the Manifold*, 96.

57 In this volume, 56: "What is new is that in Nietzsche, the concept of a multiple subject makes it *impossible to retain the idea of a substantive subject* as for the metaphysicians."

58 Ibid., 57.

59 Nietzsche, *eKGWB/NF*-1887,9[98], cited in this volume, 55; Schürmann, "Legislation-Transgression," 96.

60 Schürmann, "On the Philosophers' Release From Civil Service," *Kairos* 2 (1988), 136.

of humanity, as Schürmann observes)[61] but also, we might add, to the political militant operating in his or her shadow. Whether in thought or in politics, the founding public service consisted in securing an ultimate ground for civilization, a "mooring" for all that is.[62] Yet where life appears as "without a goal, without *telos*," we perceive "the impossibility of rendering that foundational service to our civilization" today.[63]

At the same time, Schürmann glimpses in this systematic and historical *closure* something distinct from the destitution of this or that metaphysical First: a *dessaisie* or "peremption"[64] of the *archē*, a "relinquishment of any representation functioning as plainly and simply normative."[65] Whereas Schürmann uses the term 'destitution' to refer to the collapse of legislative referents, he reserves the term *dessaisie* to describe the quashing or annulment of hegemonic, nomothetic validity as such: a time in which the entire cycle of institution/destitution finds itself concluded, having lost its condition of possibility. In so doing, he names our site as that out of which a *divestment* from hegemonic order, and a *recovery* from the tragic denial of its double binds, first becomes possible.[66]

The obscenity of our current political order must be placed against the backdrop of this closure and dispersion of the *archē*. The meanness and cruelty of our anomic order represents a hollow effort to "reinstitute figures of some authoritative First that in fact have been lost for good."[67] The various resurgent fundamentalisms of our time—from religious zealotry to right wing Constitutional-

---

61 *BH*, 601.

62 Schürmann, "On the Philosophers' Release From Civil Service," 135.

63 *HBA*, 10; Schürmann, "On the Philosophers' Release From Civil Service," 135.

64 For a detailed account of Schürmann's "hypothesis of closure" and the key notion of *dessaisie* or "peremption," see Malte Fabian Raunch and Nicolas Schneider, "Of Peremption and Insurrection: Reiner Schürmann's Encounter with Michel Foucault," in Schürmann, *Tomorrow the Manifold*, 151–181.

65 Schürmann, "'Only Proteus Can Save Us Now': On Anarchy and Broken Hegemonies," eds. Francesco Guercio and Ian Alexander Moore, *Graduate Faculty Philosophy Journal 41*, no. 2 (forthcoming).

66 *BH*, 546: "*Dessaissie* signifies the loss of every hegemony." On this point, see Schürmann, "'Only Proteus Can Save Us Now.'"

67 Schürmann, "On the Philosophers' Release From Civil Service," 137.

ism—comprise a vast work of *archē*-mourning, so many efforts to conjure up a principle capable of shoring up the authority of commandments.

Archē-mourning of this sort affects not only ruling elites, but all those activisms that are content to oppose to power merely another title of legitimacy. Just as the vocation of the philosopher in the West was to place his time under the authority of a normative standard affording "private consolation" and "public consolidation," too many political militants today still understand their vocation as that of repairing the "attributive-participative schemas" of reigning institutions, by restoring to them the legitimacy ('consensus') that they allowed to wither and decay.[68] A desperate yet farcical effort to resuscitate withering institutions by subordinating them to a will above and beyond them permeates radical political thought of all stripes.[69] Whereas the right looks beyond the laws of the *Rechtsstaat* toward the sovereign decision that rejuvenates it, the left scours uprisings for "the smallest grain of constituent power."[70] The will has become the principle sustaining every "enterprise of legitimation," restoration and rebellion alike.[71] So long as all political opposition can be translated into competing claims to a single symbolic center, the system can perpetuate itself through its own opposition. *The voluntarist political project of modernity guides our response even to its own decline.* Schürmann here invokes a striking formulation of Arendt: "the will acts like 'a kind of coup d'état.'"[72] As he explains,

> When, in the closing age of philosophy, the human will becomes absolute, willing nothing but itself, it shows forth its insurrectional nature. It is that force which seeks to establish the self as permanent and time as lasting. If

---

68 Ibid., 134; *HBA*, 5.

69 *BH*, "there is something comical about those beautiful urges to force a solution wherein one resorts to an ultimate authority so as to escape from the double bind."

70 Marcello Tarì, *There is no Unhappy Revolution*, Trans. Richard Braude (New York: Common Notions, 2021), 19.

71 *HBA*, 288.

72 Arendt, *Life of the Mind*, Vol. I, 213, cited in this volume, 71.

'justice' means for each thing to arrive and depart in accordance with the economies, 'will' is the name for rebellion against that justice.[73]

This link between the establishment of the 'self as permanent' and the so-called 'injustice' toward presencing deserves to be emphasized. Injustice disjoins us from the ontic flow of absencing-presencing-absencing, while denying the ontological "structure of hiding-showing."[74] Faced by a withering capacity to unify itself, threatened by the hollowing out of its unifying referents, voluntarism reacts by feverish action. In this way, the endless agenda of crisis management today, combined with our perpetual "busy-ness," ensures that the insistence on presence becomes a veritable *injunction to absence*. In our frenetic attempts to 'mechanize' our contact with the world, we 'harden' ourselves against "the epoch-making disjunctive decisions," refusing to face the truth of our transitional situation. It is in this hardening, Schürmann suggests, that we find the "source of all thoughtlessness."[75]

An-archic ethics

Nothing is to be repaired or done over. Just let be. Not abandon. Let be so that everything may be. Lay hands neither to the past nor to the images. The origin bides its time. At least unlearning possession. Letting go all holds.[76]

If a space of ethical decision is left, it cannot assume the thetic form of a postulate or maxim set *against* the given. Yet what does it mean for practical philosophy to quit the "enterprise of legitimation" as such? What does it mean to subvert the principial relationship between being and acting, to cease imposing on inner and outer phenomena the stamp of normative Firsts and instead to *release* ourselves into our an-archic epoch?

---

73 In this volume, 71.
74 *HBA*, 142.
75 In this volume, 71.
76 Schürmann, *Origins*, trans. Elizabeth Preston (Zurich: diaphanes, 2016), 104.

Schürmann cautions us against any simplistic temptation to supplant the fractured subject with a positive or pragmatic concept of activity. To do so would only reinstate its operating principle under a different guise, substituting one form of depth outside of consciousness for another. While such a substitution might succeed in relegating 'being' to a derivative concept, this alone is not enough to exit the terrain of metaphysics more generally.

If it is true that each age confers a distinctive responsibility on its thinkers, today this task can be stated simply: to drive whatever is left of the West's idols "into their tomb."[77] This means helping people to "unlearn the normative phantasms that are alien to everydayness," and in this way, to "release life, both public and private," from the "standards whose grip becomes all the more brutal and irrational *as they fade*."[78]

The emptying out of founding principles opens onto a space of ethical decision that is genuinely epochal. The great advantage of transitional ages such as ours lies in the practical *a priori* of releasement that their implosion facilitates. Once the "hubris of principles has lost its credibility for an entire civilization," it is finally possible "to will non-willing."[79] For Schürmann, action can take as its sole measure or verticality its *situation* or site, the varying alethic constellations. If there is a legacy of Heidegger's thought that belongs within a destituent lineage, it resides in his call to remain faithful to phenomena:

> Heidegger understands *dikē*, justice, as a harmony in presencing, as the jointure (*Fuge*) between arrival and withdrawal. *Adikia*, then, is disjointure. [...] Both Hölderlin and Nietzsche dared to 'let'—to abandon—themselves to the movement of transition in which the modern age, and perhaps the metaphysical age, comes to an end.[80]

The immediate effect of unlearning metaphysical postulates is not amnesia or ignorance of what the tradition offered; rather, "hege-

---

77 Schürmann, "On the Philosophers' Release From Civil Service," 141
78 Ibid., 144, 138, our emphasis.
79 In this volume, 72, our emphasis.
80 Ibid., 71.

monic posits would show themselves to be broken from within."[81] The principle of anarchy—if such a strained formulation can be sustained—directs us to dwell within, and thus fulfill, the closure of epochal history by *exhibiting* the "destitution of man, the legislator of presence" through a fidelity to our singular situation.[82] These two features of the principle are indissociable: it is precisely through our fidelity to our situatedness that we best exhibit the brokenness of "standards turned hollow and brutal."[83] In question is not a new "decisive" act of the will that would command us to "settle happily in a place deprived of principles,"[84] but a practice of *refusing to unstick ourselves from the unruly coming-into-form of the sensible.* Only in this way do we avoid betraying phenomena "in their place of manifestation."[85] If we can still speak here of a principle, this is because there is "only one rule": to "heed the modality in which phenomena come about in any given economy," and to act so as to release ourselves into an an-archic economy "freed from ordering principles."[86] Fidelity to the anarchy of our time renders any effort to metaphysically derive acting from being "non-operational."[87] The impulse to legitimate this or that practice by referring back to a stable subject beneath them must be systematically unlearned: let "normative *consciousness* collapse."[88]

That ours is an "age without a beyond" certainly means that "we lack all models."[89] And yet, as Schürmann reminds his hasty critics, the fact that "our heritage is preceded by no testament"[90] is not a formula for nihilism or relativism. That the situation offers the only verticality does not mean there *is none.* On the one hand, ethical *compliance* with epochal decisions as expressed in the unstable presencing of our situation must first pass through a moment of

---

81   Schürmann, "'Only Proteus Can Save Us Now'."
82   *HBA*, 302–303.
83   Schürmann, "On the Philosophers' Release From Civil Service," 141.
84   *BH*, 630.
85   Schürmann, "'Only Proteus Can Save Us Now'."
86   *HBA*, 286, 289.
87   Ibid., 296.
88   *BH*, 514.
89   *HBA*, 292; in this volume, 100.
90   Char, *Fureur et mystère*, 106, cited in this volume, 105.

"non-attachment" [*Abgeschiedenheit*] to schemas of foundation. A Schürmannian ethics would take shape through the revocation of any claim on the part of actors to be rooted in firm foundations, origins, or teleocratic principles. In this way, it seeks to turn "our estrangement from experience into a detachment from the self that guards and objectifies it"; or, in other words, "to abandon oneself and let the world be."[91] Such an ethics is, from a first vantage point, an "apprenticeship to undoing, to nothingness—the only asceticism still available."[92] On the other hand, if there is a 'law' to anarchic economies, it originates not in the legislative subject, but in the sensible becoming of nature, in the fissured pull of situated existence. As Schürmann writes, "what makes the law is *phuein*, unstable presencing."[93] Ethics consists in a paradoxically simultaneous movement of *departing* from grounds in order to *stay* with the given, deposing our predicates in order to be as the situation calls us to be: "[to take leave,] *Abschied nehmen*, is what those detached always do."[94]

In conclusion, *Modern Philosophies of the Will* provides us with a conceptual toolbox to question, and even to undo the imperative that 'we' constitute ourselves as a *willing subject*, whether personal or popular. By inviting us to unlearn the desire to legislate "in regard to our existence,"[95] Schürmann's an-archic ethics announces not a new and brighter epoch to come, but another way of inhabiting our own:

> I am not asking for the start of a new age. I know very well that it would stink. No tomorrows, but a today effervescent with levity. So that I can look this arbitrary past in the eye, without floundering.[96]

---

91 Michele Garau, "Senza perché: l'apriori esistenziale dell'agire destituente," *Qui e Ora* (online), June 2021. Our translation.

92 Schürmann, *Origins*, 147.

93 *HBA*, 290.

94 In this volume, 99.

95 Kant, *Critique of Pure Reason*, B 430, cited in *BH*, 501.

96 Schürmann, *Origins*, 238.

Remarks on this edition

This volume is based on a 106-page numbered typescript by Reiner Schürmann containing his incomplete lecture notes for a semester-long course titled *Modern Philosophies of the Will*.[97] The typescript is conserved in the Reiner Schürmann papers, NA.0006.01, box 5, folder 1–22 (New York: The New School Archives and Special Collections).[98] Although mostly written and annotated in English, the typescript contains a considerable number of pages in French.[99] The latter were sourced from Part V, "Agir et Anarchie," of *Le principe d'anarchie: Heidegger et la question de l'agir*, and used as lecture notes for sections of the course on Heidegger. Since Christine-Marie Gros' English translation of *Heidegger: On Being and Acting*

---

97 *Modern Philosophies of the Will* was conceived and taught as a 'seminar' (coded GH 384). In the 1986–1987 bulletin, the following description of the seminar is provided:
A study of key texts tracing the rationality and irrationality of the will, its ontological scope, and its functions in theories of legitimation: I. Kant, *Groundwork of the Metaphysics of Morals*; F W. J Schelling, *Of Human Freedom*; A. Schopenhauer's *The World as Will and Representation*; F. Nietzsche, *The Will to Power*; M. Heidegger, "Letter on Humanism" and *The Question Concerning Technology*.
Interestingly, Arthur Schopenhauer's *The World as Will and Representation*—indicated as "optional reading" in the 1992 course description—is mentioned here as a core text to be analyzed. In the 1991–1992 bulletin, a broader description of the seminar is instead given:
The relation between the will and the law will be traced through Kant, Schelling, Nietzsche, and Heidegger. Issues include: the will as principle of morality, of life-forms, and of technicity; the will's rationality and irrationality; the ontological turn in the conception of will; the will's megalomania and teleology; from obligation to self-overcoming, to 'decision'; a formal identity of legislation and transgression.
98 The original typescript of *Modern Philosophies of the Will* was preserved by Pierre Adler, who—after Schürmann's premature death in 1993—assembled the latter's *Nachlass* and helped render it available for research at the NSSR archive. The rigor and dedication Adler has shown in preserving and indexing Schürmann's notes, thus laying the material conditions for our editorial work, have been inspirational to us.
99 This plurilingualism is continuously found all throughout Schürmann's lecture notes (sometimes even in the same sentence). Perhaps jarring for readers unfamiliar with the author, it would appear less surprising, should one consider Schürmann's poliedric intellectual biography. Being perfectly fluent in German, English, and French, (as well as mastering ancient Greek and Latin) Schürmann—instead of preparing written translations of his non-English writings and lecture notes—often translated them orally into English as he was lecturing to his students.

was prepared in close collaboration with Schürmann himself, we included the relevant passages here rather than retranslating them anew. However, the French typescript not only differed slightly from both the French and English print versions, but also included a considerable number of hand- and type-written marginal notes by Schürmann. The current edition integrates all three versions, while remaining as close as possible to a translation Schürmann himself approved. Divergences and marginalia are noted in curly brackets in the endnotes.[100]

By contrast, the English pages in the typescript were prepared by Schürmann specifically to serve as lecture notes. Thirteen of the sixteen pages constituting Part II, sect. 2, "Nietzsche: being as 'imposed' by the will" were typed in a different font than the rest and clearly show an alternative—yet successively crossed-out and formatted—pagination. It is reasonable to assume that those thirteen pages pertained to another set of lecture notes and had been redacted either for a now-lost version of *Modern Philosophies of the Will* or, perhaps, for an unretrieved course partially or wholly dedicated to Nietzsche.[101]

---

100 For a detailed explanation of all editorial marks please refer to the Editorial guidelines in this volume, 15.

101 Schürmann's engagement with Nietzsche begins at least as early as his time at the French Dominican school of Le Saulchoir, during which he participated in "L'interprétation par Martin Heidegger du mot de Nietzsche 'Dieu est mort'," a meeting held at La Chaux castle in September, 1967, as indicated by the event proceedings conserved at Le Saulchoir library. In the Spring of 1975, during his professorship at Duquesne University (1973–75) Schürmann taught a course entitled *Nietzsche and the Problem of Time*. In the same period, and at the same institution, he also addressed Nietzsche—alongside several others—in a course titled *Philosophy and Literature*; see "Duquesne University—Undergraduate Catalogs 1972–1975" (Pittsburgh, PA: Duquesne University, 1972–1975). Schürmann's first course at the NSSR in the Summer of 1975, was initially entitled *Nietzsche and the Problem of Truth*, and later retitled *The Philosophy of Nietzsche*. In a NSSR course bearing the title *Philosophical Anthropology II: Its Contemporary Crisis*, Schürmann devotes two lectures to Nietzsche. Here Schürmann also makes explicit reference to his "Duquesne lectures" on Nietzsche; see Reiner Schürmann papers, NA.0006.01, box 4, folder 1–7 (New York: The New School Archives and Special Collections), original typescript, 26. The reader is also referred to the recently published lecture course, *The Philosophy of Nietzsche*, ed. F. Guercio (Zurich: diaphanes, 2020), as well as the invaluable reconstruction by Michel Haar, "The Place of Nietzsche in Reiner Schürmann's Thought and His

Page 1 of the *Modern Philosophies of the Will* lecture notes is dated 'Fall 1980' whilst the 'course description'—two extra pages numbered '1' and '2'—bears the date 'Spring 1992.' The presence of successively adjoined materials would seem to indicate that Schürmann regarded the structure and core argumentation of the 1980 course as sound, being content to edit it and integrate other materials into it over time until 1992, without ever fully discarding it.

Additionally, the whole typescript presents handwritten notes, glosses, erasures, re-editings as well as significant integrations and terminological shifts added through the years. Hence, in order to enable readers to ponder this osmotic process or, as it were, to grasp how Schürmann's classroom allowed for the emergence of (his) thinking—while being, at the same time, its first proving ground—we decided to supply all significant marginalia within curly brackets in the endnotes.

Editorial interventions are signaled in the volume by square brackets within the text as well as in the endnotes. Typos and misspellings in the original typescript have been silently amended, while abbreviations of names, works, and concepts have been fully spelled out. When, in rare instances, syntactically as well as semantically ambiguous sentences occur, they have been rearranged for readability, and their original form provided in the endnotes. All conjectures and interventions not of a strictly editorial nature have also been clearly demarcated.

In his lectures, Schürmann often modifies existing English translations or provides his own renditions from the original texts. Wherever possible, we have indicated where Schurmann diverges from standard English translations, as well as tracked down and provided the original sources for cited materials within square brackets in the endnotes. Bibliographical references have been unified and updated when necessary.

As Schürmann's 'course description' indicates, *Modern Philosophies of the Will* was to be divided into three parts, preceded by an historical introduction, as follows:

Reading of Heidegger." *Graduate Faculty Philosophy Journal*, Vol. 19, No. 2 – Vol. 20, No. 1, (New York: New School for Social Research, 1997), 229–245.

Historical Introduction
Rationality and Irrationality of the Will
The Ontological Turn in the Philosophy of the Will
Legislation and Transgression[102]

Unfortunately, the typescript shows a few sections missing. Whereas the Historical Introduction and Part I of the typescript are complete, Part II, sect. 1: on Schelling, is missing,[103] and Part III lacks both sect. 2: on Nietzsche, and sect. 3: on Heidegger; only its sect. 1: on Kant, has been partially retrieved.

The editors wish to thank Ian Alexander Moore, Malte Fabian Rauch, and Nicolas Schneider for their insightful comments on this afterword, and to express our gratitude to Christine-Marie Gros, Indiana University Press, Springer, Michael Heitz and the Schürmann estate for their cooperation in letting us bring out this volume.

July 2021

---

102 Or "Will and Law," as the 1992 course description has it.
103 Schürmann's marginalia suggest that Part II, sect. 1 was likely to have dealt with Heidegger's 1936 lecture course, *Schelling's Treatise on Human Freedom (1809)*, trans. Joan Stambaugh (Athens: Ohio University Press, 1985).

Tentative Chronology of Reiner Schürmann's Courses at the New School for Social Research

Year	Term	Course Title	All Instances
1975	Summer	*Nietzsche and the Problem of Truth* [The Philosophy of Nietzsche]	*1975, Summer* *1977, Fall* *1984, Spring* *1988, Spring*
	Fall	*Augustine's Philosophy of Language* [Augustine's Philosophy of Mind]	*1975, Fall* *1979, Fall* *1984, Fall* *1991, Fall*
		Aristotelian & Neoplatonic Elements in Late Medieval Philosophy [Medieval Neoplatonism and Aristotelianism]	*1975, Fall* *1981, Spring* *1987, Spring*
		Karl Jaspers' Philosophy of Existence	*1975, Fall* *1979, Spring*
1976	Spring	*Plotinus –* *A Study of the Enneads with Particular Emphasis on En. IV and VI* [Plotinus—The Philosophy of Plotinus]	*1976, Spring* *1978, Fall* *1983, Fall* *1988, Fall* *1992, Fall*
		The Scope of Hermeneutics [Hermeneutics]	*1976, Spring* *1979, Fall* *1986, Fall*
	Fall	*The Contemporary Crisis in the Philosophy of Man* [Philosophical Anthropology II: Its Contemporary Crisis]*	*1976, Fall** *1981, Spring* *1990, Spring*
		*Medieval Philosophy I: Neoplatonism**	*1976, Fall** *1979, Spring* *1980, Fall* *(ver. II)* *1990, Spring* *(ver. I)*

Year	Term	Course Title	All Instances
1977	Spring	*Heidegger's Destruction of Metaphysics** [The Phenomenology of the Later Heidegger]	*1977, Spring** *1980, Spring* *1984, Fall* *1994, Spring* †
		Kant's Critique of Pure Reason – Part II*	*1977, Spring* *1980, Spring* *1988, Spring* *1988 Fall*
	Fall	*Reading Marx*	*1977, Fall*
		The Philosophy of Nietzsche [The Philosophy of Nietzsche]	*1975, Summer* *1977, Fall* *1984, Spring* *1988, Spring*
		Medieval Concepts of Being	*1977, Fall* *1982, Fall*
1978	Spring	*Medieval Philosophy II:* *Neo-Aristotelianism* *(13th–14th centuries)*	*1978, Spring;* *1991, Spring*
		Heidegger as an Interpreter of Kant	*1978, Spring* *1985, Spring* *1991, Spring*
	Fall	*The Philosophy of Plotinus* [Plotinus—The Philosophy of Plotinus]	*1976, Spring* *1978, Fall* *1983, Fall* *1988, Fall* *1992, Fall*
		Contemporary French Philosophy [From Transcendentalism to "Post-Structuralism"; Systems and Breaks: Foucault and Derrida †]	*1978, Fall* *1983, Spring* *1994, Spring* †
		Heidegger's Being and Time*	*1978, Fall** *1982, Spring* *1986, Fall;* *1993, Spring*

Year	Term	Course Title	All Instances
1979	Spring	*Medieval Philosophy I: Neoplatonism*	1976, Fall* 1979, Spring 1980, Fall (ver. II) 1990, Spring (ver. I)
		Karl Jaspers' Philosophy of Existence	1975, Fall 1979, Spring
		*Kant's Practical Philosophy** *	1979, Spring**
	Fall	*Augustine's Philosophy of Mind* [Augustine's Philosophy of Language]	1975, Fall 1979, Fall 1984, Fall 1991, Fall
		Kant's Critique of Pure Reason – Part I	1979, Fall, 1982, Fall 1987, Fall 1988, Spring*
		Hermeneutics [The Scope of Hermeneutics]	1976, Spring 1979, Fall 1986, Fall

Year	Term	Course Title	All Instances
1980	Spring	*Kant's Critique of Pure Reason – Part II*	*1977, Spring** *1980, Spring* 1988, Spring *1988, Fall*
		The Phenomenology of the Later Heidegger [Heidegger's Destruction of Metaphysics]	1977, Spring *1980, Spring* 1984, Fall 1994, Spring †
	Fall	*Medieval Philosophy I: Neoplatonism (ver. II)*	*1976, Fall** 1979, Spring *1980, Fall* *(ver. II)* *1990, Spring* *(ver. I)*
		Modern Philosophies of the Will	*1980, Fall* 1987, Spring *1992, Spring*
		Philosophical Anthropology	*1980, Fall* *1989, Spring*
1981	Spring	*Aristotelian & Neoplatonic Elements in Late Medieval Philosophy* [Medieval Neoplatonism and Aristotelianism]	1975, Fall *1981, Spring* *1987, Spring*
		The Contemporary Crisis in the Philosophy of Man [Philosophical Anthropology II: Its Contemporary Crisis]	*1976, Fall** *1981, Spring* *1990, Spring*

Year	Term	Course Title	All Instances
1982	Spring	*Kant's Political Philosophy*	*1982, Spring* *1992, Fall*
		Heidegger's Being and Time	*1978, Fall** *1982, Spring* *1986, Fall* *1993, Spring*
		Seminar in Methodological Problems *[X-listed Econ J323s; co-taught with* *Prof. R. L. Heilbroner]*	*1982, Spring*
	Fall	*Medieval Concepts of Being*	*1977, Fall* *1982, Fall*
		Kant's Critique of Pure Reason – Part I	*1979, Fall,* *1982, Fall* *1987, Fall* *1988, Spring**
1983	Spring	*From Transcendentalism to* *"Post-Structuralism"* *[Contemporary French Philosophy;* *Systems and Breaks: Foucault and Derrida †]*	*1978, Fall* *1983, Spring* *1994, Spring †*
	Fall	*The Philosophy of Plotinus* *[Plotinus – A Study of the Enneads* *with Particular Emphasis on En. IV and VI; Plotinus]*	*1976, Spring* *1978, Fall* *1983, Fall* *1988, Fall* *1992, Fall*
		Kant's Critique of Judgment	*1983, Fall* *1990, Spring*

Year	Term	Course Title	All Instances
1984	Spring	*Medieval Practical Philosophy* [Latin Metaphysics of Nature]	*1984, Spring* *1988, Spring*
		The Philosophy of Nietzsche [Nietzsche and the Problem of Truth]	1975, Summer *1977, Fall* 1984, Spring *1988, Spring*
	Fall	*Augustine's Philosophy of Mind* [Augustine's Philosophy of Language]	1975, Fall 1979, Fall 1984, Fall *1991, Fall*
		Heidegger's Destruction *of Metaphysics* [The Phenomenology of the Later Heidegger]	1977, Spring* *1980, Spring* 1984, Fall 1994, Spring †
1985	Spring	*Greek and Latin Philosophies of Time*	*1985 Spring* *1989, Spring*
		Heidegger as an Interpreter of Kant	*1978, Spring* 1985, Spring 1991, Spring
1986	Fall	*Hermeneutics* [The Scope of Hermeneutics]	*1976, Spring* *1979, Fall* *1986, Fall*
		Heidegger's Being and Time	*1978, Fall* *1982, Spring* *1986, Fall* *1993, Spring*
		Parmenides	*1986, Fall* *1991, Fall*

Year	Term	Course Title	All Instances
1987	Spring	*Medieval Neoplatonism and Aristotelianism* [Aristotelian & Neoplatonic Elements in Late Medieval Philosophy]	1975, Fall 1981, Spring 1987, Spring
		Modern Philosophies of the Will	1980, Fall 1987, Spring 1992, Spring
	Fall	*Kant's Critique of Pure Reason – Part I*	1979, Fall 1982, Fall 1987, Fall 1988, Spring*
1988	Spring	*Latin Metaphysics of Nature* [Medieval Practical Philosophy]	1984, Spring 1988, Spring
		The Philosophy of Nietzsche [Nietzsche and the Problem of Truth]	1975, Summer 1977, Fall 1984, Spring 1988, Spring
		Kant's Critique of Pure Reason – Part I	1979, Fall, 1982, Fall 1987, Fall 1988, Spring*
		Kant's Critique of Pure Reason – Part II	1977, Spring 1980, Spring 1988, Spring 1988, Fall
	Fall	*Plotinus* [The Philosophy of Plotinus; Plotinus—A Study of the Enneads with Particular Emphasis on En. IV and VI]	1976, Spring 1978, Fall 1983, Fall 1988, Fall 1992, Fall
		Kant's Critique of Pure Reason – Part II	1977, Spring* 1980, Spring 1988, Spring 1988, Fall

Year	Term	Course Title	All Instances
1989	Spring	*Greek and Latin Philosophies of Time*	*1985, Spring* *1989, Spring*
		Philosophical Anthropology: *An Introduction*	*1980, Fall* *1989, Spring*
	Fall	*Heidegger's Thinking in the 30s*	*1989, Fall*
1990	Spring	*Medieval Philosophy I* *(Neoplatonism; version I)*	*1976, Fall** *1979, Spring* *1980, Fall* *(ver. II)* *1990, Spring* *(ver. I)*
		Kant's Critique of Judgment	*1983, Fall* *1990, Spring*
		Seminar on Philosophical Anthropology *II: Its Contemporary Crisis* [The Contemporary Crisis in the Philosophy of Man]	*1976, Fall** *1981, Spring* *1990, Spring*
1991	Spring	*Medieval Philosophy II:* *Neo-Aristotelianism* *(13th–14th centuries)*	*1978, Spring* *1991, Spring*
		Seminar on Heidegger *as an Interpreter of Kant*	*1978, Spring* *1985, Spring* *1991, Spring*
	Fall	*Parmenides*	*1986, Fall* *1991, Fall*
		Augustine's Philosophy of Mind [Augustine's Philosophy of Language]	*1975, Fall* *1979, Fall* *1984, Fall* *1991, Fall*

Year	Term	Course Title	All Instances
1992	Spring	*Luther:* *The Origin of Modern Self-consciousness*	*1992, Spring*
		Modern Philosophies of the Will	*1980, Fall;* 1987, Spring *1992, Spring*
	Fall	*Kant's Political Philosophy*	*1982, Spring* *1992, Fall*
		Plotinus *[The Philosophy of Plotinus;* *Plotinus—A Study of the Enneads* *with Particular Emphasis on En. IV and VI]*	1976, Spring 1978, Fall 1983, Fall 1988, Fall 1992, Fall
1993	Spring	*Heidegger's Being and Time*	*1978, Fall** *1982, Spring* *1986, Fall* *1993, Spring*
		Meister Eckhart	*1993, Spring*
1994 †	Spring †	*Heidegger's 'Destruction of Metaphysics'* † *[The Phenomenology of the Later Heidegger]*	1977, Spring* *1980, Spring* 1984, Fall 1994, Spring †
		Systems and Breaks: *Foucault and Derrida* † *[Contemporary French Philosophy;* *From Transcendentalism to "Post-Structuralism"]*	*1978, Fall* *1983, Spring;* 1994, Spring †

The *Chronology* is based on the NSSR Bulletin and cross-referenced with the Lecture Notes

— the underlined years/terms—e.g. 1980, Spring—are the ones mentioned in the Lecture Notes
— * = Course *is not* mentioned in the NSSR Bulletin although Lecture Notes, with specific years/terms, have been found
— ** = Course *is* mentioned in the NSSR Bulletin but *no* Lecture Notes linked to the former have been found
— [ ] = alternative title for different years/terms
— † = Course *is* mentioned in the NSSR Bulletin but was never taught due to death.

Lecture Notes of Reiner Schürmann at the NSSR— Pierre Adler's Inventory (1994)

Volume I: Ancient Philosophy	Volume II: Medieval Philosophy	Volume III: Early Modern Philosophy
• Parmenides • Greek and Latin Philosophies of Time • The Philosophy of Plotinus • Augustine's Philosophy of Mind • Medieval Practical Philosophy	• Medieval Philosophy I: Neoplatonism • Medieval Philosophy I: Neoplatonism Version II • Medieval Philosophy II: Neo-Aristotelianism (13th/14th centuries) • Medieval Concepts of Being • Aristotelian and Neo-Platonic Elements in Late Medieval Philosophy • Meister Eckhart	• Luther: The Origin of Modern Self-consciousness • Kant's *Critique of Pure Reason* Part I • Kant's *Critique of Pure Reason* Part II • Kant's *Critique of Judgment*

Volume IV: **Philosophy in Modernity**	Volume V: **Heidegger**	Volume VI: **20th Century Philosophy**
• Kant's Political Philosophy • Reading Marx • The Philosophy of Nietzsche • Modern Philosophies of Will • Karl Jaspers' Philosophy of Existence	• Heidegger's *Being and Time* • Heidegger's Destruction of Metaphysics • Heidegger as an Interpreter of Kant • Heidegger's Thinking in the 1930s	• Hermeneutics • Philosophical Anthropology • Philosophical Anthropology II, Its Contemporary Crisis • Methodology of Social Sciences (co-taught with Prof Heilbroner) • Contemporary French Philosophy

Reiner Schürmann
Selected Writings and Lecture Notes

Edited by
Francesco Guercio, Michael Heitz,
Malte Fabian Rauch, and Nicolas Schneider

This edition aims to provide a broader perspective on the prolific, multifaceted, and still largely unrecognized body of work produced by Reiner Schürmann (1941–1993). It brings together a selection of Schürmann's as yet unpublished lecture notes, written for the courses he delivered at the New School for Social Research in New York between 1975 and 1993, with previously uncollected essays.

These works offer an additional avenue into the repertoire already available—including recent re-editions of his major philosophical works and of his only novel. The printed works will be complemented by a digital edition of Schürmann's typescripts, along with transcriptions and an extensive critical apparatus.

We hope that the *Selected Writings and Lecture Notes* will contribute to a renewed appreciation of the scope of Schürmann's philosophical endeavor and help to establish him as one of those thinkers who are indispensable for the understanding of our present—or, rather, to show our present as the moment of legibility for Schürmann's work. We are grateful to the Reiner Schürmann Estate for entrusting us with the responsibility of this work and for their full endorsement.